Climbing Mount Laurel

Climbing Mount Laurel

The Struggle for Affordable Housing and
Social Mobility in an American Suburb

Douglas S. Massey
Len Albright
Rebecca Casciano
Elizabeth Derickson
David N. Kinsey

Princeton University Press
Princeton and Oxford

Copyright © 2013 by Princeton University Press
Published by Princeton University Press, 41 William Street, Princeton, New Jersey 08540
In the United Kingdom: Princeton University Press, 6 Oxford Street, Woodstock,
Oxfordshire OX20 1TW

press.princeton.edu

Library of Congress Cataloging-in-Publication Data

Massey, Douglas S.
    Climbing Mount Laurel : the struggle for affordable housing and social mobility in an
American suburb / Douglas S. Massey, Len Albright, Rebecca Casciano, Elizabeth Derick-
son, David N. Kinsey.
        pages cm
    Includes bibliographical references and index.
    ISBN-13: 978-0-691-15729-0 (cloth : alk. paper)
    ISBN-10: 0-691-15729-4 (cloth : alk. paper) 1. Low-income housing—New Jersey—
Mount Laurel (Township) 2. Housing—New Jersey—Mount Laurel (Township)
3. Zoning, Exclusionary—New Jersey—Mount Laurel (Township) 4. Social mobility—
New Jersey—Mount Laurel (Township) I. Title.
    HD7287.96.U62N552 2013
    363.5'83—dc23   2012047549

British Library Cataloging-in-Publication Data is available

This book has been composed in Sabon LT Std and Helvetica Neue

Printed on acid-free paper. ∞

Printed in the United States of America

10 9 8 7 6 5 4 3 2 1

Dedicated to the memory of Ethel R. Lawrence

Contents

Illustrations

Tables

Preface

In a very real way, this book culminates and affirms the vision of Ethel R. Lawrence, who was a founding member of the 1960s-era Springville Community Action Committee of South Jersey and lead plaintiff in the case of *South Burlington County NAACP et al. v. Mount Laurel Township et al.* This case produced the landmark State Supreme Court decision establishing the "Mount Laurel Doctrine" within the State of New Jersey. Not only did the decision clearly articulate an "affirmative obligation" on the part of each municipality to accommodate its "fair share" of the regional need for affordable housing, it also provided a model for affordable housing litigation and development elsewhere, and offered an inspiration to fair housing advocates throughout the country. Throughout her life, Ethel Lawrence steadfastly defended the right of people to live in whatever community they wished irrespective of color or economic status, and she staunchly believed in the virtues of promoting greater racial and class integration for the benefit of all citizens, not just the poor and the disenfranchised.

This book vindicates the vision of Ethel Lawrence and we are honored to dedicate it to her memory. Although she began working to bring affordable housing to Mount Laurel Township in 1967, and her right to do so was affirmed by the State Supreme Court in 1975 and 1983, the affordable housing development that now bears her name did not open its doors until November 2000, six years after she died. Moreover, until now it has been difficult to assess what effect the opening of the Ethel R. Lawrence Homes had on tenants, neighbors, and township residents, either to vindicate or challenge her original vision of integration and inclusion. In this book we describe the organization, implementation, and results of a special data collection effort implemented in 2009–2010 to achieve these goals. The "Monitoring Mount Laurel Study" was funded by a generous grant from the John D. and Catherine T. MacArthur Foundation (Grant No.08-92834-000-HCD) whose purpose was to assess how the opening of the Ethel Lawrence Homes affected the surrounding community and the lives of project residents.

Consistent with Ethel Lawrence's vision, in this book we show that an affordable, predominantly minority housing project can be developed within an affluent white suburb to further the goals of racial and class integration without negatively affecting property values, crime rates, or tax burdens in the surrounding community. Indeed, we show that such a project can blend into the wider community to the point where many neighbors do not even know of its existence. We also show that moving into the Ethel Lawrence Homes was achieved without lowering the degree of interaction that residents had with friends and relatives, and without sacrificing access to daily needs and critical services. As a matter of fact, the move likely produced a higher level of socialization with neighbors.

Beyond continued access to social networks and necessary services, living in Mount Laurel enabled project residents to lower their exposure to neighborhood disorder and violence and to experience fewer negative life events. In their new neighborhood, project residents evinced better mental health and achieved higher rates of employment, more abundant earnings, and greater economic independence than they would otherwise have achieved. It also gave residents more time and energy to devote to the education of their children, and enabled their children to attend much higher quality and safer schools while earning grades that were as good or better than what they would have earned in their old schools. For these reasons, we see the construction and management of the project not only as a vindication of Ethel Lawrence's dream, but as a model for promoting greater integration and a pathway out of poverty for disadvantaged minority families throughout the United States.

This book and the research underlying it reflect the contributions of many people. In addition to the financial support provided by the MacArthur Foundation, we owe a debt of gratitude to the foundation's Director of Policy and Housing, Michael A. Stegman, for his strong support of the project from start to finish. A portion of the qualitative research was also funded by the Department of Housing and Urban Development, Grant H-21567SG (2009-2011). We also wish to thank the many people affiliated with Fair Share Housing Development, Inc., the nonprofit agency that developed and currently manages the Ethel Lawrence Homes, especially Peter J. O'Connor, its Founder and Executive Director and co-counsel for the plaintiffs in the Mount Laurel case. In addition to giving us his time to provide guidance, answer questions, and explain the subtleties of affordable housing development, he graciously offered us free access to the files and support staff of Fair Share Housing Development, thereby making the design and implementation of the research project possible. Interviews with Kevin Walsh, Esq., Associate Director of Fair Share Housing Center, and Carl S. Bisgaier, Esq., counsel for the plaintiffs in the Mount Laurel case, proved to be invaluable in helping us to reconstruct the time line and trajectory of the litigation.

We also thank the staff of the offices of the Fair Share Housing De-velopment, Inc., which are located on-site at the Ethel Lawrence Homes, including Michelle Baraka, Cindy Haas, Debbie Del Grande, and Andrea Cardwell. All of these people provided invaluable assistance with archi-val records and helped facilitate access to subjects and research materials. The project could not have been done without the able assistance, sup-port, and guidance of staff from the Princeton Survey Research Center, especially the Associate Director of the Center, Edward Freeland, who shepherded our surveys through the various stages of design, planning, programming, and implementation. We also owe a great debt to the Field Manager, Margaret Orlando, who coordinated the details of sampling, surveying, and interviewing in weekly conference calls that lasted many months. Within the community, we offer thanks to Marie Reynolds of the Mount Laurel school district for sharing archival data and historical in-formation, and to the many civic, political, police, and educational lead-ers for their observations and reflections. We also thank Peter O'Connor, Adam Gordon, John Goering, and an anonymous reviewer for their crit-ical reading of earlier versions of the manuscript. Most of all, we thank the residents and neighbors of Ethel Lawrence Homes and the many other people we surveyed throughout the region for opening their doors and sharing their perspectives on affordable housing in South Jersey.

Climbing Mount Laurel

CHAPTER 1

Location Cubed

THE IMPORTANCE OF NEIGHBORHOODS

Any Realtor can tell you that "the three most important things about real estate are location, location, location." This oft-repeated refrain, which we might label "L³," or "location cubed," underscores the importance of place in human affairs. Everyone needs somewhere to live, of course—a dwelling that confers protection from the elements and a private space for eating, sleeping, and interacting with socially relevant others. Naturally the quality of a dwelling has direct implications for the health, comfort, security, and well-being of the people who inhabit it, and matching the attributes of housing with the needs and resources of families has long been a principal reason for residential mobility in the United States (Rossi 1980). As income and assets rise, households generally seek to improve the housing they inhabit to match it more closely with their changing familial needs, either by moving elsewhere or by investing to modify the current dwelling.

When people purchase or rent a home, however, they not only buy into a particular dwelling and its amenities but also into a surrounding neighborhood and its qualities, for good or for ill. In contemporary urban society, opportunities and resources tend to be distributed unevenly in space, and in the United States spatial inequalities have widened substantially in recent decades (Massey and Fischer 2003; Reardon and Bischoff 2011). Where one lives is probably more important now than ever in determining one's life chances (Dreier, Mollenkopf, and Swanstrom 2001; de Souza Briggs 2005; Sampson 2012). In selecting a place to live, a family does much more than simply choose a dwelling to inhabit; it also selects a neighborhood to occupy. In doing so, it chooses the crime rate to which it will be exposed; the police and fire protection it will receive; the taxes it will pay; the insurance costs it will incur; the quality of education its children will receive; the peer groups they will experience; the goods, services, and jobs to which the family will have access; and the relative likelihood a household will be able to build wealth through home appreciation; not to mention the status and prestige, or lack thereof, family members will derive from living in the neighborhood.

For these reasons, real estate markets constitute a critical nexus in the American system of stratification (Massey 2008; Sampson 2012). Housing markets are especially important because they distribute much more than housing; they also distribute education, security, health, wealth, employment, social status, and interpersonal connections. If one does not have full access to the housing market, one does not have access to the full range of resources, benefits, and opportunities that American society has to offer (Massey and Denton 1993). Residential mobility has thus always been central to the broader process of social mobility in the United States (Massey and Mullan 1984; Massey and Denton 1985). As individuals and families move up the economic ladder, they translate gains in income and wealth into improved residential circumstances, which puts them in a better position to realize even greater socioeconomic gains in the future. By interspersing residential and socioeconomic mobility, over time and across the generations, families and social groups ratchet themselves upward in the class distribution. In a very real way, therefore, barriers to residential mobility are barriers to social mobility.

Historically, the most important barriers to residential mobility in the United States have been racial in nature (Massey and Denton 1993; Massey, Rothwell, and Domina 2009). Before the civil rights era, African Americans, especially, but also other religious and ethnic minorities, experienced systematic discrimination in real estate and mortgage markets and were excluded from federal lending programs designed to promote home ownership (Jackson 1985; Katznelson 2005). In addition, the practice of redlining, which was institutionalized throughout the lending industry, systematically denied capital to black neighborhoods (Jackson 1985; Squires 1994, 1997). Poor black neighborhoods were often targeted for demolition by urban renewal programs, displacing residents into dense clusters of badly constructed and poorly maintained public housing projects that isolated families by class as well as race (Hirsch 1983; Goldstein and Yancy 1986; Brauman 1987; Massey and Bickford 1992; Massey and Kanaiaupuni 1993; Jones 2004).

The end result was a universally high degree of urban racial segregation in mid-twentieth-century America that only began to abate in the wake of landmark civil rights legislation passed in the 1960s and 1970s (Charles 2003; Massey, Rothwell, and Domina 2009). Progress in eliminating racism from real estate and lending markets was slow and halting, however, and desegregation was only achieved slowly through a multitude of individual efforts undertaken in cooperation with civil rights organizations (Patterson and Silverman 2011). One such effort occurred in the New Jersey suburbs of Philadelphia in 1969, when a group of lower-income, predominantly minority residents joined together to form the Springville Community Action Committee (Haar 1996; Lawrence-Haley 2007).

Dismayed at their inability to find decent housing at a price they could afford in their hometown of Mount Laurel, New Jersey, committee members teamed up with a local contractor to build thirty-six units of affordable housing for themselves and other low-income families in the region.

Not surprisingly given the history of race and housing in America, the response from township officials to the proposed development of clustered town houses for low-income minority families was a firm and resounding "no." The proposed project, they said, would violate Mount Laurel's zoning policies and land-use regulations, which as in many suburban communities, favored large single-family dwellings set back from the street on large lots (Rose and Rothman 1977). In response, members of the Springville Action Committee joined with local chapters of the NAACP and Camden Regional Legal Services in 1971 to file suit against the township, arguing that its zoning rule effectively prohibited the construction of affordable housing and thus, in de facto if not de jure terms, excluded poor, predominantly minority families from living in the township and enjoying its resources and benefits.

After a prolonged legal battle, the New Jersey Supreme Court in 1975 found for the plaintiffs and handed down a decision that came to be known as Mount Laurel I. In it, the court defined a new "Mount Laurel Doctrine," which stated unequivocally that municipalities in the state of New Jersey had an "affirmative obligation" to meet their "fair share" of the regional need for low- and moderate-income housing (Kirp, Dwyer, and Rosenthal 1995). The decision and its associated doctrine provided a blueprint for fair-housing advocates and affordable-housing developers elsewhere to launch similar efforts on behalf of low-income residents, and in the ensuing years Mount Laurel I was cited frequently in housing litigation around the country (Burchell 1985; Haar 1996).

Although some community members supported the project from the beginning, such encouragement was not popular. In general, public officials, township inhabitants, and neighbors near the proposed development were none too pleased with the court's decision and decried it in vitriolic demonstrations, raucous public hearings, and vituperative letters to local newspapers. Ordered to amend its zoning to accommodate its fair-share housing obligations, Mount Laurel Township officials stalled for time and after a year begrudgingly rezoned three unsuitable properties while they appealed the initial court decision.

A second drawn-out court case ensued and in 1983 the Supreme Court reaffirmed its earlier ruling in a decision that came to be known as Mount Laurel II, ordering the township to recalculate its fair share of affordable housing and to redo its zoning amendments quickly. Two years later, Township officials and the plaintiffs reached a settlement that permitted multifamily zoning in the area and provided partial funding to enable the project finally to move forward (Haar 1996). Plans were submitted to local authorities but this action triggered another round of acrimonious public hearings attended by angry citizens who vehemently expressed fears that the development would bring vexing urban problems into their suburban utopia (Kirp, Dwyer, and Rosenthal 1995). Areas of specific concern were the perceived potential for rising taxes, increasing crime, falling property values, and a general disruption of the suburban ethos (Smothers 1997a, 1997b, 1997c).

The hearings and public protests dragged on for more than a decade, and it was not until 1997 that the Mount Laurel Planning Board finally approved plans for the project to begin construction. Even then, architectural blueprints had to be finalized, permits solicited, and numerous details negotiated with local officials before the project's nonprofit developer could break ground. It was not until the year 2000 that the project was finally completed and its developers could accept applications for entry into the project's one hundred units. Late in the year the first tenants began moving in—thirty-one years after the Springville Community Action Committee originally sought to launch the project, twenty-nine years after the filing of the lawsuit, twenty-five years after Mount Laurel I, and seventeen years after Mount Laurel II. Unfortunately it was also six years after the death of the lead plaintiff, Ethel Lawrence, and the project was duly named in her honor (Lawrence-Halley 2007). In 2004, forty additional units were added to the Ethel Lawrence Homes (ELH) and leased to a new set of tenants, bringing the development to its current size of 140 units.

ELH is unusual in that it is 100 percent affordable. Many affordable housing projects in New Jersey and elsewhere simply require setting aside a percentage of units for low-income families within larger market-rate developments, typically 20 percent. In contrast, ELH from the start was designed and built entirely for low- and moderate-income families. The project presently contains one-, two-, and three-bedroom apartments located within two-story town houses that are affordable to households lying between 10 percent and 80 percent of the regional median income. These criteria yield a remarkably broad range of "affordability," with units in ELH going to families with incomes that range from $6,200 to $49,500 per year. Given New Jersey's high-income economy and pricey real estate market, however, no inhabitant of ELH could be considered well-off or affluent, though obviously not everyone is abjectly poor either.

As the project's first residents moved in, a host of observers looked on with curiosity and no small amount of apprehension. Local officials braced for possible negative reactions from citizens and disruptions arising from the incorporation of poor, minority families into the community's social fabric. Neighbors, while hoping for the best, nonetheless feared that their premonitions about rising tax rates, declining property values, and increasing crime rates might indeed come true. Fair housing advocates in New Jersey and around the country mostly crossed their fingers and prayed that the disruptions would be few and that the development would enable the new tenants to forge a pathway out of disadvantage. The residents themselves entered with a combination of hope for the future and trepidation about how they would fit into a white suburban environment whose residents had made abundantly clear their skepticism and rancor about the development they were entering.

It is within this contradictory and contentious context that we undertake the present analysis, the first systematic, comprehensive effort to determine as rigorously as possible the degree to which the manifold hopes and fears associated with the Mount Laurel project were realized. In the next chapter we describe in greater detail the Mount Laurel court case and the controversy it generated. We then go on in chapter 3 to describe the construction, organization, and physical appearance of the Ethel Lawrence Homes and to assess the project's aesthetics relative to other housing in the area. In chapter 4 we outline our study's design and research methodology, describing the specific data sources we consulted to determine the effects of the project on the community and the multiple surveys and in-depth interviews we conducted to gather information on how the opening of the homes affected residents, neighbors, and the community in general.

Having set the stage in this fashion, we begin our analysis in chapter 5 by evaluating the outcomes that were of such grave concern to local residents and township officials prior to the project's construction, using publicly available data to determine the effects it had on crime rates, tax burdens, and property values. After detecting no effects of the project on trends in crime, taxes, or home values, either in adjacent neighborhoods or the township generally, in chapter 6 we move on to consider the effects of Ethel Lawrence Homes on the ethos of suburban life. Drawing on a representative survey and selected interviews with neighbors living in surrounding residential areas, we show that despite all the agitation and emotion before the fact, once the project opened, the reaction of neighbors was surprisingly muted, with nearly a third not even realizing that an affordable housing development existed right next door.

In chapter 7 we turn our attention to a special survey we conducted of ELH residents and nonresidents to assess how moving into the project affected the residential environment people experienced on a day-to-day basis. The design of the survey enables us to compare neighborhood conditions experienced by ELH residents both before and after they moved into the project, as well to compare them with a control group of people who had applied to ELH but had not yet been admitted. Both comparisons reveal a dramatic reduction in exposure to neighborhood disorder and violence and a lower frequency of negative life events as a result of the move. Chapter 8 moves on to consider whether the move—and the improved neighborhood conditions it enabled—were sufficient to change the trajectory of people's lives. Systematic comparisons between project residents and members of the nonresident control group indicated significant improvements in mental health, economic independence, and children's educational outcomes as a result of moving into the project. In chapter 9 we recap the foregoing results and trace out their implications for public policy and for social theory. We argue that neighborhood circumstances do indeed have profound consequences for individual and family well-being and that housing mobility programs constitute an efficacious way both to reduce poverty and to lower levels of racial and class segregation in metropolitan America.

Before turning to our analyses, however, in the remainder of this chapter we situate the Mount Laurel controversy in a broader theoretical and substantive context. Theoretically, we develop a conceptual understanding of the political economy of place to underscore the distinct character of real estate markets. In doing so, we shed light on the motivations and behaviors of the various participants in the Mount Laurel controversy—project developers, prospective residents, potential neighbors, and local officials, as well as ancillary actors such as housing advocates, civil rights leaders, and suburban politicians. Substantively, we describe the evolving spatial ecology of race and class in the United States, outlining recent trends in racial and economic segregation nationally and in New Jersey, and reviewing the role that housing policies have played in structuring these trends over the past several decades. We also review the evidence adduced to date on the role played by neighborhoods in determining the social and economic welfare of individuals and families.

Although the Mount Laurel controversy was fraught with much anger and animosity, and charged with an abundance of positive and negative emotion, we hope that our theoretical and substantive framing of the issues, along with our empirical analyses of the project and its consequences, will bring needed facts and reason to the debate, enabling citizens to reflect more calmly and policy makers to evaluate more objectively the efficacy of affordable housing developments such as the Ethel Lawrence Homes as social policy. We believe our empirical findings validate the use of affordable housing projects as a tool to address the pressing problems of housing scarcity, poverty alleviation, and residential segregation. We also believe that the study's methodology and data will be of interest to social scientists, enabling them to assess more definitively than hitherto possible the influence of neighborhood circumstances on individual and family outcomes.

The Political Economy of Place

In a capitalist society such as the United States', homes are exchanged through markets. Dwellings are offered for sale or rent by owners, land-lords, or agents who seek to maximize monetary returns while renters and home buyers seek to obtain highest-quality housing at the lowest possible price. Americans often celebrate "the free market" and denigrate "government interventions" and their correlate "bureaucracy." But markets are not states of nature. They are social constructions, built and elaborated by human beings for the instrumental purpose of exchanging goods and services (Carruthers and Babb 2000). They do not arise spontaneously and they do not somehow spring into existence in a free and unfettered condition until disturbed by an intrusive state (North 1990; Evans 1995). Instead they are self-consciously constructed by human actors within specific societies and assume a variety of different institutional forms or "architectures," depending on how they are embedded within surrounding and often preexisting social structures (Hall and Soskice 2001; Fligstein 2001; Guillen 2001; Portes 2010).

In reality, governments create markets and markets cannot exist without government regulation (Massey, Behrman, and Sanchez 2006). Governments create and support a medium of exchange, define property rights, enforce contracts, specify the rights of buyers, delineate the obligations of sellers, and create infrastructures—social, physical, and virtual—to enable market exchanges to occur (Massey 2005a). Many Americans who believe they attained their suburban homes by pulling themselves up by their bootstraps, in fact received significant government help along the way from federally backed loan programs, mortgage interest deductions, subsidies for freeway construction, and other government actions. The issue is not whether governments are involved in markets or not, but whose interests are served by government actions taken to constitute the markets and how these actions influence market performance and the economic outcomes experienced by market participants. These are empirical and not philosophical questions.

For most of human history the things that people needed were exchanged outside of markets, through networks of reciprocal exchange, through inheritance within kinship systems, or by fiat within authoritarian regimes (Massey 2005b). It is only in the past two hundred years that markets have come to dominate human societies; and they did not spring to life fully formed, but emerged gradually over time as economies industrialized, monetized, and expanded to become more fluid, dynamic, and widespread. Compared with markets for goods, commodities, capital, and labor, real estate markets emerged relatively late in the capitalist game because, as we shall see, they are unlike other markets in many ways, making for a unique political economy of place in which the material stakes for market participants are high and emotion plays a salient but often unappreciated role in structuring transactions.

The exchange of homes through real estate markets entails a commodification of place in which market participants seek to maximize the value of property for private use or monetary exchange (Logan and Molotch 1987). A property's *use value* is determined by its suitability for carrying out the daily activities of life—eating, sleeping, and interacting with others inside the dwelling while consuming retail, educational, recreational, religious, social, and economic services in the surrounding neighborhood. A property's *exchange value* is determined by the amount of money it can command in the short run from rent or sale, or over the long term by the capital gain that can be achieved as a result of decisions made about land use, public investment, and private development in the property and its surroundings.

All places have both use and exchange values, but the relative importance of the two differs among different market participants, who often come into conflict with one another (Logan and Molotch 1987). The relative balance of use versus exchange values can even change over time for the same market participant. Renters are generally more concerned with the use value of places. Although they seek to minimize the rents they pay for their housing, they do not have a long-term interest in the exchange value of the places they inhabit and are more concerned with the daily quality of life than property values per se. Homeowners are concerned with both exchange and use values. Not only do they have a strong stake in the quality of daily life and an emotional bond to the local geography; they also have a long-term interest in property values. At the moment they decide to put their home up for sale, however, use value diminishes, and exchange value assumes paramount importance in their calculations. Real estate agents and property developers are the most focused on exchange values, of course, and seek to maximize the short-term returns from the rent or sale of properties and the long-term possibilities for wealth creation through development. They are less concerned with the quality of daily life within the neighborhood, except as it affects the returns on their investments.

It is government that must adjudicate between the competing, conflicting, and changing interests of renters, owners, sellers, buyers, developers, and agents, and somehow accommodate the shifting mix of use and exchange values they present (Logan and Molotch 1987). Naturally, government actors also pursue their own self interests in adjudicating policies, generally seeking to get reelected while promoting local prosperity and well-being for constituents. Early on, Charles Tiebout (1956) proposed a simple conceptual model of the metropolitan political economy in which separate municipalities offer different packages of costs (taxes) and benefits (services) to attract consumers (renters and home buyers), who then "vote with their feet" to yield a housing market that, at equilibrium, maximizes utility for all concerned, matching families with the housing they need and the services they desire at taxes they can afford.

The Tiebout model, however, has been criticized for not sufficiently taking into account the distinctive features of markets for real estate, as opposed to other goods and services (Logan and Molotch 1987). Perhaps the most distinctive feature of real estate markets is that people tend to be emotionally attached to places where they live. Within homes and neighborhoods they devote large amounts of time pursuing the fundamental activities of human existence—sharing food, sleeping, growing up, getting married, giving birth, raising families, and interacting with friends, relatives, and neighbors. These activities involve deep emotions and as a result humans acquire strong sentimental attachments to homes, schools, and neighborhoods (Logan and Molotch 1987). Emotions unconsciously color what humans like to think of as "rational" decisions (LeDoux 1996; Kahneman 2011), and for this reason, discussions and debates about land use, real estate practices, and neighborhood development are usually emotive and often fraught with intense feelings that color debate and decision-making.

Economic theory teaches us that incentives matter and that people tend to act rationally to maximize utility subject to informational and budget constraints. Based on these principles, the neoclassical economic model leads to strong theoretical predictions about the structure and organization of urban areas, and these are generally borne out in empirical research (Alonso 1964; Mills and Hamilton 1997; O'Sullivan 2008). Nonetheless, recent work in behavioral economics, psychology, and neuroscience indicates that human rationality is highly imperfect and subject to a variety of contradictions and limitations (Ariely 2009; Kahneman 2011). Moreover, human rationality, such as it is, is highly conditioned by emotional states rooted deep within the brain that may or not be consciously appreciated, but which strongly influence the formation of needs, wants, and desires and can interfere with or derail strict logic in making decisions (Ledoux 1996, 2002; Goleman 2006).

In addition to being imbued with emotion, places to live are different in another way: they are indispensable and not readily substitutable. Whereas one can decide not to purchase a new television or postpone buying a new car until one can afford it, one cannot decide to forgo housing. Likewise, whereas one might substitute a reliance on public transport for the purchase of a new car, there is no alternative for a place to live. As a result, if markets do not provide housing to families at prices they can afford, the result is homelessness, an outcome that is not simply a private consumer decision to substitute one product (a home) for another (the streets) but a structural imposition that is foisted on individuals by a fundamental mismatch between the distribution of income and the distribution of rents (O'Flaherty 1996).

Families are willing to go to extraordinary lengths to avoid homelessness, yielding a strong asymmetry in market power between the suppliers and consumers of housing. In addition, real estate agents and developers usually have greater access to information than renters or home buyers, and developers often collude with one another, acting collectively to form "growth machines" that influence markets, constrain competition, and manipulate government policies in self-serving ways (Logan and Molotch 1987). Although homeowners may also act collectively, their political power and influence is weaker and their mutual self-interest is held together by the fragile glue of shared use value rather than the strong cement of shared exchange value, and among renters, of course, the ability to act collectively is even more limited.

Within America's political economy of place, developers, investors, and other "place entrepreneurs" are also more mobile than renters, homeowners, and governments—able to shift investments across space with less friction than other market participants. Although renters are theoretically free to pick up and move on short notice without much sacrifice, when decent housing is scarce, as it is at the low end of the socioeconomic distribution, moving becomes difficult. Housing options for poor families are often quite limited, and their freedom of movement is generally more theoretical than real. Even homeowners are not so free to pack up and move if events within the political economy reduce property values below those that prevailed when they purchased their homes; and selling a home is certainly not a cost-free endeavor in any event.

Thus housing markets are unique in a variety of ways: the goods they trade are indispensable and not substitutable; consumption is collective in the sense that one acquires a neighborhood along with a dwelling; exchange and use values are unevenly distributed among buyers and sellers and often come into conflict; emotions are involved and people acquire strong sentimental bonds to specific places; the stakes in the exchange are usually high either financially or emotionally or both; and asymmetries of power, information, and mobility between buyers and sellers are common.

The foregoing characteristics produce a distinct political economy of place in which markets tend to be highly regulated and government actions and policies—particularly land use policies—play a huge role in determining outcomes. In the federal system of the United States, decisions about land use and construction fall to states, and through states to counties and municipalities, yielding a highly decentralized system of

decision-making (Schwartz 2006). To the extent that the federal government wishes to influence housing outcomes, it must act through state and
local governments (Rabinowitz 2004; Glaeser and Gyourko 2008). Until
well into the twentieth century, however, land use, building standards,
and housing markets were largely unregulated at all levels of government.

With the advent of industrialization and urbanization, however, land
uses proliferated, competition for space grew, and demographic diversity
and socioeconomic heterogeneity rose, leading to political demands for
the control and regulation of development. In the demographic realm,
certain socially defined subgroups were seen early in the twentieth
century as inherently "incompatible" with the prevailing white, Anglo
Saxon, Christian stock, leading to governmental efforts to separate black
and white, rich and poor, Jew and Christian in space. In response to the
rising tide of black migration from the rural South and immigration from
abroad, early in the twentieth century cities throughout the United States
passed ordinances to establish racially and ethnically separate neighborhoods within their municipal boundaries, essentially enacting the equivalent of the Group Areas Act that prevailed in the Union of South Africa
under its apartheid system (Massey and Denton 1993).

The first municipal segregation ordinance was passed by the Baltimore
City Council in 1910, legally demarcating separate areas of the city for
black and white occupation (Massey and Denton 1993). Thereafter segregation ordinances spread rapidly from city to city throughout the United
States. The movement toward legal apartheid was decisively stopped in
1917, however, when the U.S. Supreme Court decided in *Buchanan v.
Warley* that racial segregation ordinances were unconstitutional, not because they victimized blacks but because they deprived white owners of
their right to dispose of their property as they saw fit (Massey and Denton 1993). Thereafter, collective efforts to promote and maintain racial
segregation were carried out mainly in the private sector, through such
mechanisms as deed restrictions, restrictive covenants, and redlining, as
well as institutionalized practices of discrimination in the real estate and
lending industries that persisted openly through the 1960s and covertly
thereafter (Massey and Denton 1993).

At the same time that city authorities sought to legislate the residential separation of "incompatible" racial groups, they also passed laws to
enact the spatial separation of incompatible land uses, and in this effort,
local authorities had greater success in the courts. The movement toward land-use regulation began in response to the rapid rise in building
heights in New York City early in the twentieth century. The curtail-
ment of access to sunshine and air irritated nearby residents and business owners, who naturally sought a means of controlling the spread of
skyscrapers. In 1916, in response to popular demands for action, New

York's City Council enacted the nation's first zoning law, enforcing a height limitation in Manhattan and establishing setback requirements for high-rise buildings.

These actions provided a foundation for the steady accumulation of zoning rules and regulations, which ultimately evolved to comprise a complex code that was emulated in other towns and cities throughout the United States. In contrast to regulations that prescribed racially separate neighborhoods, however, in 1926 the Supreme Court affirmed the constitutionality of local zoning ordinances in the case *Village of Euclid, Ohio v. Ambler Realty Co* (Rabinowitz 2004). Since that date, local zoning has served as the primary means of local land-use regulation in the United States (Pendall 2000; Fischel 2004).

"Zoning" embraces a variety of different kinds of rules and regulations. Prohibitions on the mixing of land uses are common in American suburbia and have led to the spatial separation of commercial, administrative, industrial, residential, and civic functions (Duany, Plater-Zyberk, and Speck 2000). Containment regulations have been used to establish geographic boundaries limiting development within a specified suburban ring to reduce sprawl (Nelson, Sanchez, and Dawkins 2004). Some jurisdictions use ordinances or impact fees to restrict new development unless the developer pays for school infrastructure and other amenities (Pendall, Puentes, and Martin 2006). Other localities offer pro-development incentives, such as density bonuses in exchange for affordable housing and expedited permitting for the construction of affordable housing; and virtually all municipalities have building codes of one sort or another (Glaeser and Gyourko 2008). Gyourko, Saiz, and Summers (2008) have developed an overall index of the regulatory burden imposed on developers by zoning in different jurisdictions.

Although zoning regulations assume many forms and have been shown to influence both the supply and price of housing across areas (Malpezzi 1996; Glaeser and Gyourko 2003; Glaeser, Schuetz, and Ward 2006), the most widespread and powerful kind of land-use regulation is density zoning, which seeks to manage and control the number of residential units built per acre of land (Pendall, Puentes, and Martin. 2006). Glaeser, Gyourko, and Saks (2005) argue that homeowners and homeowner associations generally work to limit local development in order to foster the growth of home values and, hence, wealth. In contrast, Fischel (2004) points to class exclusion as the primary motive for zoning, whereas Fogelson (2005) underscores racist motivations that have permeated housing policy throughout American history. Whatever their motivation, density zoning rules have been found to exert the strongest effects on the cost and supply of housing relative to other forms of regulation (Glaeser and Ward 2006; Glaeser, Schuetz, and Ward 2006; Pendall, Puentes, and Martin

2006). As we outline below, it also has a very powerful effect in determining racial and class segregation. Density zoning, of course, lies at the heart of the Mount Laurel controversy.

The Ecology of Inequality

Human ecology is the study of how people distribute themselves in space, focusing on how different features of social structure and the built environment selectively channel people having different social, economic, political, and psychological traits into distinct segments of the urban geography. It also concerns itself with how residence in different ecological settings, in turn, shapes individual and family well-being along a variety of social and economic dimensions. The key point, originally made by theorists of the Chicago School of Sociology during the 1920s, is that social status and spatial location are very closely interconnected, and that to comprehend individual and group outcomes fully we must take both variables into account (Burgess 1925; Park 1926).

Although an appreciation of the close connection between social and spatial status lay at the core of American sociology for many decades, this linkage was submerged during the 1960s and 1970s as household surveys proliferated, computers came into widespread use, and statistical methods advanced to take advantage of the new abundance of data and computing power (Massey 2001). Detailed, nationally representative surveys, high-powered statistics, and complex methodologies allowed social scientists to undertake sophisticated analyses of social and economic processes unfolding among individuals and within households, the sampling units for most social surveys. Initially the surveys did not contain information on the neighborhoods in which respondents lived, and, as a result, quantitative research in social science became progressively disconnected from the ecological context within which decisions were made and social processes expressed.

The event that reintroduced space forcefully back into the mainstream of research, not just in sociology but in all of social science, was the publication of William Julius Wilson's 1987 book, *The Truly Disadvantaged*, in which he argued that whatever disadvantages individuals might experience by virtue of growing up and living in a poor family, they incurred *additional* penalties for growing up and living in a poor neighborhood. In other words, ecological context mattered in a very fundamental way that went well beyond individual characteristics or family circumstances. Wilson was the first American social scientist to realize that the world was changing in the 1970s and 1980s, and that poverty was becoming more *geographically concentrated.*

After 1987, space suddenly mattered a great deal to social scientists, and across disciplines, there was a sudden rush to measure ecological circumstances and estimate multilevel models that took into account the influence of neighborhoods on socioeconomic outcomes (see Sampson, Morenoff, and Gannon-Rowley 2002). Although the requisite contextual data files were initially scarce (Jencks and Mayer 1990), the situation soon improved, and research on housing, spatial segregation, and human ecology shifted from the back- to the front burner of social science research (Small and Newman 2001). In addition to the study of segregation by race, which had a long, unbroken history in the United States (Burgess 1928; Duncan and Duncan 1957; Taueber and Taueber 1965; Massey and Denton 1993; Iceland 2009), investigators took a new look at segregation by class and quickly discovered that accompanying the rise of income inequality was a simultaneous increase in the degree of residential segregation between rich and poor, and that it was not just poverty that was concentrating spatially, but affluence as well (Massey and Eggers 1990, 1993; Massey and Fischer 2003; Fischer et al. 2004; Reardon and Bischoff 2011).

Indeed, the past four decades have witnessed a remarkable surge in the degree of socioeconomic inequality within American society (Morris and Western 1999; Piketty and Saez 2003; Smeeding 2011). Since 1970, distributions of income and wealth have grown increasingly skewed as the affluent and wealthy have steadily pulled away from the rest of American society. According to statistics from the U.S. Census Bureau (2011a), the share of income earned by the top 5 percent of households grew from 17 percent in 1969 to 22 percent in 2009, and the Gini Index, which is the standard measure of income inequality, rose from 39.1 to 46.8 on a scale in which 0 indicates complete equality where all households exhibit the same income and 100 indicates complete inequality where one household earns all the money. The distribution of wealth is even more skewed, and from 1977 to 2007 the percentage of national wealth held by the top 1 percent of households went from 20 percent to 35 percent (Wolff 1996, 2010).

As economic inequality steadily increased, rich and poor households progressively sorted themselves into different kinds of neighborhoods to create a new ecology of poverty and privilege in the United States. Segregation is typically measured using the index of dissimilarity, which computes the percentage of two social groups (e.g., poor and affluent) that would have to exchange neighborhoods to achieve an even residential distribution (Massey and Denton 1988). When Massey and Fischer (2003) computed affluent-poor dissimilarity indices using census tract data for sixty metropolitan areas from 1970 to 2000, they found that the index rose from 29 to 37 over three decades, an increase of around 28 percent. Likewise when Reardon and Bischoff (2011b) computed an

alternative measure of income inequality known as the rank-order information theory index, they found that the value had risen by 24 percent between 1970 and 2007, going from 0.115 to 0.143 in metropolitan
areas of 500,000 or greater.

The uneven residential distribution of rich and poor across neighborhoods was accompanied by a growing spatial concentration of both affluence and poverty. The spatial concentration of people with any given
trait is customarily measured using the P* isolation index (Massey and
Eggers 1990). In measuring the concentration of poverty, the index gives
the percentage of poor families in the neighborhood of the average poor
person. When Massey and Fischer (2003) computed this index for the
sixty largest U.S. metropolitan areas, they found that the spatial concentration of poverty had risen from 14 to 25 between 1970 and 2000,
while the concentration of affluence had grown from 31 to 34. In other
words, at the turn of the millennium, the average poor person lived in a
neighborhood that was 25 percent poor and the average affluent person
lived in a neighborhood that was 34 percent affluent.

Using more recent data on 287 metropolitan areas broken down by
race and ethnicity, Rugh and Massey (2012) found a somewhat more
complicated story in which the concentration of poverty among whites
fell from 16 to 12 between 1970 and 1980 and then rose to 23 between
1980 and 1990 before declining slightly over the next seventeen years to
reach 21 in 2007. The concentration of poverty among blacks similarly
fell from 26 to 21 between 1970 and 1980 and then surged to 40 in
1990 before dropping back to 34 by 2007. Despite the modest declines
from 1990 to 2007, however, the level of poverty concentration in 2007
remained well above its 1980 nadir for both blacks and whites. As of
2007, the average poor white person lived in a neighborhood that was 21
percent poor and the average poor black person lived in a neighborhood
that was 34 percent poor.

Rugh and Massey (2012) found that the rise in the concentration of
affluence was even more impressive than the growth in the concentration
of poverty, beginning at a higher level in 1970 and rising more consistently in the ensuing years. Although the upward trend reached a plateau
between 1980 and 2000, the increases from 1970 to 1980 and from 2000
to 2007 were sharp, and over the whole period the index of concentrated
affluence went from 36 to 44 among whites and 19 to 34 among blacks,
figures well above their original values. In general, the concentration of
poverty rose most sharply for whites while the concentration of affluence
rose most sharply for blacks.

In the end, however, racial differentials remain quite large with respect
to the spatial concentration of both affluence and poverty. As of 2007 the
typical poor black household lived in a neighborhood that was 34 percent

poor compared with a figure of 21 percent for the typical poor white household, meaning that despite a narrowing of the gap, poor blacks still experienced a much greater concentration of poverty than poor whites. Likewise, in 2007 rich whites continued to enjoy a higher concentration of affluence than rich blacks, with the typical affluent white household inhabiting a neighborhood that was 44 percent affluent compared to a figure of 34 percent for the average affluent black household. Although the relative position of blacks improved in both cases, the improvement was disproportionately greater for affluent blacks than poor blacks. Thus the relative size of the black-white gap in concentrated affluence fell from 86 percent to 30 percent but the racial gap in concentrated poverty dropped only from 88 percent to 58 percent.

As class segregation increased and the spatial concentrations of both affluence and poverty rose in recent decades, however, the degree of black-white segregation steadily fell to create a more complex urban ecology characterized by a new interaction between race and class. Average black-white dissimilarity in the sixty largest metropolitan areas fell from 77 in 1970 to 60 in 2000 while the black P* isolation index dropped from 53 to around 30 (Massey, Rothwell, and Domina 2009). Whereas the average black person lived in a neighborhood that was majority black in 1970, by 2000 the typical African American lived in a neighborhood that was less than a third black.

Likewise, in their analysis of *all* metropolitan areas from 1980 through 2000, Iceland, Weinberg, and Steinmtez (2002) found that black-white dissimilarity dropped from 73 to 64 and black isolation fell from 66 to 59. Despite these declines, however, black segregation remains quite high in the United States, especially relative to other multiracial societies such as Canada (Fong 1994, 1996, 2006; Fong and Shibuya 2005) and Brazil (Telles 1992, 2004). Indeed, in 2000 roughly half of all urban blacks lived in metropolitan areas that could be defined as hypersegregated according to Massey and Denton's (1988) criteria, with African Americans living in ghettos characterized by exceptionally high levels of unevenness, isolation, clustering, centralization, and concentration (Massey 2004).

At the same time as these trends in black-white segregation were unfolding, the racial taxonomy of the United States was being radically transformed by immigration, shifting the nation from a binary division of people into black and white into a more variegated mosaic of hues that included Asians, Latin Americans, Caribbean Islanders, Africans, and Pacific Islanders, with many new and different phenotypes. Although other things equal, a rise in the number of Asian and Hispanics within U.S. metropolitan areas would tend to increase the demographic potential for segregation, the degree of Hispanic-white dissimilarity remained flat after 1980, rising from 50 in that year to just 51 two decades later;

and Asian-white dissimilarity likewise went from 40 to 41 over the same period (Iceland, Weinberg, and Steinmetz 2002). Although the degree of residential unevenness remained constant, however, rising numbers of Hispanics and Asians crowding into neighborhoods nonetheless brought about an increase in the degree of spatial isolation of both groups, with the P* isolation index for Hispanics rising from 45 to 55 and that for Asians going from to 23 to 31 (Iceland, Weinberg, and Steinmetz 2002). At the end of the twentieth century, in other words, the average Hispanic lived in a neighborhood that was 55 percent Hispanic and the average Asian lived in a neighborhood that was 31 percent Asian.

The foregoing trends were mirrored in the state of New Jersey. From 1970 to 2010, the number of Asians grew from around 23,000 to around 726,000 while the Hispanic population went from 310,000 to 1.555 million.[1] Over the same period, the black population grew from 770,000 to just 1.142 million, meaning that Hispanics surpassed them as the state's largest minority group. Black-white dissimilarity across New Jersey's census tracts peaked at 74 in 1980, and by 2010 had fallen to 67, while black isolation dropped from 56 to 43. Over the same period, Hispanic-white dissimilarity fell from 65 to 58; but owing to the huge increase in the number of Latinos, Hispanic isolation rose from 16 to 40. With respect to class, affluent-poor residential dissimilarity fluctuated around a value of 45 between 1970 and 2010, but because the number of poor and affluent surged as inequality rose, the poor isolation index rose from 15 to 21 while the affluent isolation increased from 39 to 52. Thus, in the Garden State the typical affluent person lives in a neighborhood where more than half of that person's neighbors are also affluent.

In both New Jersey and the nation as a whole, after 2000, U.S. urban ecology was increasingly characterized by declining black-white dissimilarity, falling black isolation, steady levels of Hispanic-white and Asian-white dissimilarity, and slowly rising levels of Hispanic and Asian isolation. These racial trends were accompanied by rising class segregation and growing spatial concentrations of affluence and poverty. In sum, whereas the old ecology of inequality was structured by modest differences in income and purchasing power that produced low levels of class segregation, combined with high levels of prejudice and racial discrimination that produced high levels of black-white segregation, the new urban ecology was characterized by falling levels of racial discrimination and sharper differences in purchasing power to yield a trend of falling black-white segregation and rising class segregation. Moreover, although the moderation in discrimination produced flat trends in Hispanic and Asian

---

[1] The authors thank Jacob Rugh for the calculations reported in this paragraph.

segregation, their increased numbers nonetheless produced more spatial isolation for both groups.

As a result, purchasing power, rents, and housing prices increasingly dominate locational decisions and increasingly condition segregation patterns in the United States. Although real estate markets by definition discriminate on the basis of price and the ability to pay, high levels of class segregation do not necessarily follow from this fact alone. Whereas racial discrimination necessarily brings about the exclusion of minority groups from majority residential areas, price discrimination will do so only if expensive and affordable housing units are located in different neighborhoods. Everyone would like to live in a desirable residential area, of course, and the price of land in desirable locations is generally bid up to produce high land values (Mills and Hamilton 1997; O'Sullivan 2008). Nonetheless, even if land is expensive developers can still satisfy the demand for housing emanating from lower-class households by using it more intensively. Instead of building large single-family homes on large lots, they can simply buy a lot and erect a multi-unit structure to amortize the high cost of land over a larger number of buyers or renters.

In a totally "free" real estate market, therefore, developers—especially nonprofit developers—could buy land in affluent, desirable areas and erect apartment buildings containing affordable units for lower-income families; but of course real estate markets do not work this way in practice. As noted above, housing markets are not "free" but instead are structured by zoning and land-use regulations. Affluent residents in desirable areas, in order to preserve their privileges and maximize property values, enact government policies to prevent unwanted land uses (e.g., toxic waste facilities) and unwanted population groups (e.g., poor minorities) from entering the privileged confines of their enclaves (Orfield 2002; Fischel 2004; Fogelson 2005; Glaeser, Gyourko, and Saks 2005; Levine 2005; Massey 2008).

The more decentralized the system of government, the easier it is to enact this kind of exclusion. A locally concentrated population of economically homogenous people naturally share common use and exchange values and possess similar attitudes toward social and economic outsiders, and they can easily use their local majority to gain effective control over municipal government and compel local planning authorities to maintain a low maximum allowable residential density, thereby restricting the supply of housing and raising home values to prevent the entry of lower-income households (Massey 1996). Because Hispanics and blacks generally evince lower incomes than whites, this class-based exclusion perforce also forestalls the entry of minority households. With the municipality dominated by affluent households with few social problems, its affluent residents can give themselves lavish services while paying modest taxes (Massey 1996).

Density zoning uses regulations of various sorts to limit the number of dwelling units allowed per unit of land. These regulations may explicitly set a maximum allowable density, but they may also achieve low residential densities by less direct means, such as enforcing lot size restrictions, enacting setback requirements, and writing expensive and burdensome building codes. Although density zoning was sparingly deployed in the United States before 1970, since then it has risen to become increasingly prominent throughout the United States, especially in suburbs surrounding older central cities (Pendall 2000; Fischel 2004). In New Jersey, especially, a recent study found that land use has become substantially more exclusionary since the mid-1980s (Hasse, Reiser, and Pichacz 2011). As a result, half of all residential development since 1986 has occurred on lots of an acre or more, and two-thirds has occurred on lots of at least one-half acre.

Density zoning is now the most important mechanism promoting class and racial segregation, both in the United States generally and in New Jersey particularly (Rothwell 2011; Rothwell and Massey 2009, 2010; Hasse, Reiser, and Pichacz 2011). The greater the maximum residential density allowed in the suburbs of U.S. metropolitan areas, the lower the degree of racial segregation, the lower the level of black isolation, the lower the degree of class segregation, the lower the spatial concentration of poverty, and the lower the concentration of affluence. At the same time, higher allowable densities predict more rapid shifts toward racial and class integration; and instrumental variable regression estimates suggest these relationships are not simply associational, but causal (Rothwell 2011; Rothwell and Massey 2009, 2010).

Spatial Polarization and Public Policy

The simultaneous rise of zoning and the decline of racial discrimination in the production and maintenance of housing segregation is largely a product of the post–civil rights era. As already noted, local governments sought to achieve racial segregation by fiat early in the twentieth century, but in 1917 the Supreme Court held that laws mandating separate black and white residential areas were unconstitutional. Between 1920 and 1970 private discrimination replaced public policy as the principal motor of segregation (Massey and Denton 1993). During the 1920s the real estate industry developed devices such as deed restrictions and restrictive covenants to prevent the entry of blacks into white neighborhoods. The former attached a clause to property titles that forbade subsequent sale to

African Americans and other unwanted groups (e.g., Jews), whereas the latter were contracts between homeowners within a specific geographic area in which residents mutually agreed not to rent or sell properties to African Americans and other unwanted groups. The contracts became enforceable when a majority of owners had signed, and thereafter those within the area who violated the contract could be sued in civil court.

Although the Supreme Court declared restrictive covenants to be unenforceable in its 1948 *Shelly v. Kramer* decision, the FHA continued to require them for several years more (Massey and Denton 1993). Individual and institutional refusals to rent or sell to minority-group members remained perfectly legal for decades thereafter, and racial discrimination was widely practiced throughout the United States into the 1960s. It was the passage of four laws late in the civil rights era that finally turned the tide against housing discrimination and segregation (Metcalf 1988). In 1968 Congress passed the Fair Housing Act to outlaw racial discrimination in the sale and renting of housing. In 1974 it enacted the Equal Credit Opportunity Act to ban discrimination in mortgage lending; and it followed up in 1975 with the Home Mortgage Disclosure Act requiring lenders to publish data on the race and ethnicity of applicants, thereby enabling enforcement of the 1974 act. Finally in 1977 Congress passed the Community Reinvestment Act to prohibit the practice of redlining, which historically had cut off the supply of mortgage capital to black neighborhoods.

After the 1970s, overt discrimination declined and institutionalized practices to exclude minorities largely disappeared from view. Nonetheless, audit studies reveal that covert racial discrimination continues in real estate and lending markets in a variety of guises (Squires 1994; Yinger 1995; Turner et al., 2002; Charles 2003; Ross and Turner 2004; Squires 2007). In an audit study, researchers organize a series of encounters between minority and majority group auditors, who are trained to pose as buyers with equivalent characteristics, and sellers in some market of interest. Over a series of encounters, investigators keep track of systematic differences in the treatment of minority and majority auditors to reveal hidden patterns of discrimination. Audit studies indicate that new, surreptitious, and more subtle forms of discrimination have been invented in the wake of the civil rights era (Massey 2005). These include name discrimination against people with stereotypically "black" names (Bertrand and Mullainathan 2004), linguistic profiling against people with "black" accents (Purnell, Idsardi, and Baugh 1999; Massey and Lundy 2001; Fischer and Massey 2004; Squires and Chadwick 2006), predatory lending that targets black borrowers for subprime loan products (Lord 2004; Squires 2004), and reverse redlining that targets entire black neighborhoods to be sold risky financial instruments (Smith and DeLair 1999;

Turner et al. 2002; Friedman and Squires 2005; Brescia 2009; Rugh and Massey 2010).

Despite the covert continuation of discrimination in real estate and lending markets, however, black-white segregation has nonetheless steadily declined over the past decades (Massey, Rothwell, and Domina 2009). As overt discrimination has declined, moreover, differences in purchasing power have become more salient in determining where people live and density zoning rises as a key mechanism promoting and sustaining segregation on the basis of income and race (Rothwell 2011; Rothwell and Massey 2009, 2010). Although private fair housing groups, public authorities, and aggrieved individuals continue to combat discrimination by suing developers, lenders, and real estate agents in court, over time these actions have become weaker arrows in the quiver of antisegregation measures. In a world where overt discrimination has largely vanished from public view, subtle forms of discrimination are hard to detect, and density zoning now functions as a principal cause of segregation. In response, fair housing advocates have sought new ways to promote residential integration.

The most salient and visible of the new tools to which they have turned are programs designed to promote housing mobility for minorities and the poor. Indeed, housing mobility policies have been proposed not simply as a means to promote racial and class integration, but as a way to combat poverty and promote socioeconomic mobility more generally (de Souza Briggs, Popkin, and Goering 2010). Rather than striving to change real estate marketing and lending practices, housing mobility programs offer poor households the chance to escape distressed, disadvantaged neighborhoods and move into more attractive, advantaged areas, thus reducing threats to well-being and offering greater access to social and economic resources such as jobs and education (Goering and Fines 2003; de Souza Briggs 2005). Very often but certainly not always, the affluent neighborhoods are located in suburbs of large metropolitan areas (Rosenbaum and Rubinowitz 2000).

Historically, residential mobility programs have taken one of two forms: either they have supported the construction of subsidized housing projects containing affordable units and made these units accessible to poor families currently living in substandard units elsewhere; or as an alternative they have given poor families a direct subsidy, usually in the form of a housing voucher, that allows them to move into a better but more expensive unit in an advantaged residential area with some public authority covering the difference between the market rent and what the household can afford (Schwartz 2006; Varady and Walker 2007).

The construction of affordable housing and its allocation to poor families dates back to the New Deal and the National Industrial Recovery Act of 1933, which created the Public Works Administration. Under its authority, federal authorities razed slum neighborhoods and replaced them with low-cost public-housing projects, initially to house PWA workers. When the Supreme Court ruled that the PWA lacked the right of eminent domain and could not engage in the wholesale clearance of neighborhoods, Congress responded by passing the Housing Act of 1937, which authorized the creation of local public-housing authorities and set aside federal funds to allow these authorities to construct low-income housing projects (Hirsch 1983; Schwartz 2006).

Owing to the persistence of the Great Depression and the Second World War, however, little housing was constructed under the 1933 and 1937 Acts, and it wasn't until 1949 that amendments to the Housing Act increased its scope and funding sufficiently to launch large-scale urban-renewal projects and massive public-housing construction. Although federally funded housing projects were initially seen as providing temporary dwellings to deserving but poor working families who were temporarily down on their luck, during the 1950s and 1960s public housing was increasingly combined with large-scale urban renewal in an effort to contain the spread of black ghettos, reinforce the residential color line, and isolate families on the basis of class as well as race (Hirsch 1983; Turner, Popkin, and Rawlings 2008; Hunt 2009). Instead of temporary housing, by the 1970s, public housing had become home to a spatially immobile, quasi-permanent underclass living within new, high-rise ghettos (Hirsch 1983; Massey and Denton 1993).

As it became increasingly obvious that public housing was being used in discriminatory ways to perpetuate rather than ameliorate race and class isolation, in the late 1960s civil rights leaders took to the courts to challenge the policies of local housing authorities (Polikoff 2006). In 1966 Dorothy Gautreaux launched such a challenge by filing suit against the Chicago Housing Authority (CHA) and the U.S. Department of Housing and Urban Development (HUD) on behalf of herself and other public-housing tenants, alleging that the CHA and HUD had violated federal law by racially discriminating in the selection of project sites and in the allocation of people to projects (Hirsch 1983; Varnarelli 1986). In 1969 the U.S. Supreme Court decided in favor of the plaintiffs in *Hill v. Gautreaux*, but as was the case in Mount Laurel, a series of appeals delayed final resolution of the case until 1981, when a federal judge finally approved a consent decree under which CHA and HUD accepted responsibility for past racial discrimination and agreed to allocate some 7,100 subsidized rental vouchers to public-housing residents for use in securing private rental units in the city and surrounding suburbs (Rosenbaum et al. 199; Kaufman and Rosenbaum 1992).

Once the *Gautreaux* ruling put a stop to the selective razing of black neighborhoods and the systematic targeting of high-density family housing to adjacent areas, local authorities ceased proposing urban-renewal projects and ended the construction of high-density public housing (Massey and Denton 1993). The *Gautreaux* decision coincided with the end of Lyndon Johnson's War on Poverty and led to a scaling back of government programs and a shift toward market-based policy solutions under Richard Nixon. With public housing construction at a virtual standstill but housing needs still pressing, in 1974 Congress amended Section 8 of the 1937 National Housing Act to create two new housing voucher programs that relied on private markets rather than public housing authorities to make housing available to the poor. One program was "project based" and the other "tenant based." In the former, cooperating landlords and developers agreed to reserve a certain share of units for low-income families who were given "Section 8 Certificates" to cover the difference between the market rent and a third of their income. In the latter, these certificates were given directly to individuals or families to use in private rental markets, where they could apply the voucher toward a portion of the market rent demanded by a private landlord (Varady and Walker 2007).

By the 1980s, even liberals had come to see high-density housing projects for the poor as perpetuating rather than alleviating the endless cycle of urban poverty (Venkatesh 2000; Husock 2003; Polikoff 2006; Hunt 2009; Cisneros and Engdahl 2009). In this context, voucher-based residential mobility programs became increasingly attractive, despite their Republican origins. Notably, the remedy in the *Gautreaux* settlement required participating families to use Section 8 vouchers to move into integrated and suburban neighborhoods (Rubinowitz and Rosenbaum 2000). Some *Gautreaux* families, however, were allowed to move into predominantly black neighborhoods in Chicago if it was determined that they were "revitalizing" communities (Marelli 1986; Keels et al. 2005).

The Gautreaux Demonstration Project was set up after the fact to follow city versus suburban movers and to compare their subsequent socioeconomic trajectories (Rubinowitz and Rosenbaum 2000). Results indicated that city movers ended up in tracts that averaged 47 percent black and 27 percent poor whereas suburban movers ended up in tracts averaging 6 percent black and 5 percent poor (Keels et al., 2005). Although the two groups initially appeared statistically identical, once removed from the inner city, suburban movers were found to earn higher wages and to display higher employment rates while their children achieved better grades, lower dropout rates, and higher rates of college attendance than families who remained behind in the city (Rosenbaum, Kulieke, and Rubinowitz 1987; Rosenbaum and Popkin 1990, 1991; Rosenbaum 1991; Rosenbaum et al., 1991). Mendenhall, DeLuca, and Duncan (2006) also showed that women placed in predominantly white neighborhoods with resources evinced significantly higher earnings than those placed in predominantly African American neighborhoods with low resources.

Although results such as these suggested the efficacy of voucher programs in promoting both desegregation and socioeconomic mobility, the Gautreaux Demonstration Project was not based on an experimental design, and critics quickly questioned the validity of its conclusions. Nonetheless its findings were promising enough to help justify two new HUD housing initiatives in the 1990s. The first was the HOPE VI Program, authorized by Congress in 1993 to demolish distressed public-housing projects in cities around the country and construct new housing developments through public-private partnerships. HOPE VI also repealed federal regulations that had required housing authorities to replace demolished housing units on a one-for-one basis. It also rescinded the requirement that housing authorities give preference to extremely poor families, leading to a decline in the number of heavily subsidized units throughout metropolitan America (Popkin et al., 2004). In the course of redevelopment under HOPE VI, some of the displaced residents would be housed in new units rebuilt on-site whereas others would receive assignments to other housing projects or Section 8 vouchers to use in the private market (Schwartz 2006).

Although the original goals of HOPE VI were to reconstruct public housing at lower densities and to empower project residents, over time the program broadened to embrace the goals of economic integration, poverty deconcentration, inner-city revival, and social mobility (Popkin et al., 2004; Schwartz 2006; Cisneros and Engdahl 2009). Unfortunately the HOPE VI initiatives—and mobility programs more broadly—appear not to have adequately met the needs of the most troubled residents of the public-housing projects that were taken down, whatever their effects on other residents (Popkin et al 2004). The forced relocation of households disrupted families' social networks and support systems and disempowered residents—particularly the elderly, residents with disabilities, and children (Crowley 2009). Assessing the consequences of HOPE VI for public-housing residents, Crowley (2009) concluded that more people were harmed than were helped.

The second initiative was the Moving to Opportunity Demonstration Project (MTO). Unlike the Gautreaux Demonstration Project, it was designed as an experiment from the outset, with random assignment of public-housing residents in five urban areas to one of three comparison groups. Those in the experimental group were assigned Section 8 vouchers and required to use them to move into a neighborhood with a poverty rate of 10 percent or less; those in the traditional voucher group were given Section 8 vouchers but could use them to move wherever they wanted; and those in the control group were not offered vouchers and experienced no experimentally induced change to their residential circumstances (de Souza Briggs, Popkin, and Goering 2010).

The five cities targeted for the MTO experiment were Baltimore, Boston, Chicago, Los Angeles, and New York. To be eligible for participation in MTO, tenants had to live in high-poverty census tracts (greater than 40 percent poor), have children under the age of eighteen, and agree to go through Section 8 eligibility determination. Built into the program's design was a longitudinal survey of study participants that interviewed them prior to moving, kept track of subsequent moves, and surveyed them afterward (de Souza Briggs, Popkin, and Goering 2010). Although the project was designed as an experiment, in practice the experimental design didn't hold up for very long into the study (Clampet-Lundquist and Massey 2008).

Among those randomly assigned to be experimental subjects and move into low-poverty neighborhoods, only half accepted the proffered vouchers and moved, yielding a selective uptake process that was decidedly nonrandom (Clampet-Lundquist and Massey 2008). An additional layer of selection occurred after experimental subjects had relocated to nonpoor neighborhoods because they were under no obligation to remain in those neighborhoods for more than a year. Over time there was widespread and nonrandom movement of experimental subjects back into poor areas (Clampet-Lundquist and Massey 2008).

In addition to these departures from experimental control, the MTO Demonstration Project suffered from other drawbacks. The study's design, for example, confounded the effects of moving with the effects of living in a low-poverty neighborhood. Moves are always disruptive, and study participants necessarily experienced a rupture of their social networks in addition to entering new and unfamiliar social environments within neighborhoods that were not necessarily close to jobs, transportation, or services. Although the neighborhoods that experimental subjects occupied before moving may have been poor and disadvantaged, they were often centrally located close to public transportation and downtown job centers. In addition, most project residents were deeply embedded within extensive social networks of support after several generations of project residence (Clampet-Lundquist 2004a, 2004b, 2007, 2010). As a result, even those experimental subjects who would ultimately go on to forge a path out of poverty initially suffered setbacks and required an extended period of adjustment to come back from the shock of relocation. For most families, the required year of residence did not offer enough time to recover, and even for those who remained in low-poverty neighborhoods the benefits only accrued gradually whereas the costs of moving were immediate and powerful (Clampet-Lundquist and Massey 2008). After any move, even a beneficial one, it takes time to reconstruct the social networks and daily routines that make life easier.

Another problematic element of the MTO design was that experimental subjects were not required to use their vouchers to enter racially integrated or suburban neighborhoods (just low-poverty neighborhoods), as had been true of participants in the Gautreaux Demonstration Project. As a result nearly three-quarters simply traded locations within the ghetto by moving between high- and low-poverty black, inner-city neighborhoods; and the decision to enter an integrated versus segregated neighborhood was highly selective, as were later moves back into segregated, high-poverty circumstances (Clampet-Lundquist and Massey 2008). As a result of widespread selective migration after assignment, most experimental subjects accumulated relatively little time in low-poverty settings, and the time spent within low-poverty neighborhoods that were also racially integrated was particularly limited. By the time of the interim evaluation, nearly half of all experimental subjects who had moved were already living back in a poor, racially segregated neighborhood (Clampet-Lundquist and Massey 2008).

Possibly as result of these design problems, the MTO project yielded a mixed set of results. Although analyses indicated that MTO was indeed successful in moving people out of poor neighborhoods and that the move led participating adults to feel safer and more satisfied with their housing and neighborhood, which yielded positive effects for their mental health, over the longer term, investigators could detect no effect on labor-market outcomes or social-program participation. In addition, among children the move did not improve educational outcomes or math and reading scores; and although the move improved the mental health of girls and reduced the likelihood of their engaging in risky behaviors, it had the opposite effect among boys (Kling, Liebman, and Katz 2007; Ludwig et al., 2008).

Despite the mixed record of results, housing mobility programs continue to be discussed actively both as a remedy for racial and class segregation and for poverty reduction and social mobility. Indeed, the salience of such increased after a 2009 federal court decision (*Anti-Discrimination of Metro New York, Inc., v. Westchester County*) found a white suburban New York county guilty of falsely representing its efforts to overcome segregation on HUD funding applications. For many years HUD has required its grantees to exhibit "affirmative efforts" to overcome the legacy of housing segregation as a condition of funding (see Termine 2010). In the New York case, the court found that although Westchester officials had indeed been working to develop affordable housing in the county, they were doing so in a way that did not advance the goal of desegregation. HUD withheld an estimated $15–$20 million of funding to the county until it could develop a suitable integration plan. The Westchester controversy is ongoing.

In its settlement with the court, the county agreed to build 750 units of affordable housing at the cost of $52 million, with 750 of the units to be located in communities containing little ethnic and racial diversity. The decision mirrors an earlier 1985 desegregation case against Yonkers, New York, in which the city was found guilty of developing nearly all of its 700 units of affordable housing in areas that already had high percentages of poor racial and ethnic minorities. As a remedy, the town was ordered to desegregate its housing through the development of scattered site units throughout the municipality (Briggs et al., 1999).

Mount Laurel in Context

The mantra "location cubed" underscores the importance of place in human affairs. Dwellings are inevitably tied to neighborhoods, which in turn define a social, economic, cultural, and political environment that shapes life trajectories to affect individual and family well-being along a variety of dimensions (Sampson 2012). Urban housing markets are complex because homes and neighborhoods evince both use and exchange value to market participants, yielding divergent motivations across actors that often come into conflict. Places are also imbued with emotion, and living space is nonsubstitutable, producing a high-stakes arena for intense struggles over land use and market outcomes. Land-use decisions are controversial precisely because place does matter—indeed it matters a lot, and its importance only appears to be rising in the current political economy.

It is hardly surprising, therefore, that the Mount Laurel study occurs against a backdrop of controversy and debate both inside and outside the academic community. Outside the academy, the use of Section 8 certificates and the construction of affordable housing projects for poor families continue to constitute a "third rail" in suburban politics—too hot to touch without a politician getting shocked and burned. Whenever plans for an affordable housing project are announced, or the entry of Section 8 Certificate holders is projected, a firestorm of protest and opposition tends to erupt in suburban areas, as it did in Mount Laurel. The issue of affordable family housing is especially fraught in New Jersey, since it is the nation's most densely populated state in which property taxes are high, open space is scarce, and many communities see themselves as fully "built out."

Prior to the mid-1990s there was little systematic, methodologically defensible research to draw on in deciding how affordable housing actually influenced surrounding neighborhoods and communities; but since then a growing number of statistically sophisticated evaluations have been done, focused primarily on how affordable housing affects local property values (see Galster 2004; Nguyen, 2004; Koebel, Lang, and Danielsen. 2004). These studies generally focus on affordable housing for poor families rather than housing for the elderly, as the latter rarely spark significant controversy, and most examine central city areas rather than suburban areas, as in Denver (Santiago et al., 2001), Memphis (Babb et al., 1984), Minneapolis (Goetz et al., 1996), Philadelphia (Lee et al., 1999), and Portland (Rabiega et al., 1984). An exception is Funder-burg and MacDonald's 2010 study of Low-Income Housing Tax Credit (LIHTC) developments in Polk County, Iowa, which includes portions of suburban Des Moines. Their study found that clustered LIHTC housing developments were associated with a 2–4 percent slowing of property-value appreciation among nearby single family homes that were matched with comparable homes elsewhere in the same county; but they also found that this effect was negligible when the housing was high quality and mixed-income.

The results of studies conducted through 2008 were summarized by Ahrentzen (2008) in a report to the Housing Research Synthesis Project at Arizona State University's Stardust Center for Affordable Homes and Families. Her review suggests that no one comprehensive answer exists to the question of whether affordable housing lowers property values. Instead, the size and direction of effects depends on five factors: whether the project replaces existing blighted property or is built on vacant land; the degree to which the housing is dense and geographically concentrated; whether the project is surrounded by a stable, low-poverty neighborhood or a vulnerable, high-poverty neighborhood; the quality of the project's management and maintenance; and the quality and aesthetics of the project's architecture and its compatibility with the surrounding stock of suburban housing. Although little work has been done on how tenant characteristics affect surrounding property values, three other characteristics of affordable housing projects have been found not to matter—namely type of ownership, type of subsidy, and whether the project consists of single family, multifamily, or town house units (Ahrentzen 2008).

Studies have long linked the construction of high-density family projects in inner cities to increased crime and social disorder in surrounding neighborhoods (Newman 1972; Roncek, Bell, and Francik 1981; Sampson 1990; Bursick and Grasmick 1992; Holzman 1996; McNulty and Holloway 2000: Popkin et al., 2000), but to date little research has considered the effect of low-density affordable housing projects in suburbs. In their study of affordable family housing projects in Baltimore and Denver, Galster et al. (2003) found no effect on crime rates, except in those cases where a development was constructed near an existing high-density housing project. In their study of affordable family housing developed under the federal Low-Income Housing Tax Credit Program, Freedman and Owens (2011) found that affordable housing developments were actually associated with a reduction in violent crime.

The relationship between affordable housing and crime has recently become the subject of extensive speculation and contentious debate in the non-academic arena. In a 2008 article in *The Atlantic*, Rosin (2008) suggested a direct causal link between public housing deconcentration under HOPE VI and a dramatic increase in violent crime in inner suburbs of Memphis and other cities, but her article was more anecdotal and impressionistic than analytical and has been strongly criticized by social scientists (see Briggs and Dreier 2008). In contrast to the attention paid to property values and crime rates, virtually no work has been done to consider the effect of affordable housing developments on property tax burdens experienced by residents of surrounding neighborhoods and the host municipality.

As evidenced by the foregoing citations, academics and not just suburban dwellers and politicians are keenly interested in the effects of affordable housing on communities and neighborhoods, though the issue and the results have been less emotional and not as controversial for scholars as for suburban homeowners faced with the prospect of affordable housing in their backyards. Rather than obsessing about the effects of poor people on neighborhoods, academics have spent more time and energy debating the effects of neighborhoods on poor people and the resulting "neighborhood effects" literature, largely spawned by Wilson's 1987 book, remains quite controversial.

Although it is now well accepted that exposure to neighborhood advantage and disadvantage significantly and often strongly predicts individual and family outcomes with respect to a variety of key outcomes, including health, cognitive skills, education, labor-force participation, earnings, family formation, fertility, crime, and delinquency (Sampson, Morenoff and Gannon-Rowley 2002; Sampson, Sharkey, and Raudenbush 2008; Sampson and Sharkey. 2008; Sampson 2009, 2012), the controversy lies in whether these relationships are causal, stemming directly from neighborhood circumstances themselves, or spurious, emanating from some unmeasured endogenous variable associated with both neighborhood circumstances and social outcomes, or from a selective process of migration between neighborhoods in which poor people with serious problems concentrate themselves in space (Tienda 1991).

Many scholars hoped that MTO would settle the debate, but in the end it only extended the controversy. As already noted, however, MTO suggested that neighborhood conditions did influence the mental health of adults but had no effect on adult economic independence, leading some to conclude that, when it comes to the reproduction of urban poverty, "neighborhoods don't matter." In response, critics listed a variety of reasons why broader socioeconomic benefits may not have been detected: only the *offer* of a voucher was randomized; exposure to the experimental treatment was selective; residential mobility after assignment was widespread and nonrandom; low-poverty neighborhoods were still racially segregated; the design confounded improved neighborhood circumstances with the disruptions of moving; and in the end most experimental subjects spent relatively little time in advantaged settings before moving back to high-poverty neighborhoods (Clampett-Lundquist and Massey 2008).

Although ongoing debates about the effect of affordable housing on people and neighborhoods have yet to be resolved, the issues are critically important for the United States given the sharp polarization of America's urban ecology in recent decades. The racial diversification of metropolitan America, combined with rising class segregation and the moderation of racial segregation, has produced a complex social ecology in which density zoning plays a leading role in determining levels and trends in both racial and class segregation, which brings us back to the central issue in the Mount Laurel case. In filing suit against the township, plaintiffs argued that Mount Laurel's zoning regulations effectively prohibited the entry of poor minorities, in violation of New Jersey's Constitution. From the viewpoint of township residents and local officials, they were only protecting their hard-won piece of the American Dream by blocking the entry of land uses (multi-unit developments) and populations (poor families) that imperiled their community by threatening to raise taxes, increase crime, lower property values, and generally disrupt their suburban way of life.

From our discussion of the political economy of place, we can see that neighbors and community members were simply mobilizing in defense of the projected exchange value latent in their homes (fearing a decline of property values) and the perceived use value of their neighborhoods (fearing a rise in crime rates). Prospective tenants, in contrast, were mobilizing to improve the use value of their residential environment (upgrading the quality of housing and improving neighborhood conditions) while having little stake in the exchange value either at their places of origin or in the proposed place of destination (since they were renters and not property owners). Affordable-housing developers and fair-housing advocates, meanwhile, were seeking a mechanism to combat the powerful forces that enforced racial and class segregation in New Jersey and thus heaped disadvantage on poor minorities. Township officials, for their part, were compelled to adjudicate these conflicting values and interests and naturally sided with the township residents who had elected them (in the end, vigorously opposing the proposed development in court).

Given the strong bonds and sentimental attachments of Mount Laurel residents to their homes and neighborhoods, as well as the large financial stake they had in home ownership and property values, the conflict proved divisive, acrimonious, and highly emotional. In the next chapter we take a closer look at the emotion and controversy surrounding Mount Laurel's opposition to the Ethel Lawrence Homes as a prelude to our systematic study of the project's effects on neighbors, the community, and tenants.

CHAPTER 2
━━━━━━━

Suburban Showdown

THE MOUNT LAUREL CONTROVERSY

Mount Laurel Township is located eight miles east of Camden, New Jersey, a decaying industrial suburb of Philadelphia that once housed dozens of factories owned by blue-chip firms such as RCA, Campbell's Soup, and New York Shipbuilding, Inc. At its peak in 1950, the city of Camden housed 125,000 people who comprised a vibrant middle- and working-class community. During the 1960s, however, the city entered a spiral of urban decline as factories closed, stores departed, services evaporated, and working families exited for better opportunities in surrounding areas. As of 2010, Camden's population stood at just 77,000 and was half black and 42 percent Hispanic, mostly Puerto Rican, with 38 percent of families living in poverty (U.S. Census Bureau 2011b). In 2009 the city achieved the dubious distinction of having the highest crime rate in the nation, with 2,333 violent crimes per 100,000 persons (Hirsch 2009). Three of the city's recent mayors have been jailed for corruption, and in 2005 the State of New Jersey was forced to assume control over the City of Camden, including both the school system and the police department. To people throughout the region, Camden—even more than Philadelphia, its neighbor across the Delaware River—epitomizes urban dysfunction.

One of the places that white working families left Camden for was Mount Laurel Township. When Camden reached its peak population of 125,000 inhabitants in 1950, Mount Laurel was still a sleepy rural hamlet of just 2,800 persons. In the ensuing decades, however, the township was radically transformed from an isolated farming community into a sprawling suburb within the greater Philadelphia area. The construction of two superhighways, the New Jersey Turnpike in the 1950s and Interstate 295 in the 1960s, provided local residents with four on-ramps that offered a quick link to job centers throughout the region. With excellent highway accessibility, Mount Laurel's farms were soon transformed into four large Planned Unit Developments projected ultimately to house ten thousand families, along with a number of smaller residential subdivisions as well as numerous retail centers, office complexes, and light industrial parks offering thousands of jobs. By 1960 the population had nearly doubled to 5,200, and by 1970 it had doubled again to 11,200 residents, growing rapidly thereafter to reach 18,000 in 1980, 30,000 in 1990, 40,000 in 2000, and 45,000 by 2010 (U.S. Census Bureau 2011b).

As the new superhighways sliced through local farms they displaced low-income, mostly African American, tenant–farm workers, who comprised a substantial portion of Mount Laurel's population and often had multiple generations of residence in the township. With few local housing choices available, many of these longtime residents moved into the township's Springville neighborhood, a ramshackle area of converted farm structures, modest summer cottages not fit for year-round use, and shacks lacking indoor plumbing. Township officials quickly began to step up code enforcement in the neighborhood, however, often condemning the housing as unfit for habitation and tearing it down whenever they could. In some cases, they simply waited for families to get tired of living in squalor and move out. Then the township would condemn the property and raze the dilapidated structures without having to assume responsibility for rehabilitating the housing or relocating the residents. One family who lived in a converted chicken coop said they were considered lucky because they had a concrete floor. Many other converted structures were built over hard-packed dirt floors, with leaky roofs and raw sewage regularly backing up into the house through whatever plumbing it had (Lawrence-Haley 2007).

New Jersey's landmark Mount Laurel Doctrine on exclusionary zoning and affordable housing arose from the actions of Springville residents to deal with this dire situation (Kirp, Dwyer, and Rosenthal 1995; Fair Share Housing 2011). With no realistic alternative other than moving into the slums of Camden or Philadelphia, residents grew increasingly concerned about the rising pressure to leave. Many foresaw a systematic displacement of the township's historical black community, achieved through the vice grip of deteriorating housing that spurred abandonment and condemnation by township authorities leading to displacement—a "kinder, gentler" form of the ethnic cleansing then unfolding in cities such as Philadelphia through massive urban renewal, large-scale redevelopment, and monumental public-housing construction (Jones 2004).

One resident with these concerns was Ethel Lawrence, a sixth-generation African American resident of Mount Laurel, certified day-care teacher, mother of nine, and member of the Burlington County Community Action Program. She immediately realized that unless deliberate actions were taken, Mount Laurel would not be home to the next generation of her family. According to her daughter, she "saw other family, neighbors, and friends who had lived in the Mount Laurel community for many generations being displaced, because while Mount Laurel officials were condemning and tearing down the substandard homes in which many of these 'lower income' people lived, no efforts were being made to assist them in relocating elsewhere in the community" (Lawrence-Haley 2007).

In 1967 Ethel Lawrence joined with other local residents to form the Springville Community Action Committee, which was established with the explicit goal of bringing subsidized housing to Mount Laurel. The nonprofit obtained seed money from the State of New Jersey and in 1968 optioned a 32-acre parcel in Springville, along Hartford Road, and began drawing up plans to build thirty-six two- and three-bedroom garden apartments affordable to low-income renters. This was the genesis of the suburban showdown that became regional and then national news and led to the landmark New Jersey Supreme Court ruling establishing what became known as "the Mount Laurel Doctrine" (Kirp, Dwyer, and Rosenthal 1995).

The Road to Mount Laurel I

Developing the proposed multifamily affordable housing required Springville committee members to obtain three key approvals from the Township of Mount Laurel. First, since local zoning ordinances prohibited multifamily housing except within the four Planned Unit Developments, which exclusively provided for middle- and upper-class home development, the 32-acre parcel would either have to be rezoned or granted a variance by local officials to permit construction of the proposed low-income, multi-unit project. Second, the Springville Community Action Committee required township approval to obtain a "resolution of need" in order to obtain necessary federal and state housing subsidies so that the apartments, when constructed, would be affordable to low-income families. Finally, the site for the proposed housing project needed to be connected to the township's public water and sewage systems, which obviously required its concurrence.

Figure 2.1 offers readers a time line to summarize the Mount Laurel case from start to finish in order to facilitate following the complex story of the Ethel Lawrence Homes. As noted in the prior chapter, the Springville Community Action Committee's request on these three matters went over like a lead balloon with township officials, and in October 1970, Mount Laurel Mayor Bill Haines delivered the township's response at a Sunday meeting held at the Jacob's Chapel AME church, stating infamously to the black, poor congregation "if you people can't afford to live in our town, then you'll just have to leave" (Kirp, Dwyer, and Rosenthal 1995, p. 2). The congregants were initially shocked into stunned silence, but as they were leaving the church, one member of the

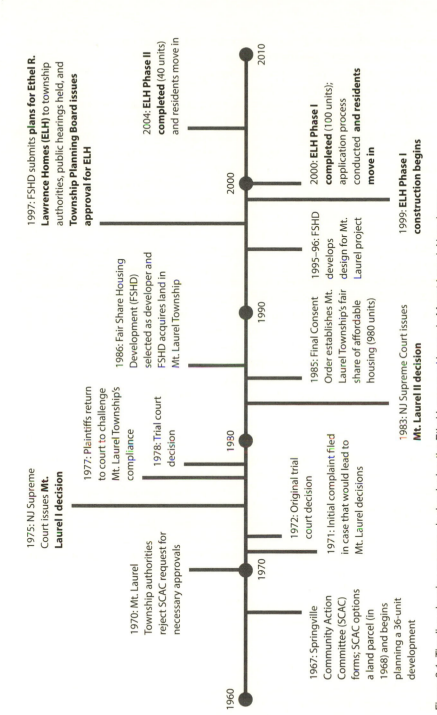

1967: Springville Community Action Committee (SCAC) forms; SCAC options a land parcel (in 1968) and begins planning a 36-unit development

1970: Mt. Laurel Township authorities reject SCAC request for necessary approvals

1971: Initial complaint filed in case that would lead to Mt. Laurel decisions

1972: Original trial court decision

1975: NJ Supreme Court issues **Mt. Laurel I decision**

1977: Plaintiffs return to court to challenge Mt. Laurel Township's compliance

1978: Trial court decision

1983: NJ Supreme Court issues **Mt. Laurel II decision**

1985: Final Consent Order establishes Mt. Laurel Township's fair share of affordable housing (980 units)

1986: Fair Share Housing Development (FSHD) selected as developer and FSHD acquires land in Mt. Laurel Township

1995–96: FSHD develops design for Mt. Laurel project

1997: FSHD submits **plans for Ethel R. Lawrence Homes (ELH)** to township authorities, public hearings held, and **Township Planning Board issues approval for ELH**

1999: **ELH Phase I construction begins**

2000: **ELH Phase I completed** (100 units); application process conducted **and residents move in**

2004: **ELH Phase II completed** (40 units) and residents move in

1960   1970   1980   1990   2000   2010

Figure 2.1. Timeline showing progress in developing the Ethel Lawrence Homes in Mount Laurel, New Jersey

Springville Committee, Ethel Lawrence, was heard to vow, "I'm not done with Mount Laurel" (Getlin 2004).

Unbeknownst to the mayor and Springville Committee members, attorneys at Camden Regional Legal Services, an NGO representing poor families living in five South Jersey counties, had already been researching exclusionary zoning ordinances and Planned Unit Developments in the region and were looking for plaintiffs to challenge exclusionary policies in state court. A white minister active with the Springville Community Action Committee connected Ethel Lawrence with Legal Services attorney Carl S. Bisgaier, who, together with Kenneth E. Meiser, Thomas J. Oravetz, and Peter J. O'Connor, filed the resulting lawsuit, *Southern Burlington County NAACP. et al. vs. Township of Mount Laurel, et al.*, on May 1, 1971.[1]

The complaint alleged that Mount Laurel Township had, in effect, systematically excluded people on the basis of class and race through its zoning ordinances and preferential treatment of middle-class housing in its Planned Unit Developments. It further asserted that under the New Jersey Constitution the township, in fact, had an affirmative obligation to create realistic opportunities for people of all races and incomes to live within its boundaries and enjoy its benefits. From the attorneys' perspective, the facts were open-and-shut and overwhelmingly favorable to their case: a pre–Civil War indigenous black community living in rural poverty was being denied the opportunity to build low-income family housing to stay in their hometown.

The carefully conceived lawsuit included four classes of plaintiffs: indigenous residents of Mount Laurel, such as Ethel Lawrence, who faced displacement unless zoning ordinances changed and funding was available to build affordable housing; former residents of the township who had moved or been forced to leave Mount Laurel for Camden or other locations for lack of affordable housing; low-income residents of Camden and other poor communities who had been prevented from living in Mount Laurel because of the high rents and home prices created by exclusionary zoning; and three institutional plaintiffs that signed on in support of the litigation, including civil rights groups such as the Southern Burlington County NAACP and the Camden Congress of Racial Equality as well as the Camden County NAACP. The civil rights groups joined in the complaint partially to shield individual plaintiffs from the heated emotional reaction of township officials and residents that many feared would erupt after the brief was filed.

---

[1] This account relies on remarks by Carl S. Bisgaier, Esq., at a seminar on land-use policy and planning at Princeton University, March 5, 1999, as well as subsequent communications with him.

Despite the effort at institutional shielding, the individual plaintiffs were indeed subject to a rough ride in the months and years that followed, and the burden fell especially hard on the lead plaintiff, Ethel Lawrence. According to her daughter, after the complaint was filed, "she was severely harassed, received death threats and had to explain to her children why they were being called names and harassed at school. Yet she still took on the onus to fight against the 'exclusionary zoning' practices of Mount Laurel (and many other suburban communities in NJ). She did so because she saw a need and knew that a lot of people could be helped by it" (Lawrence-Haley 2007).

The Mount Laurel litigation did not occur in a social and legal vacuum, of course. In the late 1960s and early 1970s, concern was growing in liberal circles around the country about the pervasive economic and racial exclusion that suburbs in large metropolitan areas were then engineering through zoning and other legal mechanisms (Danielson 1976). New Jersey, in particular, was a hotbed of litigation against suburban municipalities, which routinely welcomed firms bringing jobs, and developers bringing middle class housing, but used their zoning powers to block the entry of lower-class residents and the construction of affordable, low-income housing. These actions attracted the attention not simply of civil rights leaders and advocates for the poor, but for-profit real estate developers as well.

In 1971, for example, a major developer in New Jersey challenged the zoning policies of the upscale community of Bedminster Township, filing a lawsuit that was later joined by the American Civil Liberties Union. Bedminster lay in the heart of Somerset County's wealthy fox-hunting countryside, and its zoning ordinances forbade the construction of *any* dwelling—whether town house, apartment, or single-family home—on less than five acres of land. Also in 1971 two developers joined with low-income plaintiffs in sprawling, rapidly growing Madison Township in Middlesex County to challenge zoning policies that set aside minimal acreage for multifamily housing. Meanwhile, Mahwah, in Bergen County, hosted a huge Ford automobile assembly plant, but its workers could not afford to live anywhere in the community, prompting the United Auto Workers to challenge its zoning policies as exclusionary in a 1971 civil rights complaint and later lawsuit.

The trial court in the Mount Laurel litigation initially ruled in 1972 that Mount Laurel Township, through its exclusionary zoning ordinances, was indeed practicing an illegal form of economic discrimination under the state constitution, one that deprived the poor of adequate housing within the municipality. It also found that township officials had illegally deprived developers of the opportunity to build subsidized housing, even though they regularly used federal, state, county, and municipal resources

to benefit middle- and upper-income households in the Planned Unit Developments (*South Burlington County NAACP et al. v. Mount Laurel
Township et al., 119 N.J. Super.* 164 1972). In rendering its decision, the
court concluded that the township, "through its zoning ordinances, had
exhibited economic discrimination in that the poor had been deprived of
adequate housing and the opportunity to secure construction of subsidized housing and [that] the municipality had used federal, state, county
and local finances and resources solely for the betterment of middle and
upper-income persons."

To remedy this breach of New Jersey constitutional law, the trial judge
invalidated the township's zoning ordinance and directed it to prepare a
new land-use plan that identified specific housing needs within the township and then to implement an "affirmative program" to satisfy these
needs, subject to court approval. The ruling required local officials explicitly to identify *all* substandard housing within township boundaries
and then to enumerate the number of families that would be displaced
by an effective program of housing-code enforcement, regardless of their
present income. In addition to counting the number of families currently
living in dilapidated township dwellings, the court also required officials
to identify the housing needs of other low- and moderate-income people,
whether or not they occupied substandard housing, as well as the needs
of all persons who presently worked in the township or were projected to
work there in the near future, and then to take these needs into account
in formulating the new zoning plan.

Both the plaintiffs and the township appealed this trial-court decision,
the former hoping to expand the ruling to apply a region-wide remedy
for the provision of affordable housing in Mount Laurel, and the latter
to void the ruling in its entirety. The New Jersey Supreme Court agreed
to hear the appeal, along with the lawsuit that had been filed in Madison
Township, which raised similar issues of exclusionary zoning. After oral
arguments in the Madison case were postponed, however, the Mount
Laurel appeal became the lead case and gave its name to the final decision
and the resulting doctrine.

In 1975 the New Jersey Supreme Court handed down a bold, original
opinion, which came to be known as Mount Laurel I. The sweeping ruling issued an unprecedented directive to municipalities throughout the
state to end their exclusionary zoning practices. In doing so, the court
interpreted the general welfare provisions of the New Jersey Constitution
to require that municipalities enact land policies that made "realistically
possible the opportunity for an appropriate variety and choice of housing" and that would address regional, and not just local, housing needs
(*South Burlington County. NAACP et al. v. Mount Laurel Township et
al.,* 67 N.J. 151 1975). The court went on to establish an "affirmative

obligation" on the part of "developing municipalities" such as Mount Laurel to allow for the construction of their "fair share" of regional needs for low- and moderate-income housing. The mandate explicitly included the needs not only of families presently inhabiting substandard housing within the townships, but also the projected need for affordable housing among families in the surrounding region. These principles became known as "the Mount Laurel Doctrine."

Beyond its statement of constitutional principle, the Supreme Court specifically directed authorities in Mount Laurel to amend the township's zoning ordinance within ninety days so as to permit the construction of multifamily housing, without limiting the number of bedrooms, and also to allow the building of small houses on small lots. In addition, it ordered township officials to eliminate other provisions that artificially drove up the cost of housing, such as minimum lot sizes and overly demanding building-code regulations. The opinion went so far as to articulate a "moral obligation" on the part of New Jersey municipalities to establish local housing agencies to provide decent housing for poor residents presently living in substandard conditions within their areas of jurisdiction.

In this startlingly comprehensive opinion, the Supreme Court thus overruled the trial court on two critical points. First, it required Mount Laurel Township to address its fair share of the regional need, and not just the need for affordable housing within its boundaries, in effect linking the needs of poor households in Mount Laurel with those of poor households in Camden and elsewhere, as the plaintiffs had originally sought. Second, it lifted the trial court's requirement that the township prepare and implement an affirmative plan to identify and satisfy housing need within the township. Instead, the Supreme Court entrusted the township to make necessary zoning amendments and take whatever other actions were necessary to fulfill its fair share of regional affordable housing needs. Rather than specifying concrete actions, in other words, the court trusted Mount Laurel to live up to the spirit of the ruling. Unfortunately, this trust proved to be misplaced.

The Path to Mount Laurel II

From the outset, township authorities took every opportunity to drag their feet in complying with the court's directive, and when it finally did amend the zoning ordinance, the effort was halfhearted, at best. It wasn't until thirteen months after the Supreme Court ruling that the township finally adopted amendments to its zoning regulations that declared three small residential areas eligible for multifamily housing, totaling a minuscule twenty acres or less than 0.2 percent of the township's twenty-one square miles. The plaintiffs returned to trial court in 1977 to challenge the township's compliance with the Supreme Court ruling, and a local developer joined the litigation by proposing to erect a 585-unit, 107-acre mobile-home park in the township, in which 20 percent of the units would be set aside as affordable.

The trial court's initial 1978 ruling proved to be a setback for the plaintiffs, however, as the lower court approved the township's half-hearted zoning amendments as being consistent with the higher court's directive. In coming to this decision, the court relied, in part, on a 1977 New Jersey Supreme Court ruling in the Madison Township case that retreated somewhat from the lofty principles of Mount Laurel I (*Oakwood at Madison, Inc. v. Township of Madison*, 71 N.J. 481 1977). Although the trial court did grant the mobile-home developer's request for rezoning, the plaintiffs challenged the decision and once again appealed it to the New Jersey Supreme Court.

The court agreed to rehear the case, and on this appeal consolidated it with other cases that had by then been filed around the state by public-interest groups and home developers seeking to overturn similar restrictive zoning ordinances. Throughout the long, drawn-out legal process Ethel Lawrence remained steadfast in her dedication to the goal of bringing affordable housing to Mount Laurel and other townships. Unlike typical class-action plaintiffs who watched the proceedings from afar, she attended every hearing and sat in court day in and day out, not only observing the unfolding litigation, but providing historical research and practical advice to the lawyers who were arguing the case (Lawrence-Haley 2007).

Oral arguments were heard in 1980 and this led to an extended period of in-camera deliberation during which time the justices carefully drafted the final opinion, seeking to avoid the ambiguities that had become apparent in the earlier ruling. More than two years later, in 1983, a unanimous Supreme Court finally handed down its ruling, known as Mount Laurel II, which not only clarified but reinvigorated Mount Laurel I in even more sweeping terms (*South Burlington County NAACP et al. v. Mount Laurel Township et al.*, 92 N.J. 158 [1983]). Determined to transform the admittedly vague principles of the initial ruling into concrete reality and to enforce the State Constitution strictly, the Supreme Court adamantly reaffirmed the soundness of the Mount Laurel Doctrine and narrowed its coverage to focus specifically on the needs of low- and moderate-income households.

To encourage compliance with the court order, the ruling offered municipalities six years of immunity from exclusionary zoning litigation once their ordinances had been brought into line with the new doctrine. In order to ensure prompt compliance with their fair-share housing obligations under the state constitution, the justices sought to create incentives for private agents to enforce the doctrine. Specifically, the Supreme Court created a potential remedy for builder plaintiffs, offering them the possibility of securing court-ordered, higher-density zoning if the municipality did not comply with its housing obligations and if the proposed building site and project offered a substantial percentage of affordable housing and were consistent with sound land-use planning principles and environmental regulations.

In order to manage potential litigation arising from the ruling and translate Mount Laurel principles into workable definitions, standards, and housing allocations, the Court also undertook a series of unusual initiatives. First, it designated three judges to hear all Mount Laurel–related lawsuits. Second, it authorized the widespread use of special court-appointed "masters," who would serve as experts and negotiators for the trial judges. Third, it set up mechanisms and procedures for vigorous case management. Fourth, it remanded pending litigation back to trial courts to determine what the townships' fair share of regional affordable housing needs might be, and to approve whatever zoning amendments and other actions might be required to create the long-delayed opportunities for building low- and moderate-income housing in Mount Laurel and other municipalities throughout the state. Finally, it invited the state legislature to address the issue of fair-share housing while making clear its commitment to continue enforcing the constitutional obligations it saw as lying at the core of the Mount Laurel Doctrine.

In undertaking these initiatives, the Supreme Court firmly rejected Mount Laurel Township's patently weak and disingenuous efforts to comply with Mount Laurel I, calling the amended zoning ordinance "little more than a smoke screen that attempts to hide the Township's persistent intention to exclude housing for the poor" (*South Burlington County NAACP et al. v. Mount Laurel Township et al.*, 92 N.J. 295 1983). The strong spirit of the ruling is indicated by the court's statement that "we may not build houses, but we do enforce the Constitution" (*South Burlington County NAACP et al. v. Mount Laurel Township et al.*, 92 N.J. 352 1983).

In the end, the state legislature and governor finally heeded the court's invitation to legislate on the issue of affordable housing and in 1985 enacted New Jersey's Fair Housing Act, which created a new state agency known as the New Jersey Council on Affordable Housing, commonly identified by its acronym COAH. This body was assigned the task of resolving exclusionary zoning issues and assisting municipalities devise and implement plans to satisfy their constitutional low- and-moderate income housing obligations (*State of New Jersey P.L. 1985, c. 222; N.J.S.A. 52:27D-301 et seq*). In 1986 the Supreme Court ruled that the new law was indeed constitutional (*Hills Development Corporation v. Bernards Township*. 103 N.J. 1, 65 1986). In subsequent decisions (in 1990, 1993, and 2002) the high court has continued to clarify and reaffirm the Mount Laurel Doctrine (see *Holmdel Builders Association v. Township of Holmdel*, 121 N.J. 550 1990; re *Township of Warren*, 132 N.J. 1 1993; *Toll Brothers v. West Windsor Township et al.*, 173 N.J. 502 2002; and *Fair Share Housing Center, Inc., et al. v. Township of Cherry Hill*, 173 N.J. 393 2002).

With the jurisprudence on affordable housing firmly settled and the enabling legislation passed, the newly formed public bodies acted quickly to turn Ethel Lawrence's dream of affordable housing into a statewide reality. During 1983–85, the three judges and court-appointed special masters, together with municipal planners, developers, affordable housing groups, civil rights organizations, and individual plaintiffs, developed institutional mechanisms by which the goal of fair-share housing might be realized in the State of New Jersey, developing (1) a workable methodology to estimate regional low- and moderate-income housing needs and a formula to allocate those needs, reasonably and fairly, to municipalities throughout the state to determine their "fair shares;" (2) procedures and criteria for determining whether municipalities had met their allocated fair-share obligations; and (3) standards for evaluating sites, projects, and compliance mechanisms proposed by builder-plaintiffs and municipalities to rehabilitate substandard housing and build new affordable housing.

Tempest in a Suburban Teapot

At this point, the quest for affordable housing in Mount Laurel returned to the trial court, which was in remand charged with overseeing and approving a new zoning regime and action plans for bringing affordable housing into the township. Two additional Mount Laurel lawsuits had been filed in 1984 and these were consolidated into the remand. In the first of these two additional cases, the original Mount Laurel plaintiffs sued developers of the township's Larchmont neighborhood, one of the four large Planned Unit Developments, for failing to provide or even plan for low-to-moderate-income housing. Second, another developer filed a builder's remedy lawsuit against the township to begin construction of affordable housing sooner rather than later. With the assistance of the special judge for southern New Jersey and a court-appointed master, the parties avoided another trial by reaching a comprehensive settlement agreement, which the trial court approved in September 1985.

The Final Consent Order established the township's fair share affordable housing at 950 units based on the newly minted methodology, with the units to be split evenly between low- and moderate-income house-holds. At that time Mount Laurel included around 8,500 dwelling units in addition to extensive nonresidential development, with more housing on the drawing board in the four Planned Unit Developments, so the affordable housing units would comprise a little more than 10 percent of all dwellings in the township. This settlement finally created the long-sought "realistic opportunity" for construction of affordable housing in Mount Laurel Township. As Ethel Lawrence herself observed in 1988, "the court said this: poor people have the right to the opportunity to live in any community" (DePalma 1988).

Thus the stage was finally set for the project to move forward. All parties agreed that a nonprofit developer designated by the original plaintiffs would build 255 units of affordable rental housing up to a maximum of ten units per acre, to be located on at least two sites anywhere in Mount Laurel of the plaintiffs' choosing, subject to township review and binding arbitration, if necessary, by the special master. A contribution of $3.2 million and additional payments for water- and sewer-connection fees from planned unit developers would help fund the initiative. Apart from the housing project originally sought by the Springville Community Action Committee, the township would fulfill the remainder of its fair share obligation by relying on the incentive of higher allowable densities, up to fourteen units per acre, to entice private builders to develop projects at other sites. With 20 percent set aside for low- and moderate-income units, developers could use profits from the market-rate housing to subsidize the affordable units internally.

Mount Laurel II, the Fair Housing Act, and ensuing moves toward affordable housing construction created a firestorm of political and municipal opposition across New Jersey. One group of New Jersey municipalities appealed unsuccessfully to the U. S. Supreme Court, which declined to hear the case because it raised no identifiable federal issue. Another group of state legislators made an unsuccessful attempt to amend the state constitution to repeal the Mount Laurel Doctrine; and moderate Republican Governor Tom Kean went so far as to label the doctrine a "communist concept" and proposed a moratorium on the builders' remedies that had been authorized by the court (Hanley 1984). Within Mount Laurel, plans for the project were submitted to township authorities in 1997 and were subject to a long series of acrimonious hearings before the township's Planning Board, ultimately attended by a total of more than five hundred agitated citizens.

Political opposition to the proposed development in Mount Laurel was fierce. "We need this like Custer needed more Indians," said one resident of the community (Smothers 1997a). Witnesses before the board offered up images of urban dysfunction coming to Mount Laurel and disrupting its tranquil suburban way of life; and as one would expect given the scholarly literature on opposition to affordable housing, their testimony made frequent invidious references to poor, minority communities in the region. After all, one resident raged, "we don't want this place to become another Camden." One opposition attorney called the proposed project a "low-income plantation of poverty" (Smothers 1997b). With words like "plantation" and "Camden" juxtaposed, the underlying racial references were hard to miss.

Typical of the opposition was an older white witness who considered himself a refugee from urban dysfunction elsewhere in the metropolitan area, and told the audience: "I am 55 years old and I lived in Philadelphia . . . . near two low income housing projects; and during the fifteen years that I lived there as a child, those two projects were razed to the ground . . . . and eventually . . . . they became slums. I haven't seen one project yet that is successful. I've only seen ones that are not" (Albright 2011, p. 40). Another resident agreed with this sentiment and offered up his own experiences with urban blight, stating that "I went to law school in Newark. We had a wall of low income and moderate income projects that within ten years went into such disrepair that they all had to be boarded up and eventually were torn down. I would hate for the same thing to happen to our fair town of Mt. Laurel" (Albright 2011, p. 41).

One resident couched his opposition more obliquely by critiquing the proposed building site's unsuitability, arguing that "low-income residents can't afford cars, and there is no public transportation near the site. They will be all dressed up with no place to go. Our low-income neighbors will be stranded. On that basis alone, it's the wrong site" (Albright 2011, p. 46). Other opponents were more direct and objected to affordable housing on principle. A resident from one of the neighboring subdivisions wrote in a letter to the editor of the *Burlington County Times* that "the outrageous idea of creating a 100 percent low-income neighborhood is simply not desired anymore, since towns opt instead for set asides, enabling better integration and socialization with other residents" (Fox 1997).

Whereas these residents based their opposition on the characteristics of the project, others focused on the presumed moral defects of the residents. At one planning-board meeting, a resident testified that "it would be lovely to think that all the folks moving into Fair Share will be model citizens. I know Fair Share shares this hope. We always feel this way. But the experience with other types of developments tells us this may not be so" (Smothers 1997b). As noted in the prior chapter and discussed more fully in the next, the affordable housing project ultimately came to be named in honor of Ethel R. Lawrence, and a lawyer for the adjacent retirement community worried about the stigma that a project so named would bring to the area and its tenants, predicting that "the majority of the citizenry will look upon a development with the name Ethel R. Lawrence Homes as a low-income housing project, and it will be like painting a bold 'P' for poverty on the tenants' foreheads" (Smothers 1997b).

One tenant of the project experienced moral opprobrium on this issue after the fact, when, after moving into the project, she called to initiate electrical service on her new unit:

> When I first moved here, and I was, you know changing my electric bill, and all my bills, the guy on the phone said to me, where will you be moving to? And I said I'll be going to Ethel Lawrence. He says, those new houses over there? I said yeah. He said, how dare you? He was nasty. How dare you? How dare you, put a house up of that value, across the street from my two hundred thousand dollar home. (Albright 2011, p. 42)

Apart from the moral character of the presumed tenants, others who testified before the planning board framed public-housing construction as a breach of an implicit moral contract in which people worked hard, played by the rules, saved their money, and were duly rewarded by society with residence in a nice suburb like Mount Laurel. By implication, prospective project residents had not worked hard, played by the rules, and saved their money or they would already have been rewarded with suburban residence and not in need of outside intervention. In this framing, witnesses typically lauded the responsibility and rectitude of people like "us," leaving unsaid the implicit characterization of project residents as a "them" lacking the same positive attributes. In the self-righteous words of one person, "[W]e are not subsidized. We get up every day and we earn a living. We pay our taxes, we pay our car insurance, we pay for our children to do things, to do activities. If we want to go out to dinner, we pay for that. Nobody subsidizes us" (Albright 2011, p. 43).

In an extended peroration, the same man went on to list the attributes that "they" (the presumed residents of the project) would need to exhibit (but presumably didn't) if they were to be accepted in Mount Laurel:

> If this community is going to come into our neighborhood, and these people are going to live inside our community, I don't care what their income is, as long as they are going to make an effort to get up and go to work every day if they can, if they are not disabled, and if they are going to take care of their property and have respect for themselves and people around them, then that is what I think this entire group is looking for. I welcome anybody into our neighborhood that wants to be that same kind of person. (Albright 2011, p. 43)

The implicit "us and them" comparison was likewise in clear evidence in the statement of another witness, who told the planning board:

I personally worked fifty years to save money. Nobody subsidized me. If my mom couldn't make it on what my pop was making, she would say, papa you got to get more money. Papa got another job. He worked to 11 o'clock at night. We didn't ask for subsidy. Harry Truman was probably one of the best presidents we ever had. He said if you want to do something for a hungry man, teach him how to fish and how to grow crops. Don't give him food because you destroy his initiative. (Albright 2011, p. 45)

Some people offered solutions to assuage the concerns of residents about the moral character of likely residents, such as the lawyer who said he "would ask the developer to consider having concerned residents of nearby neighborhoods to serve as screening committee members along with you so they can lend the benefit of their advice and wisdom to your organization and to help you screen tenants." The mayor at the time echoed these sentiments, telling fellow citizens, "I'm going to insist on a couple of conditions with approval which is provided. One of the conditions is that the applicant must establish a tenant selection committee. . . . [T]he criteria should include personal interviews with prospective occupants, credit history checks, criminal checks, review of five years of previous residential history, a home visit of prior residence, and written verification of income."

As these statements suggest, negative sentiment against the project generally ran very high, so high that at times the emotions exceeded the bounds of civil discourse. In two instances, for example, emotions boiled over into actions that were symbolically and in some respects literally quite violent. Twice the sign erected by Fair Share Housing to advertise the site of the proposed housing project was destroyed by vandals—one using a chainsaw to cut it to pieces and another using a vehicle to run it down (Bell 1997). Such strong emotions are only to be expected, of course, when residents in stereotypical fashion perceive the new arrivals as morally suspect, undeserving, and likely to bring urban problems such as crime into the community, thereby lowering property values and increasing tax burdens in their suburban utopia. Indeed, fears about crime, property values, and increased taxes were repeatedly mentioned in testimony before the planning board (Haar 1996; Kirp, Dwyer, and Rosenthal 1997).

For example, one witness rose to state, "[M]y concern is the impact this will have on the community as a whole. Have we talked with anyone from the police department?" He then went on to reference a nearby development in which affordable housing units had been set aside for rental to low-income families:

Speaking of Stonegate, which has one of those mini-condo units, they had I think four buildings which had three low income units for sale to be sold to low income, and one building that was rental. In that whole development of Stonegate, all problems that derive out of Stonegate come from that one condo building. And you are talking about eight families. Now how many people live in Stonegate never had a problem? They put one rental building in Stonegate; that is where the police department responds to that one building. (Albright 2011, p. 43)

Given their expectation that rising crime rates would emanate from the project, township residents naturally saw declining property values as following close behind. As one resident put it, "I would like to stay in Mt. Laurel and continue to live at my present address without the fear that my property values are going to deteriorate" (Albright 2011, p. 41). Another expressed his concern that stigmatization of neighborhoods adjacent to the proposed project would spur a cycle of out-migration and decline to undermine not only property values, but sociality itself. Referring to the proposed project, he said, "[I]t will guarantee that this part of the Township will be stigmatized as bad and an exodus will occur, property values will deteriorate, and a constant state of anger between parties will create an atmosphere of hate and retaliation" (Albright 2011, p. 41).

Concomitant with their concerns about property values and crime rates, residents also voiced concerns that their taxes would exorbitantly increase. As one resident caustically put it, "I don't feel we should pay taxes that they will not pay, nor do we have to pay their sewer and water and all the streets. I think that's a big consideration the township has to take into account when they come to discuss with the developers what is a fair contribution to Mount Laurel. As it stands now, I see nothing but trouble for . . . a property owner" (Albright 2011, p. 43). Senior citizens in the nearby retirement village claimed a special mantle of victimization, with one witness arguing:

> [S]enior citizens are being asked to pay taxes for people that will be earning more than they are earning. . . . A person on a fixed income that's trying to get along and that has to really make ends meet is in jeopardy of losing their home because we have to pick up school taxes for people who will be earning more money than we are. This is justice? (Albright 2011, p. 42)

Comments by another senior citizen likewise exposed the undercurrents of generational as well as racial and class conflict by focusing on school taxes:

> We must do something for the people who are on fixed incomes. They will be asked to be paying a higher burden on taxes because certainly the school taxes will go up. And what I am afraid of when we leave this forum tonight that they will be left paying more taxes and they will have no forum to express that concern. And I am asking if Fair Share would be willing to offer

some time or some people on his staff to try to help senior citizens with the tax issue. (Albright 2011, p. 42)

Although the drift of prevailing sentiment about affordable housing expressed at the planning-board hearings was decidedly antagonistic, not all those who rose to speak were negative, as indicated by the witness who warned that "if we, the citizens of Mt. Laurel, do not accept this change with an open mind, and do our best to integrate and welcome these residents into our community, then we ourselves will most certainly shoot ourselves in the foot" (Albright 2011, p. 41). Another woman drew on her thirty years of experience working in Mount Laurel, and framed her support in terms of resolving the social-justice issue and its long history in the township:

> Thirty years ago I was the community health nurse in Mt. Laurel. Although I had other responsibilities, I spent many days in rural Mt. Laurel in the early '60s and early '70s. My responsibility here was to see that every child had the opportunity to receive the necessary immunization, exams, and appropriate follow-up. Who lived in Mt. Laurel then? Aside from Ramble-wood which had recently been developed, rural Mt. Laurel was home to people with low and moderate incomes who needed our clinic services. On Hartford Road I visited families living in the converted chicken coops. Some of the small side streets I remember have disappeared. But I remember people who worked hard and raised their children well. We did not see neglected children. When Ethel Lawrence and others developed a plan to build apartments way back in 1970 so that those living in deteriorating housing would have a better place to live, the Township refused, although they would have been no cost to the town. The children that I helped to treat who were forced to leave their home would today be in their 20s and early 30s. Think of all the litigation and thousands of dollars that have been spent on this issue all because our Township refused to build apartments for their old time residents. It is time to correct a wrong. (Albright 2011, p. 47)

Another man rose to chide residents, most of whom were recent arrivals, about their opposition to housing for African Americans who had been in Mount Laurel for generations, noting that:

> Some of these people have been here for 70 and 80 years, some of them 100 years with family. How can someone come into this particular area where people have been living all these years, and some of them from what I've been hearing have only been here maybe ten years, fifteen years. They are new people. So let's be realistic here. (Albright 2011, p. 48)

Another woman echoed these same sentiments in a letter to the local *Burlington County Times* (April 1, 1997), in which she wrote:

I hear many comments stating that I should be so thrilled with the $300,000 and $400,000 homes that are being built because obviously it will raise the value of my home. What? Besides my taxes being raised to four times what they were seventeen years ago because of this over-development, I don't see such a thing happening. Oh, and isn't it funny that ten different developments can be going up at the same time and that won't overtax the schools with too many new children, but suddenly this lower-income development will put just such a burden on those same schools? Sounds like elitist attitudes to me.

Despite these positive views, most comments at the hearings were decidedly antagonistic to the construction of affordable housing in Mount Laurel, with residents offering both moral and material reasons for their opposition to the proposed project. Morally, they expressed concerns about the presumed character of project inhabitants, frequently drawing upon stereotypes of poor minority group members as lazy, welfare dependent, crime prone, and unable or unwilling to care properly for private property. Others referenced an implicit moral contract that rewarded hard work and good behavior with suburban residence, which they viewed as being undeserved in the case of the plaintiffs. Materially, residents repeatedly voiced fears that the project would lead to rising crime rates, falling property values, and increasing tax burdens, fears that were grounded both in impressions of other public housing projects in the region and in stereotypical perceptions about project residents.

Beyond Mount Laurel

The controversy about affordable housing in New Jersey continues to the present day. In the course of the 2009 gubernatorial race, for example, two Republican candidates sought to outdo each other in their expressions of contempt for the Mount Laurel Doctrine. Assemblyman Richard Merkt told voters that "if I am governor, I will drive a stake into COAH's heart, bury it, and make sure it never rises again," whereas former U.S. Attorney Chris Christie, more delicately but nonetheless directly, promised that "if I am governor, I will gut COAH and I will put an end to it" (Pizarro 2009). According to the reporter present, Christie's comment got a "raise-the-roof response" from the suburban crowd, prompting one local pol to predict, "[Y]ou just won the election," which Christie ultimately went on to do. Upon his election, he sought to keep his promise by abolishing COAH but was overruled by the NJ Supreme Court (Spoto 2012), whereupon he sought to have municipalities transfer affordable housing funds back to the state (DeMarco 2012).

Despite continuing controversy, the Mount Laurel II decision nonetheless succeeded decisively in changing statewide politics and policy, forcing suburban municipalities throughout New Jersey to focus on *where and how* and not *whether* to create realistic opportunities for constructing affordable housing. Within two years of the ruling, builder-plaintiffs had filed more than one hundred lawsuits challenging exclusionary zoning regulations around the state. These court actions were in addition to other previously filed cases that affected most of two counties and other scattered municipalities. Moreover, in spite of municipal foot-dragging and the vagaries of the real estate cycle and permit acquisition, some sixty-five thousand new affordable housing units have been built since Mount Laurel II and the establishment of COAH; and in addition, some fifteen thousand substandard units have been rehabilitated (Council on Affordable Housing 2010), with more units of affordable housing added per capita each year than in any other state (Keevey 2008).

The great irony in the Mount Laurel controversy is that if the township had simply approved the Springville Community Action Committee's original request, the township would have gained just thirty-six affordable housing units. Moreover, these homes would have been built in a section of the township where poor African Americans had long since established a presence. Instead, by fighting the request all the way to the State Supreme Court the township incurred an obligation to provide nearly a thousand units of affordable housing scattered throughout the entire community. At the same time, it established a new statewide doctrine that prohibited exclusionary zoning and created an affirmative obligation to provide for the housing of low- and moderate-income families that applied to *every* municipality in the state. Beyond New Jersey, the case provided a model for affordable housing litigation and judicial remedies to promote racial and class inclusion throughout the United States (Kirp, Dwyer, and Rosenthal 1997).

CHAPTER 3

Field of Dreams

ETHEL LAWRENCE HOMES COME TO MOUNT LAUREL

Bringing affordable housing to her hometown of Mount Laurel was very much Ethel Lawrence's dream. According to her daughter, she was the "Drum Major" of the case and its ensuing litigation, spurring on plaintiffs and lawyers by getting out front and leading the way with enthusiasm and verve. "Ethel Lawrence did not argue the case before the New Jersey Supreme Court," her daughter has written, "she did not write the legislation which created the NJ Fair Housing Act . . . nor through this legislation did she create the New Jersey Council on Affordable Housing. But, because she cared, fought, and never gave up, they all exist. She never gave up the fight for affordable housing in Mount Laurel and the entire state of New Jersey has benefitted from it" (Lawrence Haley 2007). Although Ethel Lawrence participated in all of the litigation and court hearings and was active in the early phases of project planning, her health declined in the 1990s and she passed away in July of 1994 at the age of sixty-eight, with her dream of affordable housing in Mount Laurel still unrealized. In her honor the future housing project was baptized the "Ethel R. Lawrence Homes."

As figure 2.1 clearly illustrated, the development of an affordable housing project is no walk in the woods under any circumstances, and readers may wish to refer back to this figure to keep the chronology of events straight. Project development is a long, drawn-out process that entails three basic components: (1) a suitable parcel of land that meets basic site-development standards and is available for purchase; (2) sufficient funding for the housing to be constructed and yet remain affordable to future low- and moderate-income residents; and (3) the organizational capacity to navigate successfully the tortuous approval process. The consent order approved in 1985 addressed all three points, setting off a chain of events that ultimately would produce the affordable housing development originally envisioned by the Springville Community Action Committee way back in 1968. Unfortunately the process would require another sixteen years to come to fruition and it was not until 2000 that it opened its doors to the first residents, seven years after Ethel Lawrence had passed away.

Suburbia by Design

To begin the long and convoluted process of project development, the consent order required plaintiffs to select a developer, and in 1986, they chose a nonprofit organization, Fair Share Housing Development, Inc., to plan, construct, and ultimately manage the affordable housing development. Fair Share Housing Development (FSHD) was founded that year by one of the plaintiff's original attorneys, Peter J. O'Connor, who had gained experience in affordable housing development when he assisted another nonprofit in building and managing a 402-unit affordable housing development in North Camden, a 50-unit affordable housing development in Deptford Township, Gloucester County, and 100 units of affordable housing for the elderly in Pennsville Township, Salem County. Armed with the Final Consent Order's $3.2 million in funding and judicial license to select an affordable housing site anywhere in Mount Laurel, he scoured the township during 1985 and 1986 to identify suitable tracts of land.[1]

Whereas it had been relatively easy for the original plaintiffs to settle quickly on a potential building site in the 1960s, by the 1980s, real estate development in Mount Laurel had become a hot industry and land markets were very competitive. In the end, FSHD had to bid on ten different sites in order to acquire suitable properties. One of the major homebuilders in Mount Laurel was acquiring land for construction at the same time, and he frequently outbid FSHD for land available on the market. Ethel Lawrence participated directly in the site selection process, which considered standard planning criteria in reviewing the various fields, farms, and woodlands that were then available for purchase. After considering issues such as street access and wetlands protection, FSHD ultimately acquired three parcels for potential development in late 1986, totaling 132 acres. At least Ethel Lawrence was able to see the site where the project named in her honor would ultimately be erected.

The first parcel was a 10-acre wooded tract adjacent to a church and across a main road from a school complex and garden center. The second was a 60-acre tract of farm fields, woods, and wetlands at an undeveloped, still somewhat rural crossroads. The third parcel was a 62-acre property known as the Hurley Tract. It consisted of a large farm field surrounded by woods, wetlands, and a narrow creek, with about one thousand feet of frontage on the Moorestown–Mount Laurel Road. This roadway traversed the township and connected its new municipal

---

[1] This account draws heavily on documents provided by Fair Share Housing Development, Inc., Mount Laurel, New Jersey, and an interview with Peter J. O'Connor, executive director and founder, Fair Share Housing Development, Inc., May 25, 2010.

complex with the eponymous Mount Laurel at a crossroads 2.5 miles away where an eighteenth-century Quaker meeting house stood.

Preserved woods and wetlands proliferated around the Hurley Tract's edges and naturally buffered the site from adjacent land uses, mostly farmland and woods. To the west a single house and barn were located on an acre of land; and to the south, across the Moorestown–Mount Laurel Road, was a partially developed, age-restricted retirement community then under construction named Holiday Village, which eventually included several hundred small, single-family duplex and triplex units. Acquired for $20,000 per acre, the Hurley tract quickly became the preferred site for the proposed housing development. FSHD had committed most of the $3.2 million in funding under the consent order to land acquisition in order to be able to develop the 255 units anticipated in the final settlement agreement. Township officials had expected that the funds would be used both for acquisition and development costs, however, and they demanded that the 60-acre crossroads site be sold to raise money. FSHD acquiesced and sold the parcel to a local developer, adding the proceeds to its pre-development fund.

Although a potential building site had finally been identified and acquired, from 1985 to 1995, FSHD focused on the development of other projects in the region while it sought to raise additional funds toward the cost of the Mount Laurel project. In Camden, for example, FSHD developed Cooper Plaza Historic Homes, sixty-four affordable family rental units that were created by renovating large Victorian homes adjacent to a downtown hospital. FSHD eventually earned a $600,000 developer's fee from this project and deposited it in the pre-development fund for the Mount Laurel project. Obtaining funding for the project was complicated by the fact that, unlike most housing developments, the Ethel Lawrence Homes were projected from the start to be 100 percent affordable.

Planning for ELH only began in earnest after Ethel Lawrence's death, and during 1995–96 Peter O'Connor, the executive director of FSHD, found himself sketching plans on napkins at a local diner, thinking, and refining his conceptions for the development. One thing he was clear about was that the development should fit into the surrounding suburban environment. Thus he sought a housing density lower than the ten units per acre permitted by the settlement. He also wanted high-quality construction with extensive landscaping and irrigation; and he wanted town houses, not apartment buildings, though he did want the size of the units to be larger than the minimum standards so as to accommodate the larger size of low-income families. Moreover, he wanted the project to avoid large and unsightly parking lots and to offer outdoor facilities for play as well as indoor facilities for recreation, education, social services, and offices for FSHD maintenance and management personnel.

Most of all, O'Connor wanted the housing to be attractive. From prior hearings and court testimony, he well knew that township officials and residents feared a repeat of the failed public housing projects that had come to blot the Camden and Philadelphia landscapes, and he thus fervently sought to avoid the stigmatizing architectural forms and building aesthetics long associated with public housing projects in the American mind. If he was successful, he felt, suburbanites would visit the project and leave complaining that the development was, if anything, too nice for poor people. The resulting configuration for what became the 140-unit Ethel Lawrence Homes is depicted in the aerial photo shown in figure 3.1, taken in 2003 as the last phase of development was being completed.

Entry to the complex occurs through a 1,000-foot landscaped boulevard that follows an old farm road through an opening in the woods, entering directly from the Moorestown–Mount Laurel Road, which cuts diagonally across the bottom of the picture. This parklike entrance leads to a one-third-acre open village green and four residential courts situated around it, each of which consists of a circular, two-way street that rings a central green and connects up with the entry boulevard. Each court has twenty-eight to forty town houses, which are small, two-story, simply detailed structures, each consisting of four attached units arrayed around the courts with their central greens. Perpendicular parking is available to residents and visitors in front of the town houses and alongside the court's central green. Sidewalks ring the courts and small front yards separate the town houses from the parked cars and pavement. In addition to front doors opening onto the courts and greens, each town house has a back door that opens onto additional common lawns and ample landscaped areas. Three large basins collect and manage the site's storm water, and a pump station conveys wastewater to the township sewer system.

In the end, ELH was developed with a low gross density of just 2.25 units per acre, far below the 10 units per acre allowed under the 1985 settlement and only slightly higher than the average density of 1.31 units per acre in the township as a whole. In addition to the town houses, the site plan also provided for a two-story, 8,000-square-foot FSHD management and maintenance building; a 4.1-acre outdoor recreation area with lighted basketball and tennis courts, handball courts, amphitheater, picnic and game areas; and a 10,000-square-foot education-recreation building. As of 2012, the outdoor recreation area and the education-recreation building still had not yet been developed.

The research we reviewed in chapter 1 revealed that the design and density of affordable housing projects, along with their aesthetic compatibility with the surrounding housing, are critically important in shaping neighbors' perceptions and determining outcomes such as property values and crime rates. A key concern raised by local residents about the

Figure 3.1. Aerial view of Ethel Lawrence Homes with Phase II addition under construction. (*Source*: Fair Share Housing Development, Inc.)

project in public hearings was that it would be unattractive and easily identified as "public housing" and that poor management would quickly lead to its becoming dilapidated, thus "bringing down the neighborhood." As a result, FSHD paid considerable attention to the aesthetics of design and layout, seeking to create a residential development that was physically and aesthetically similar to those found in surrounding neighborhoods. Rather than erecting a traditional institutional-looking public housing complex of brick and concrete buildings densely packed into a square, the developer built framed town houses on cul-de-sacs using materials and construction methods similar to those in nearby suburban homes. Figure 3.2 displays two photographs for comparison, the first of

(a) Ethel Lawrence Homes—affordable housing

(b) Market-rate housing on Chapel Hill Road, approximately one mile from Ethel Lawrence Homes

Figure 3.2. The aesthetics of (a) Ethel Lawrence Homes compared with (b) nearby market-rate housing.

town houses in the Ethel Lawrence Homes and the second of market-rate properties located in a development approximately one mile from the ELH site.

The plan for Ethel Lawrence was carefully crafted after completing a systematic, in-depth study of existing housing throughout the township. In one way, it was easy for the development to fit in, as Mount Laurel's housing stock is relatively new. According to the 2000 Census, only 15 percent of homes were built prior to 1970 whereas 33% percent were built between 1990 and 2000 (U.S. Census Bureau 2009). Single-family detached homes are the most prevalent kind of housing in the township, comprising about half of its housing stock, with another quarter of dwellings being single-family town-houses. The dominant pattern of spatial organization for housing throughout Mount Laurel is the residential subdivision. Subdivisions are typically organized into self-contained enclaves or pods, often constructed by a single real estate developer (see Duany, Plater-Zyberk, and Speck 2000). Thus the subdivision and cul-de-sac design of the ELH development match the spatial organization of most neighborhoods in the township, and the attached multifamily town-house design duplicates a quarter of the existing stock. By virtue of being newly constructed, ELH was able to match the other new housing recently developed in the town in terms of methods and materials.

In addition to assuring the compatibility of ELH with surrounding road layouts, materials, and building forms, the developers paid considerable attention to the aesthetics of landscape architecture. Indeed, the maintenance budget for ELH from the start has had a dedicated line item for landscaping; and according to FSHD managers, the final landscape design was explicitly modeled on nearby properties in Haddonfield and Moorestown, two adjoining affluent suburbs characterized by high property values. The design and maintenance of the project's grounds are contracted out to private vendors, and FSHD managers remain vigilant to make sure that these contractors deliver a quality product that is comparable to the services provided to other, higher-end developments, despite the fact that it is a subsidized housing complex. In addition, FSHD keeps a full-time maintenance person on-site, and with its administrative offices located in the development, managers are able to supervise the property actively.

Management also sought to build aesthetic control into the social structure of the complex in several ways. First, it engaged in a rigorous screening and selection process that sought explicitly to identify people who would be good tenants and respectful neighbors. All applicants were subjected to third-party verification of income and a search of public records for criminal, bankruptcy, or landlord judgments. They were also asked to supply a five-year residence history. Those who met the initial entry criteria were interviewed both in the office and at home. The latter included a home inspection to make sure that prospective tenants were likely to maintain adequate property and maintenance standards.

Second, social factors were taken into account in the design of the project itself. At the suggestion of local police, for example, a proposed wall for handball was ultimately not built to prevent it becoming a canvas for graffiti, consistent with the "broken windows" theory of crime deterrence, in which signs of social disorder such as graffiti are taken to indicate a lack of local social control and, hence, an invitation to delinquency (Wilson and Kelling 1982; Wilson 1983; Skogan 1990).

Finally, FSHD organized a neighborhood watch group for the development. It meets monthly at the administrative center in the complex and is affiliated with Mount Laurel's official Neighborhood Watch Program, which is run as part of its community policing effort. A small group of residents regularly make the meeting, which is also attended by the FSHD education coordinator and occasional speakers and guests. The meeting typically lasts about an hour and serves as a time for residents to express concerns about the complex. Each cul-de-sac in the development has one leader who offers an update on recent events and activities. In addition, FSHD officials use the meetings to distribute information about upcoming events in the complex and township, as well as to answer questions and provide contacts and information about social-service organizations and programs. Residents offer their own suggestions and ideas about future events, networking opportunities, and partnerships with local organizations.

The monthly meetings of the Neighborhood Watch provide a regular venue for bringing up issues with respect to maintenance, as well as for suggesting areas for remediation and improvement. Based on the character of resident comments, management may offer suggestions about how to best solve the problem or about who should be contacted with a complaint. At one Neighborhood Watch meeting, for example, a staff member discussed the importance of residents maintaining the appearance of their unit and exhorted tenants to avoid leaving clutter in their yards, noting that "it is especially important [for residents] to keep their backyards cleaned up, since this is the first and last area that anyone sees coming into the development and should make a good impression." A frequent topic at the meetings is the proper placement and retrieval of trash cans on garbage-collection days.

The Winding Road to Construction

After completing engineering and architectural plans, FSHD applied in late 1996 to the Mount Laurel Township Planning Board to obtain the necessary approvals for its subdivision and site-development plans. As related in the prior chapter, tempestuous public hearings were held at the local middle school during the winter and spring of 1997 before hundreds of residents. Despite strong and emotional opposition from residents, however, in the end the Township Planning Board had little discretion under the terms of the 1985 consent agreement. If the ELH plans conformed to the zoning and site-development standards previously negotiated by the plaintiffs, then the board had no choice but to approve the project, and in April of 1997, the Planning Board finally met and unanimously gave the go-ahead for construction of the Ethel R. Lawrence Homes in Mount Laurel, New Jersey, though not without a final burst of vitriol. After the vote, one of the opponents gestured menacingly toward board members, the mayor, and township council members and angrily shouted, "[Y]ou're history!" (Smothers 1997c).

Once the Planning Board had given its assent, another round of negotiations ensued between the plaintiffs, the township, and other parties to update and amend the 1985 settlement agreement. The Township Municipal Utility Authority agreed to guarantee sufficient water and sewer capacity for the project and accepted ownership and maintenance responsibility for the projected pump station and force main to be located at the site. The developer of one of the township's Planned Unit Developments reaffirmed his willingness to cover the water- and sewer-connection fees for the ELH units at $900 per unit. The township also agreed to accept dedication of the project's entrance boulevard and sewer pumping station.

Each of these agreements brought the project closer to realization. With the foregoing approvals in hand, the developer next needed approval from the New Jersey Department of Environmental Protection. To construct the landscaped access boulevard, certain encroachments on a stream and wetlands were necessary and required state permission. Although the roadway followed the route of a long-standing farm lane that for generations had allowed tractors and other farm machinery to move onto the property, satisfying environmental regulations for the wetland crossing and freshwater mitigation took two years to complete, significantly delaying the project and adding to its final cost.

Aside from the foregoing approvals, the other principal barrier to overcome on the road to construction was financing. From 1998 to 2004 the Ethel Lawrence Homes were financed and built for around $26.7 million, or $190,459 per unit for the 140 townhouses, including costs of land acquisition. Figure 3.3 shows the sources from which this investment was financed. Around half of the funds (49 percent) came from the federal Low-Income Housing Tax Credit program, which was established by the Tax Reform Act of 1986 to encourage private investment

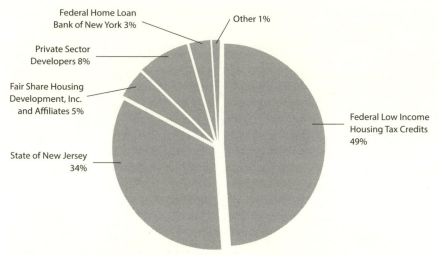

Federal Home Loan
Bank of New York 3%

Other 1%

Private Sector
Developers 8%

Fair Share Housing
Development, Inc.
and Affiliates 5%

Federal Low Income
Housing Tax Credits
49%

State of New Jersey
34%

Figure 3.3. Funding of the development of the Ethel Lawrence Homes

in low-income rental housing. Since its creation, the LIHTC program has funded the construction of some 1.6 million housing units, or about one-sixth of all multifamily housing built over the period and a number that is greater than the total number of units presently administered as public housing (Schwartz 2006).

In any given year, the total dollar amount of LIHTC credits is set on a state-by-state basis by federal authorities. In 2010, for example, states could allocate up to $2 per capita in tax credits for affordable housing construction. The total annual tax credit is thus directly pegged to the population size of each state, and given this limitation, the resulting funds are generally allocated competitively among eligible developers (Schwartz 2006). These procedures limited the dollar value of LIHTC funds accessible to FSHD developers during the years the project was being planned, compelling them to finance and build the Ethel Lawrence Homes in two distinct phases, with one hundred units constructed around three of the four central courts and opened in late 2000, and the final forty units added later around the fourth court and opened in 2004.

As always, the principal challenge in financing affordable rental housing projects is how to plug the gap between the rental income expected from low- and moderate-income tenants paying no more than 30 percent of their income for rent and utilities and the actual cost of operating the housing project. Operating costs include administrative expenses, maintenance costs, utilities, reserves for repair and replacement, payments in lieu of taxes, and debt service on funds borrowed to construct the project in the first place. This financial challenge is known housing circles as the

problem of "gap financing" (Schwartz 2006). The inability to fund operating expenses adequately from tenant revenues was a major reason for
the physical deterioration of public housing projects in inner cities during
the 1960s, 1970s, and 1980s (Hirsch 1983; Hunt 2009).

Projects developed with tax-credit equity in New Jersey are typically
affordable only to households with incomes that hover around 50 to 60
percent of the regional median income, adjusted for family size—around
$36,180 to $43,416 per year for a three-person family in Mount Laurel
in 2011. FSHD developers, however, sought to provide units to households earning a range of incomes that was unprecedented in its breadth,
going from 10 to 80 percent of the regional median income, or from
$7,230 to $57,888 annually for a three-person family in 2011. Without a
deeper range of affordability, the developer felt, many of the low-income
plaintiffs that were the original impetus for the project would not be able
afford to live in the Ethel Lawrence Homes when they were opened.

In order to build a high-quality complex of affordable town houses
and simultaneously achieve a wide range of affordability, FSHD was
compelled to cobble together an unusual package of tax credits, grants,
developer contributions, reduced township fees, and loans. As figure 3.3
indicates, most of the gap (34 percent) was plugged by loans from the
State of New Jersey, with 18 percent coming from by the N.J. Housing and Mortgage Finance Agency, 13 percent coming from the state's
Affordable Housing Trust Fund (formerly known as Balanced Housing
Neighborhood Preservation Program), and the remaining 3 percent coming mainly from a small grant made by the N.J. Department of Community Affairs.

Combining funds from the federal LIHTC program with the State of
New Jersey's contributions, we see that 83 percent of the project's total
funding came from public sources, either state or federal. The remaining
17 percent was covered by a variety of private sources, including 5 percent in contributions from Fair Share Housing Development; 8 percent in
contributions from other private developers; 3 percent from the Federal
Home Loan Bank of New York; and the final 1 percent from a number of
small, disparate sources. The symbolism of honoring the memory of the
Ethel R. Lawrence contributed significantly to the ability of developers to
assemble the necessary subsidies.

A Dream Come True

Construction finally began on phase one of the Ethel Lawrence Homes
in 1999 and the first one hundred units were ready for occupancy in late
2000. At this point, FSHD began an aggressive marketing campaign in

local newspapers and media, followed by three days during which applications were distributed to all who sought them. Applications had to be turned in on-site, and in the end, some 868 prospective tenants applied for the first one hundred units and were placed on a ranked list in the order their applications were received. One indicator of the latent demand for affordable housing in the region occurred when the second phase offered forty additional units in 2004. As word about the benefits of ELH had spread through low-income social networks in Camden and elsewhere (Molz 2003) more than 1,800 people applied, with many literally camping out in the entry roads and parking lot to be at the front of the line on the first morning that applications were accepted. At present the waiting time is between two years and five years depending on the number of bedrooms needed and the income of the applicant.

After the close of the three-day application window, FSHD staff began evaluating candidates at the top of the list and worked their way down, thus giving preference to those who applied early and yielding a rough "first come first served" decision rule. On the application form candidates reported family size, household structure, and housing needs; the number of bedrooms requested; marital status and age of family members; income; recent residential history; and the reason for making the application. As noted earlier, incomes were verified independently and public records were searched for criminal, bankruptcy, and landlord judgments. Those who passed this screening were subject to in-person and in-home visits, and if they satisfied the foregoing criteria and agreed to the terms of the lease, they were offered a place in the new development.

The first tenants began moving into their new homes in November 2000. Mostly they were single mothers who worked in medical offices, real estate and insurance firms, and other small businesses (Getlin 2004). Ironically, but not surprisingly given the three decades that had passed since the project was first envisioned, none of the original plaintiffs or their immediate family members were in a position to move to Ethel R. Lawrence Homes when they finally opened, though some residents do cite extended kinship ties to plaintiffs. Over time some families moved on after gaining a firmer foothold in the suburbs, generating new vacancies. FSHD managers went back to the ranked list, and when it became thin, the application process was repeated in 2006, 2007, and 2010 in order to refresh it.

By 2010 the Ethel Lawrence Homes had become an established feature of life in the Mount Laurel community, and the controversy had died down, though it never disappeared entirely and resurged from time to time in response to periodic threats to local order that usually had little to do with the project itself. In the regional and national press, however, the development was generally heralded as an unqualified success. When the

Ethel Lawrence Homes opened in November 2000, the local newspapers ran front-page stories on the event. South Jersey's *Courier Post* entitled its article, "Complex Provides a New Start," and featured a photo of a young woman from East Camden smiling and standing in front of her new home (Wahl and Pearsall 2000). The article went on to describe ELH as offering the resident "not just a new apartment, but a new life opening for her."

In the following year, ELH was proclaimed by an article in the *New York Times* to be "The Affordable Housing Complex That Works" (Capuzzo 2001), a far cry from earlier *Times* coverage that featured headlines such as "Low-Income Houses and a Suburb's Fears" (Smothers, 1997b). A May 2002 article that appeared in the *Courier Post* featured a photo of two children playing in front of their grandmother, and was entitled "S.J. housing project shines" (Molz and Burkhart 2002). In the summer of 2011, columnist Bob Braun in the *Newark Star-Ledger* opined that "Mount Laurel low income housing is a success story," noting that "from the road the development looks no different than the planned suburban housing communities that ring cities throughout New Jersey" (Braun 2011).

To some extent these proclamations of unqualified success reflect the low expectations that were initially held for the project. Ultimately the Ethel Lawrence Homes opened and attracted tenants, but low and behold, the sky did not fall and the suburban world did not stop. Indeed, it continued on much as before. Nonetheless the declarations of success made to date are based on few facts and little systematic evaluation. Whereas reporters' anecdotes, selective statements from residents, and FSHD management's own appraisals all coincide in giving high marks to the project, in this book we endeavor a more comprehensive and systematic evaluation. Before we can present the results of our analysis, however, we must lay out the methodology we developed to conduct the study, the epistemological issues we faced in designing it, and the problems we faced in implementing it. These issues are covered in the next chapter.

CHAPTER 4

Rhetoric and Reality

MONITORING MOUNT LAUREL

In our earlier review of the political economy of place, we presented a theoretical rationale for anticipating high levels of emotion in debates about land use, and in the specific case of the Ethel Lawrence Homes the residents of Mount Laurel certainly did not disappoint. Whether it was the majority who expressed strong misgivings about locating an affordable housing project within the township, or the minority who offered sympathy and support for the venture, emotions generally ran high. Feelings seemed to be especially raw among those who opposed the project, judging by the invective hurled at public hearings. And in many ways, who could blame them? The record of subsidized housing in the United States is hardly unblemished.

Historically, public housing projects have been used to support racial and class segregation rather than spur economic mobility, hardly an auspicious record for township residents to contemplate (Goldstein and Yancey 1986; Brauman 1987; Massey and Denton 1993; Massey and Kanaiaupuni 1993). In addition, subsidies for public housing in the past primarily went to the costs of land acquisition, demolition, and construction, leaving the projects themselves chronically underfunded with respect to operating costs (Bowly 1978; Hirsch 1983; Hays 1985). In many cities, housing-authority management practices tended to be shoddy and were frequently corrupt. The combination of poor management and underfunded operations typically led to the deterioration of both the physical and social infrastructure of projects over time (Rainwater 1970; Venkatesh 2000; Hunt 2009).

Mount Laurel residents thus had understandable reasons for their emotional opposition to what they saw as a "public housing project." Although the design, management, and financing of the Ethel Lawrence Homes would prove to be quite different than was typical for subsidized housing projects, and ELH was to be run by a private nonprofit organization rather than a ponderous public bureaucracy, residents did not appreciate these subtleties beforehand. In their minds, public housing was public housing and, apart from any racial or class prejudice they might harbor, they had good reasons to be suspicious of the motives and managerial capacity of the developers. Even affordable housing advocates would have to admit, in all candor, that the track record for public housing to that point was not encouraging, and the success of the project could hardly be assumed.

Although, in the end, the dire negative consequences foreseen by township residents did not seem to materialize, prior to the current study we did not have an objective assessment of exactly *how* the project's opening *did* affect local trends crime, property values, and taxes, or how the insertion of tenants into the community influenced the tenor of suburban life. Nor did we have any reliable information about how neighbors actually perceived the project and its residents once it was built. Most importantly, we had no way of assessing how moving into the Ethel Lawrence Homes actually affected the life chances and well-being of the tenants themselves. This book was written explicitly to address these issues, and in this chapter we describe the methods used in the "Monitoring Mount Laurel Study" to gather information about how residence in the Ethel Lawrence Homes influences the lives of tenants and neighbors, as well as the research design we developed to assess effects on the wider community.

Effects on the Community

As noted in the prior chapter, in their opposition to the construction of the Ethel Lawrence Homes township, residents repeatedly expressed their fears about rising crime, falling property values, and increasing tax burdens. In order to assess how the opening of ELH affected these outcomes we designed a multiple control-group time-series experiment (Campbell and Stanley 1963; Spector 1981). A time-series experiment involves assembling a longitudinal series of indicators before and after the advent of some policy intervention, and the basic analysis is to undertake a statistical test to determine whether there is a significant discontinuity in the time trend before and after the intervention, yielding what Galster (2004) calls a "difference in differences" study.

In order to assess the influence of the opening of the Ethel Lawrence Homes on crime rates, for example, we would examine the trend in Mount Laurel crime rates annually before 2001 and compare it with the annual trend observed afterward. If the trend beforehand was flat or declining, and afterward rising, and this difference in trajectories was statistically significant, we would be justified in concluding that the opening of the project brought about an increase in crime rates. If the trend was flat or declining before, and still flat or declining afterward, we would then conclude that the opening of ELH had no effect on crime rates. In general, the longer the number of observations before and after the intervention, the greater the strength of the causal inference, and the greater the internal validity of the design.

The principal threat to the validity of causal inference in a time series design is what Campbell and Stanley (1963) label "history," the temporal pairing of the policy intervention with some other event that also could conceivably have produced the observed break in the trend. The strength of inference is therefore greatly strengthened by the inclusion of one or more control cases for comparison. In the present instance, the addition of comparison cases would entail observing trends in crime rates for other, similar townships nearby. If the opening of ELH happened to coincide with some historical event, the happening should also have influenced trends in other townships. Thus, if we were to observe a temporal discontinuity in the time series for Mount Laurel but not in other townships, it would greatly strengthen our causal inference that the opening of the project increased crime rates. The inclusion of multiple comparison cases turns the study into a multiple control group time series experiment.

Figure 4.1 presents a map showing the geographic locations and median household incomes for Mount Laurel and three neighboring townships that we chose to serve as comparison cases—in essence, our control groups. The three townships are Cherry Hill, Cinnaminson, and Evesham. As the figure indicates, each of these municipalities lies in close proximity to Mount Laurel and has a similar median income. The figure also depicts the geography of inequality prevalent in South Jersey by showing the high degree of spatially concentrated poverty in and around the city of Camden, which is just a few miles away from the suburban townships.

The degree of similarity between the control townships and Mount Laurel is further substantiated in Table 4.1, which presents selected social, economic, and demographic characteristics of the municipalities based on the Census of 2000, around the time the ELH project first opened (U.S. Bureau of the Census 2009). At that point (and still today), all of the municipalities were overwhelmingly white, ranging from 85 percent in Cherry Hill to 91 percent in Cinnaminson, compared with 87 percent in Mount Laurel. The housing stock was overwhelmingly owner-occupied, ranging from 78 percent in Evesham to 96 percent in Cinnaminson and 84 percent in Mount Laurel. Poverty rates were universally low, varying narrowly from 2.4 to 4.0 percent, and median household incomes likewise ranged narrowly between $64,000 and $69,000 per year. Although Cinnaminson's population was much smaller than that of the other municipalities (15,000 versus 40,000–70,000), it comprises a much smaller geographic area (see figure 4.1). Compared with people in the

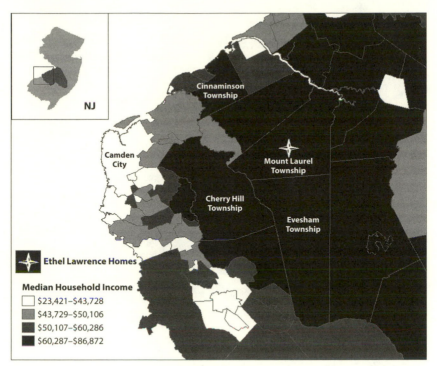

Figure 4.1. The location and median income of Mount Laurel and three comparison townships in southern New Jersey, 1999

other townships, residents of Evesham had a somewhat lower average age and income and were somewhat more concentrated in rental units than in owner-occupied housing, though the latter still overwhelmingly predominates.

In addition to their geographic proximity and socioeconomic comparability to Mount Laurel, we chose the comparison townships because of the relative absence of 100 percent affordable housing developments during the time period under observation. Utilizing COAH reports, we examined the amount, type, and timing of affordable housing developments built in each township from 1990 to 2008 (New Jersey Department of Community Affairs 2010). Compared with Mount Laurel's 140 units of 100 percent affordable housing, there were no such developments in Cinnaminson and just one16-unit project in Evesham; but in Cherry Hill a 122-unit did open in 1997. Subsidized housing was not entirely absent in Cinnaminson, which had 89 units of elderly housing. Cherry Hill also had 100 units of elderly housing and Mount Laurel itself had one small project with fewer than 100 units of elderly housing.

Table 4.1. Demographic and economic characteristics of Mount Laurel and comparison townships in South Jersey

Characteristic	Mount Laurel	Cherry Hill	Cinnaminson	Evesham
Demographic Status				
Median Age	38.9	41.8	42.0	36.0
% Family Households	66.8	74.0	81.9	72.2
% Households with Persons <18	31.9	34.0	36.3	40.1
% Households with Persons 65+	24.5	31.3	36.3	17.4
Race and Ethnicity				
% White	87.1	84.7	91.4	91.3
% Black	6.9	4.5	5.1	3.1
% American Indian	0.1	0.1	0.2	0.1
% Asian	3.8	8.9	1.9	4.1
% Two or More Races	1.4	1.2	1.0	1.0
% Hispanic (Any Race)	2.2	2.5	1.5	2.0
Economic Status				
Median Household Income (000)	$63.8	$69.4	$68.5	$67.0
Poverty Rate	3.1	4.0	2.4	2.8
Housing Cost				
Median Monthly Mortgage	$1,467	$1,538	$1,398	$1,501
Median Monthly Rent	$939	$793	$916	$886
Housing Tenure				
% Owner Occupied	83.7	83.0	96.2	77.7
% Renter Occupied	16.3	17.0	3.8	22.3
Total Population	40,221	69,865	14,595	42,275

The most common form of subsidized housing in the other townships is scattered-site housing that came about through inclusionary development projects. Rather than erecting a project composed entirely of affordable units, developers of market-rate projects agree to set aside a percentage of units for lower-income families. Cherry Hill has 398 such units, compared with 101 in Evesham and 238 in Mount Laurel. A small number of units were also made available in several townships through a program that rehabilitates existing units for occupation by low-income families, yielding 18 units in Cherry Hill, 16 in Evesham and 21 in Mount Laurel. The final category of subsidized housing in the communities is special-needs housing, containing bedrooms for people with disabilities, numbering 73 units in Mount Laurel, 21 in Cinnaminson, and 97 in

Evesham. In sum, although other townships contained subsidized housing, Mount Laurel had by far the most, and no other township had a
large number of units in 100 percent affordable projects.

As already noted, in designing our multiple time-series experiment, we
focused on three issues that were most frequently mentioned as concerns
by township residents in debates leading up to the project's approval:
crime rates, property values, and taxes. Crime data come from the FBI's
1990–2009 Uniform Crime Reports for the State of New Jersey. Each
year, the New Jersey State Police prepare a tally of crime statistics gathered from state enforcement agencies, which are then turned into the
Uniform Crime Reporting System (New Jersey Division of State Police
2009). These data include all crimes categorized by the FBI as "index
crimes," including homicide, rape, robbery, aggravated assault, burglary,
larceny-theft, and motor-vehicle theft. Among these index crimes, homicide, rape, robbery, and aggravated assault are classified as violent
whereas burglary, larceny-theft, and motor-vehicle theft are designated
as nonviolent. Manslaughter and simple assault are not considered index
crimes, and domestic violence is not counted as an index crime unless
it falls under the heading of another index crime (e.g., homicide). Each
crime is attributed to the municipality in which it was committed rather
than the municipality that received the report or responded to the crime.

Property values and tax data come from reports prepared by the New
Jersey Division of Taxation and are available at the municipal level from
1994 through 2010 (for property values, see New Jersey Division of Taxation 2010a) and from 1997 through 2010 (for property taxes, see New
Jersey Division of Taxation 2010b). Each year, the Division of Taxation
calculates the average residential sales price for each municipality and
reports the municipal-level property-tax burden (the "general tax rate"),
which is the multiplier used to calculate the tax levied on each property.
These general rates are then adjusted by assuming that all municipalities
are at 100 percent valuation to yield "effective tax rates," which are more
accurate for comparison.

In addition to township-level property-value data, we used public property records to compile neighborhood-level data for two specific areas located immediately adjacent to the Ethel Lawrence Homes, Hillside Lane
and Holiday Village, both of which were developed in the early 1990s
and predate the project. Holiday Village is located just across the street
from ELH and is an age-restricted retirement community comprised of
single-family homes and condominiums limited to persons fifty-five years
and older. Hillside Lane is a just down the road and is comprised of stand-
alone, luxury single-family homes that follow a handful of design models.

In order to gain additional insight into what transpired in Mount Laurel after the ELH complex was inhabited in 2001, we supplemented our

time-series data with qualitative data gathered from a series of in-depth interviews undertaken with forty-two inhabitants of Ethel Lawrence Homes and five members of the ELH management team. These semistructured interviews focused on social organization and individual behavior within the project, and the management practices of ELH staff. With the cooperation of Fair Share Housing, we also obtained copies of transcripts from all ELH Neighborhood Watch meetings held from 2006 to 2010.

Perceptions in Mount Laurel

In order to assess community reaction to the project, we undertook a representative survey of households located in the adjacent neighborhoods of Holiday Village and Hillside Lane. Figure 4.2 presents an aerial view of EHL that depicts its spatial location with respect to surrounding neighborhoods. The Hurley Tract, on which the project was built, is outlined in white and the development's four cul-de-sacs are identified and labeled. The entrance to the Holiday Village senior housing lies in the lower center of the photo just below the bottom corner of the tract. Detached housing along a suburban way known as Rolling Glen Court is visible just above the top border of the tract, in the top right of the photo. Hillside Lane is located just off the aerial photo to the top left.

From a private vendor, we purchased a list of all residential addresses in the postal-carrier routes adjacent to the Hurley Tract on which ELH was built, yielding a list of 1,942 addresses, around 70 percent of which also included a phone number and name of the household head. Because the survey was meant for households in two particular neighborhoods, we created a list of streets corresponding to Holiday Village and Hillside Lane and used it to generate a final sampling frame of 1,129 addresses in two strata: Holiday Village (n = 891) and Hillside Village (n = 238). To draw the sample, we randomly selected two hundred addresses from each list and approached households serially to solicit interviews, sending out personalized letters that were in most cases followed by a telephone call. Out of the four hundred addresses, 382 eligible respondents were located and of these 127 submitted to an interview, with 124 refusals and 131 nonresponses, yielding a final response rate of 33.2 percent. Of the 127 completed interviews, 57 were respondents who lived in Holiday Village and 70 were from Hillside Lane. The final sampling weight for the Holiday Village respondents was therefore 15.63 (or 891/57), whereas the weight for Hillside Lane was 3.4 (or 238/70). We report weighted tabulations when presenting our findings.

Interviewers conducted the survey by phone or in person, at the respondent's preference, and in each case undertook a computer-assisted

Figure 4.2. Aerial view of the Ethel Lawrence Homes showing its location relative to surrounding neighborhoods (*Source*: Google Earth; © 2012 Google)

interview. The neighbor questionnaire is reproduced in appendix A1. As can be seen, the survey asked nearby residents about their perceptions of trends in both the neighborhood and township in recent years, focusing explicitly on property values, crime rates, taxes, and various other indicators of quality of life. These were questions followed by a series probing awareness about the Ethel Lawrence Homes, the degree of contact with ELH residents, and impressions about the project itself. The survey was short and lasted about fifteen minutes. In addition to fielding this short survey, we also conducted in-depth interviews with fifteen respondents from the same subdivisions as well as thirty-one stakeholders from around Mount Laurel, including current and former elected officials, school administrators, teachers, librarians, clergy, and the police. The guide for these semistructured interviews is included as appendix A2.

Effects on Project Residents

To assess how entry into the Ethel Lawrence Homes affected the lives of project residents themselves, we surveyed current and former ELH residents as well as a comparison sample of individuals who had applied to the project but who, for one reason or another, either remained on the waiting list at the time of the survey or had not been accepted into the project. The survey staff sent letters explaining the study and its goals and requested the participation of all eligible respondents. Field interviewers subsequently followed up with phone calls or, if a phone number could not be identified, with home visits. The interviewers, from Princeton University's Survey Research Center, administered the sixty-minute questionnaire to all willing participants in person, either in their homes or at a neutral site of their choosing. The interviews were conducted between November 19, 2009 and March 3, 2010.

The final sample included 116 residents and 108 nonresidents. Of the 116 residents, 5 were former residents who had since moved out of the project. Table 4.2 shows response rates and a breakdown of the reasons for nonresponse in each group. Since 2001 a total of 153 families has occupied the project's 140 units. At the time of the survey, two units were vacant, yielding a universe of 138 resident households and 15 former ELH resident households. Apart from these households, some 350 families had applied but were not admitted or were still on the waiting list, and constituted our nonresident comparison population. Not surprisingly, the response rate was highest among current ELH residents who were by definition easy to locate. Whereas 80 percent of current ELH residents completed the survey, the response rate among former residents was just 33 percent and that among nonresidents was only 31 percent.

Table 4.2. Response rates and reasons for nonresponse, by resident status

	Current Residents	Former Residents	All Residents	Nonresidents
Final Sample size	111	5	116	108
Total Attempted Contacts	138	15	153	350
Response Rate	80.4%	33.3%	75.8%	30.9%
Reason for Nonresponse				
Could Not Find	3.7	70.0	21.6	64.5
Refused	96.3	30.0	78.4	34.7
Other	0.0	0.0	0.0	0.8
Total Refusals	27	10	37	242

In both of the latter groups, the most important reason for nonresponse was that the subject simply could not be located (70 percent of former residents and 65 percent of nonresidents). Among those who were successfully located and contacted, 63 percent of former residents and 56 percent of nonresidents agreed to be interviewed.

The questionnaire used to survey residents, former residents, and nonresidents is shown in appendix A3. The survey begins by asking respondents to think about their living situation back in 1999, before the opening of the Ethel Lawrence Homes. This date was easy for respondents to situate in time, given that we prompted them to think about where they were and with whom they were living at the time of the millennium celebration. We began by compiling a roster of residents in the household that respondents inhabited in 1999, noting the age, sex, educational status, labor-force participation, and duration of residence for each household member. We then asked respondents about conditions in the neighborhood they inhabited in 1999, focusing on specific instances of exposure to social disorder and violence. We also queried them about the frequency of interaction with relatives and friends and access to various public and private services.

After finishing with 1999, we went on to ask the same set of questions about current household composition and neighborhood circumstances. After establishing these, we posed a series of questions about respondents' current health, work status, and educational attainment, as well as recent experiences with crime and social disorder, visits with friends and relatives, and access to public and private services. This information was gathered from current and former residents as well as nonresident applicants.

As noted above, the applicant list was sampled in order to provide a control group that would enable us to identify more precisely the effect of living in Ethel Lawrence Homes. In our analyses we considered salient outcomes such as exposure to disorder and violence, mental and physical health, labor-force participation, earnings, and program participation, yielding a research design known as a post-test-only static-group comparison (Campbell and Stanley 1963; Spector 1981). If ELH residents (current or former) display higher rates of labor-force participation, higher earnings, better health, and lower rates of welfare receipt than nonresident applicants, it would constitute evidence that access to affordable housing in an advantaged suburb positively influences the lives of low-income individuals.

The degree to which one can attribute a causal effect to ELH residence depends on the underlying equivalence of the two comparison groups. If the groups can indeed be considered equivalent to one another in all important respects, then a causal attribution is warranted; if not, such an attribution is called into question. In the present case, membership in the resident versus nonresident samples was not randomly assigned, so equivalence cannot be tacitly assumed. In the absence of random assignment, selectivity constitutes the most important threat to a study's internal validity (Campbell and Stanley 1963; Spector 1981). If selection into the comparison group occurs on the basis of a variable or trait that is related to the outcome, it becomes a plausible alternative explanation for the effect. Usually researchers worry about self-selection on the basis of some unmeasured attribute—for instance, motivation, persistence, or gumption—such that members of the experimental group possess more of these qualities and therefore do better.

In the present case, however, both current and former residents and nonresident applicants have self-selected into the group of people seeking to leave their current homes and neighborhoods and move into the Ethel Lawrence Homes, thus holding unmeasurable traits such as motivation and gumption more or less constant. All members of the experimental and control groups revealed their gumption by showing up at the ELH management office to pick up and fill out an application form. Even among applicants, of course, not everyone has the same degree of motivation, which is why some people show up earlier than others to drop off their applications.

Since applications are processed on a first-come, first-served basis, however, we also have a direct measure of the degree of gumption by coding rank order on the list, thus enabling an additional layer of direct control. Presumably those who arrived earliest were the most motivated to secure an entry spot.

Initial assignment to the experimental group (ELH residence) was made on the basis of information contained in the residence application, which is known to us for both residents and nonresidents, thereby enabling us to control statistically for all the measured characteristics upon which assignment was made, including gumption as indicated by position on the rank-ordered list. Access to data from the application form opens up the possibility of drawing on a new statistical technique that has been developed to control for selectivity bias. Known as propensity score matching, the technique involves using data from the application to estimate a model that predicts the likelihood, or propensity, of gaining entry into Ethel Lawrence Homes (Rubin 2006; Morgan and Winship 2007; Guo and Fraser 2009). From this model we generate estimates of each individual's probability of entry and then use these "propensity scores" to create matched comparison groups of project residents and nonresidents for use in statistical comparisons.

Originally we sought to compute propensity scores for residents and nonresidents before the fact and then attempted to interview only those nonresidents who most closely matched residents. Unfortunately, given the difficulty of tracking down and locating nonresidents and the finite resources at our disposal, we were compelled simply to survey as many applicants as we could track down and interview and only estimate propensity scores after the fact. Applications to the Ethel Lawrence Homes are archived at Fair Share Housing Development's offices at ELH. With the permission of project managers we entered these data and used them to create a database that included age, household size, family composition, relationship status, sex, income, neighborhood, current living situation, and type of residence desired by each applicant. In addition to these variables, we also coded applicants' stated reason for wanting to move and, as noted above, measured the degree of their motivation to enter the project by coding position on the first-come, first-served waiting list. Descriptions of variables used to estimate the propensity models are presented in appendix A4.

Table 4.3 shows mean values for these variables as well as coefficient estimates for the propensity score model itself. Since units were allocated based on rank order on the application list, it is not surprising that residents are concentrated in the first two quartiles of the ranked list whereas nonresidents are spread predominantly through the last three quartiles. Other than this obvious difference, residents and nonresidents appear to be quite similar with respect to measured characteristics. The typical applicant, whether successful at the time of the survey or not, was an unmarried female aged 36 to 37 years with minor children and an income of around $20,000 per year. The neighborhoods in which they originated were roughly half minority (32% black and 13% Hispanic), with a poverty rate of around 14% according to 2000 census tract data. Somewhat more of the ELH residents than nonresidents cited a dissatisfaction with housing as their main reason for moving (53% versus 41%), which is consistent with fact that residents were somewhat more likely to have children present (73% versus 64%) and were slightly more likely to be living with other family members at the time of application (28% versus 23%).

Because we not only gathered information on project residents and nonresidents at the time of the survey, but also compiled more limited data on outcomes and characteristics in 1999, before any of the subjects had moved into ELH, we are in some cases able to turn to an even stronger research design known as a pre-test/post-test static-group comparison. Statistically these data enable us to conduct a within-subjects fixed-effects analysis that holds constant the effect of unmeasured individual traits as long as they are not time-varying. The existence of measures before and after ELH residence occurred allows us to assess whether moving into ELH had any effect on the variable being measured. If we observe a rise in employment rates between 1999 and the survey

Table 4.3. Mean values and estimated coefficients for variables used in estimating propensity score models

Variable	Mean Values		Propensity Model	
	Nonresidents	Residents	Coefficient	Standard Error
Position on Waiting List				
Quartile 1	0.17	0.30	----	----
Quartile 2	0.29	0.19	−0.746**	0.266
Quartile 3	0.25	0.22	−0.646*	0.269
Quartile 4	0.29	0.17	−0.944**	0.273
Not Assigned a Position	0.04	0.15	0.797+	0.448
Number of BRs requested	2.01	2.08	−0.312	0.217
Lives with Family Member	0.23	0.28	−0.048	0.232
Female	0.87	0.90	0.098	0.331
Relationship status				
Never married	0.71	0.67	----	----
Married	0.07	0.13	−0.349	0.373
Divorced/separated	0.19	0.19	−0.168	0.416
Widowed	0.02	0.03	−0.003	0.709
Age	37.2	36.4	−0.003	0.009
Has children	0.64	0.73	0.681+	0.392
Income (000)	20.6	18.9	−0.149	0.098
Income imputed	0.01	0.06	−0.208	0.721
Neighborhood Traits				
% black	32.1	32.4	0.002	0.005
% Hispanic	12.8	13.7	0.005	0.010
% vacant units	8.0	7.8	−0.020	0.025
% rental units	34.0	34.1	0.001	0.007
% poor	13.6	13.8	0.005	0.018
Reason for Applying				
Housing issues	0.41	0.53	0.503+	0.265
Safety and Opportunity	0.23	0.20	0.133	0.527
No Reason Provided	0.34	0.30	0.192	0.301
Interaction				
Children*Safety & Opportunity			−0.425	0.573
Intercept			0.705	0.736
Chi Squared			36.230**	
Number of Cases	108	116	224	

+P < .10; *p < .05; **p < .01

date for ELH residents but not nonresident applicants, for example, we have strong grounds for concluding that ELH had a significant effect in improving residents' employment prospects.

Given the fact that ELH residents entered the project at different times, with two major move-in periods in 2000–2001 and 2004, that exits from the project occur over the entire 2000–2009 period, we gain yet another design advantage. As noted in chapter 1, the MTO experiment confounded the effects of moving with the effects of inhabiting a low-poverty neighborhood. In the present case, however, we have a diversity of durations spent in the project, enabling us to disentangle the disruptive effects of moving from the benefits of inhabiting quality housing in an affluent suburban neighborhood. If the costs of moving are experienced immediately but the benefits accrue gradually over time, then we hypothesize that the duration of time spent living in ELH will be positively related to indicators of social and economic well-being.

Outcomes among Children

In addition to surveying the adults who filled out applications to enter ELH, we also undertook a special subsurvey of young people age 12–18 who were present in respondent households. Adults with adolescent children present were asked for permission to interview their offspring, and of the forty-nine eligible adolescents in this age range living in ELH at the time of the survey, thirty-seven participated in the study (response rate = 75.5 percent), whereas thirty-four of the fifty-three eligible nonresident children participated (response rate = 64.2 percent), yielding an overall response rate of 69.6 percent. By far the most common reason for not participating was not the lack of adult permission, but the failure of a young person to complete the written questionnaire. In addition, of the seventy-one surveys filled out, eight were missing data on one or more key variables, which required us to drop these cases, yielding a final sample of thirty-three resident and thirty nonresident adolescents.

The youth questionnaire is reproduced in appendix A5. As can be seen, it asks basic questions about the young person's demographic characteristics, school courses and grades; parent or guardian's involvement in school, discipline style and support for enrichment activities; number of hours spent on academic and non-academic activities outside of school; as well as a host of questions about extracurricular activities, self-esteem, views about school; and peers' views about school. In our analyses, we supplement these data with information from the adult questionnaire to control for family composition and socioeconomic status. Although most of the adult respondents were parents of the adolescents who were inter-viewed, in a few cases (N = 5) they were grandparents, aunts, or uncles. To supplement the quantitative data arising from these surveys, we also conducted in-depth interviews with fifteen adolescents to ask about their experiences in the project, at school, and in the community generally.

Conclusion

The "Monitoring Mount Laurel Study" was launched to undertake a systematic evaluation of what effect the Ethel Lawrence Homes had on crime rates, property values, and taxes in the surrounding community; the attitudes and perceptions of neighbors and township leaders about the project; the social and economic well-being of project residents ver-sus nonresidents; and educational outcomes experienced by adolescents who lived in the sampled households. To assess the project's effects on crime, property values, and taxes we designed a multiple control-group time-series experiment using publicly available data. We also carried out in-depth interviews with project managers and residents. To assess com-munity perceptions of the project we surveyed neighbors living in adja-cent neighborhoods and carried out in-depth qualitative interviews with both neighbors and stakeholders throughout the township, including elected officials, school administrators, teachers, librarians, and clergy. Finally, to assess effects on project residents we surveyed current and former project residents along with nonresident applicants to the project as well as adolescent children present in respondent households. We also undertook in-depth qualitative interviews of nonresident applicants as well as current project residents.

While the multiple control-group time-series design offers a relatively high degree of internal validity for drawing conclusions about the proj-ect's effects on crime, taxes, and property values (Campbell and Stanley 1963), in the absence of random assignment to the resident and nonres-ident comparison groups, it is impossible to make a *definitive* attribu-tion of causality with respect to the project's effects on the lives of ELH tenants and their children. We argue, however, that internal validity is strongly bolstered by several features of the present study's design: all respondents are self-selected into the group of people who wish to leave their current home and neighborhood and enter the Ethel Lawrence Homes; we have a direct measure of the strength of their motivation in position on the ranked list; access to all data from the completed appli-cations of both residents and nonresidents enables direct control of the factors that entered into allocation decision; and the same data enable estimation of a model to establish probabilities of entry into the project and thus apply the technique of propensity score-matching. Although by no means perfect, we believe these design features offer an advance over prior contributions to the burgeoning literature on neighborhood effects.

CHAPTER 5

Neighborly Concerns

EFFECTS ON SURROUNDING COMMUNITIES

Previous chapters have revealed that white suburban residents generally oppose the location of affordable housing developments within their communities, at least those intended for poor families as opposed to the elderly, and that such opposition is at least partially rooted in racial and class prejudice. Apart from prejudice, however, we also argue that suburbanites have legitimate practical reasons to be skeptical about the influence of "public housing" on their communities, given the lamentable record of the projects built throughout the country during the 1950s and 1960s. Both skepticism and prejudice were evident in the rhetoric employed by Mount Laurel residents in opposing the construction of the Ethel Lawrence Homes in their township. Although it is doubtful that many of these local critics were well grounded in the social science literature, there are nonetheless defensible theoretical and substantive reasons to expect social problems to follow from the insertion of a 100 percent affordable housing project into a white, affluent suburban setting.

Such an expectation derives from the fact that locating affordable housing units in suburban areas inevitably entails increasing the ethnic heterogeneity, residential mobility, and class diversity of the host community. In general, social disorganization theory predicts that increasing diversity will be accompanied by decreases in social control that, in turn, lead to increased rates of crime and declining home prices (Shaw and McKay 1969; Sampson 1993; Sampson and Wilson 1995). Indeed, empirical studies have documented a significant association between residential mobility, ethnic heterogeneity, and spatial inequality and lower collective efficacy within neighborhoods, where collective efficacy refers to the degree to which neighbors are socially cohesive and willing to intervene for the common good within public spaces (Sampson, Raudenbush, and Earls 1997; Sampson, Morenoff, and Earls 1999; Morenoff, Sampson and Raudenbush 2001; Putnam 2007; Sampson 2012).

Although it is well established that rates of crime and social disorder generally rise as collective efficacy falls, it is not clear that a lack of collective efficacy necessarily stems from racial and ethnic diversity. Collective efficacy is a form of social capital, and Putnam (2007) argues that public trust is undermined by racial-ethnic diversity. In his extensive analysis of the social ecology of Chicago neighborhoods, however, Sampson (2012) found that although collective efficacy was indeed associated with the degree of concentrated disadvantage, it was not really correlated with the racial or ethnic composition of particular neighborhoods. Portes and Vickstrom (2011) argue that variation in social capital is more strongly associated with racial and ethnic inequalities linked to deep historical processes rather than racial-ethnic diversity per se. Likewise, Rothwell's (2012) analysis indicates that intermetropolitan variation in public trust is associated with racial segregation rather than racial diversity.

In applying social disorganization theory to the specific case of affordable housing, researchers have tended to focus their reasoning on the characteristics either of people or of places. "Place" theories link the design of affordable housing projects to social disorganization, asserting that the built environment in most projects offers few opportunities for surveillance and social control, leading to higher rates of crime and disorder (Griffiths and Tita 2009). "People" theories focus on the allocation of poor people to confined spaces and argue that public housing isolates poor residents from "mainstream" society and concentrates poverty spatially to produce a social environment that fosters criminality and social disorganization (Wilson 1987; Massey 1995; Weatherburn et al., 1999).

Facing Community Fears

For a variety of theoretical reasons, therefore, it is by no means illogical for suburban dwellers to anticipate that rising ethnic heterogeneity, increased residential mobility, and the concentration of poverty associated with affordable housing might increase social disorganization and lead ultimately to a rise in crime rates and a decline in property values. The degree to which poor neighborhoods *automatically* may be assumed to promote social disorganization has been strongly contested, however (Suttles 1969; Small 2004). Although the potential for social disorganization is clearly latent in affordable housing developments, whether social disorder is ultimately expressed depends very much on the project's design, management, and internal organization. As noted in chapter 3, Fair Share Housing Development paid considerable attention to these issues in planning, constructing, and managing the Ethel Lawrence Homes. Although there may be historical and theoretical reasons to anticipate greater disorganization in the wake of an affordable housing development, these outcomes are by no means a given. Ultimately the effect of subsidized housing on the surrounding community is an empirical question, and this is the issue to which we now turn.

Effects on Crime

As discussed in the previous chapter, in order to evaluate the effects of the opening of the Ethel Lawrence Homes on the surrounding community, we designed a multiple control-group time-series experiment to compare trends in Mount Laurel before and after the project's opening with trends before and after within a set of comparison townships. Figure 5.1 undertakes this analysis visually by showing trends in crime rates observed from 1990 to 2009 in Mount Laurel, and comparing them with trends observed in our comparison townships of Cherry Hill, Cinnaminson, and Evesham over the same period. As a point of reference, we also show the trend in crime rates for the State of New Jersey as a whole. Given the relatively small size of the township populations, crime rates vary considerably from year to year, and to reveal the underlying trend more clearly, we computed three-year moving averages.

As seen in figure 5.1, all geographic areas experienced a significant drop in crime over the period. In New Jersey as a whole, the rate dropped

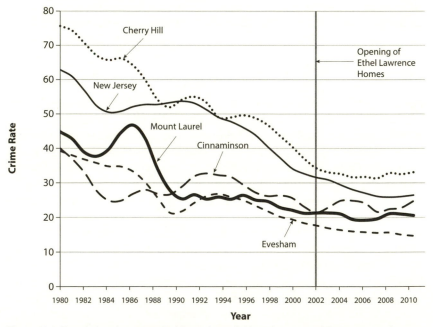

Figure 5.1. Trends in crime rates in Mount Laurel, New Jersey, and three comparison townships (*Source*: NJ Division of State Police)

from 63.1 crimes per 1,000 residents in 1990 to around 26.5 crimes per 1,000 residents in 2009. The trend in Cherry Hill closely followed the state trend though beginning at a higher level, moving from a crime rate of 75.9 in 1980 to 24.9 in 2009. Crime rates in Mount Laurel, Evesham, and Cinnaminson were much lower than the state average in 1990, so they had less room to fall and the decline was less dramatic in these townships. Nonetheless crime declined in all three townships from 1990 to 2009. The trend in Mount Laurel is indicated by the thick black line. Although the decline was flatter there than in some of the other townships, there is no evidence of any discontinuity in the trend line following the year 2000, when ELH opened, or after 2004 when it expanded by 40 percent.

In Table 5.1 we undertake a formal test of temporal discontinuities in Mount Laurel's crime rate relative to trends in the comparison cases by estimating simple Ordinary Least Squares (OLS) regressions of crime rates years for each township during two separate periods: a pre-ELH period from 1990 to 2000, and a post-ELH period from 2001 to 2009.

Table 5.1. OLS regressions of crime rates on time (year) in Mount Laurel and comparison townships

Township	Pre-ELH (1990–2000)		Post-ELH (2001–2009)		Pre v. Post
	β	$\beta \neq \beta_{\text{Mt. Laurel}}$	β	$\beta \neq \beta_{\text{Mt. Laurel}}$	$\beta_{1990-2000} \neq \beta_{2001-09}$
Total Crime					
Mount Laurel	−0.53	---	−0.12	---	Yes**
Cherry Hill	−1.71	Yes***	−0.09	No	Yes***
Cinnaminson	−0.93	No	0.15	No	Yes***
Evesham	−0.56	No	−0.32	No	No
Violent Crime					
Mount Laurel	−0.05	---	−0.06	---	No
Cherry Hill	−0.05	No	−0.06	No	No
Cinnaminson	−0.04	No	−0.03	No	No
Evesham	−0.01	Yes***	0.00	Yes**	No
Nonviolent Crime					
Mount Laurel	−0.49	---	−0.06	---	Yes**
Cherry Hill	−1.67	Yes***	−0.03	No	Yes***
Cinnaminson	−0.89	Yes*	0.19	No	Yes***
Evesham	−0.55	No	−0.31	Yes*	No
No. of Observations	11		9		

*p <. 0.01; **p < 0.05; ***p < 0.01. Based on Wald Test of hypothesis that slopes are equal.
Source: New Jersey Division of State Police 1990–2009

We also present results separately for violent and nonviolent crimes. The resulting slopes indicate the average rate of linear change in each township over the time period under consideration. If the opening of ELH caused an increase in crime, we should observe a significant difference between the 1990–2000 slope and the 2001–2009 slope, and this difference should be significantly greater than the corresponding slopes observed in the comparison townships, corresponding to Galster's (2004) "difference in differences" approach.

As the regression results very clearly demonstrate, there is no evidence that the opening of the Ethel Lawrence Homes brought about an increase in crime within Mount Laurel Township. Indeed, overall crime rates decreased during both periods under consideration. Crime rates fell everywhere before and after the opening of ELH, except in Cherry Hill. Although the rate of decline slowed or reversed in all townships after 2000 (significantly, in three cases), in none of the comparisons was the change in crime rates observed during 2001–2009 significantly different from that observed in Mount Laurel.

When we consider violent and nonviolent crime rates separately in the bottom two panels, we see that the slowing of the decline between 1990–2000 and 2001–2009 was entirely attributable to a shift nonviolent criminal activity. Across all four townships there was no statistically significant difference in the rate at which violent crime declined between the two periods; and the decline in violent crime in Mount Laurel after 2000 was no different than that observed in Cherry Hill and Cinnaminson. Although there was a significant difference compared with Evesham, this difference reflects the fact that we observe no significant decline in violent crime at all in Evesham, either before or after 2001, whereas Mount Laurel's violent crime rate continued the decline established before this date.

In contrast, the rate of decline in nonviolent crimes declined or reversed after 2000 in all townships, and this discontinuity was significant in three of the four cases. Nonetheless, the post-ELH rate of decline in Mount Laurel was no different than the post-ELH rate of decline in the other townships, with the exception again being Evesham, whose nonviolent crime rate declined more rapidly than the others. But here once again, Evesham is the outlier, not Mount Laurel. Thus, despite historical and theoretical reasons to expect an increase in crime, we find no evidence that the opening of ELH had any influence at all on crime rates in Mount Laurel, which were falling before 2001 and continued to fall afterward, just as they did in nearby townships.

Effects on Property Values

In figure 5.2 we move on to consider the project's potential effects on property values by plotting trends in home prices in Mount Laurel and the

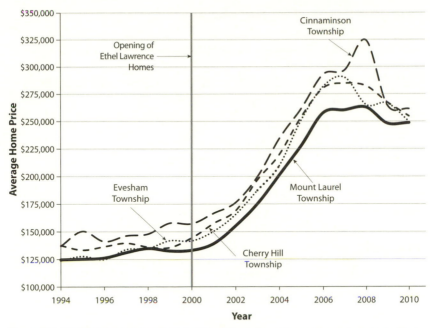

Figure 5.2. Trends in property values in Mount Laurel and three comparison townships 1994–2010 (*Source*: NJ Department of Taxation)

three comparison townships from 1994 through 2010. In keeping with the national boom in housing costs, home values rose rapidly across all townships in the years after 2000. From values in the range of $125,000 to $150,000 in 1994, average home prices in the townships rose into the range of $250,000 to $300,000 by 2006, when prices leveled off before declining when the national housing bubble burst in 2008, which was preceded by a minibubble in Cinnaminson. The trend for Mount Laurel is again indicated by the thick black line. Of the four townships, Mount Laurel tied with Evesham for the lowest average home value in 1994, and its average home values remained below those of the other three townships throughout the period, going from around $125,000 in 1994 to $260,000 on the eve of the housing bust. Over the same period, Evesham went from approximately $125,000 to around $290,000, while Cherry Hill rose from $138,000 to $285,000 and Cinnaminson grew from $137,000 to $300,000.

The price gap between Mount Laurel and the three comparison townships did increase somewhat after 2000. Thus if the opening of ELH had any possible effect on home prices, it was to slow down the escalation of home prices somewhat compared with other townships, but this scenario was not borne out by statistical analysis. In the top panel of Table 5.2, we

Table 5.2. OLS regressions of property values on time (year) in Mount Laurel and comparison townships

| Township | Pre-ELH (1994–2000) | | Post-ELH (2001–2010) | | Pre v. Post |
	β	$\beta{\neq}\beta_{\text{Mt. Laurel}}$	β	$\beta{\neq}\beta_{\text{Mt. Laurel}}$	$\beta_{1994-2000}{\neq}\beta_{2001-19}$
Comparison Townships					
Mount Laurel	$1,726	---	$13,827	---	Yes***
Cherry Hill	$867	No	$13,693	No	Yes***
Cinnaminson	$2,915	No	$13,790	No	Yes***
Evesham	$3,284	Yes**	$13,722	No	Yes***
Adjacent Neighborhoods					
Hillside Lane	$1,896	No	$29,588	No	Yes***
Holiday Village	$6,476	Yes***	$5,875	No	No
No. of Observations	7		10		

*p < .0.01; **p < 0.05; ***p < 0.01. Based on Wald Test of hypothesis that slopes are equal.

Source: New Jersey Division of Taxation 1994–2010; Asbury Park Press 1994–2010

undertake a formal statistical test of the hypothesis by using OLS regressions to estimate the average linear change in home prices across the four townships during 1994–2000 and 2001–2010. Once again there are no significant differences between Mount Laurel and the three comparison townships, either in the rate of home-price increase after 2000 or the change in slopes between 1994–2000 and 2001–2010. Simply put, we find no evidence that the opening of the Ethel Lawrence Homes had any significant effect on township home prices.

Although we found no significant effect of the project's opening on property values in Mount Laurel as a whole, it may be that the township is too large an aggregate to detect price effects. Thus in figure 5.3 we show trends in home prices in the two adjacent neighborhoods of Holiday Village and Hillside Lane. Of the two neighboring areas, Holiday Village is the most comparable to Ethel Lawrence Homes in layout and construction, though not in composition, of course. It is a retirement village composed mainly of older couples and singles without children. Nonetheless, like ELH, it is physically composed mainly of cul-de-sacs surrounded by town houses. It is also located directly across the street. In contrast, although it is adjacent to ELH property, Hillside Lane is a few blocks away and is more of a luxury-home development targeted to wealthier families, many with young children.

The luxury nature of the Hillside Lane development is clearly indicated in figure 5.3. Whereas the average home value in Hillside Lane stood at

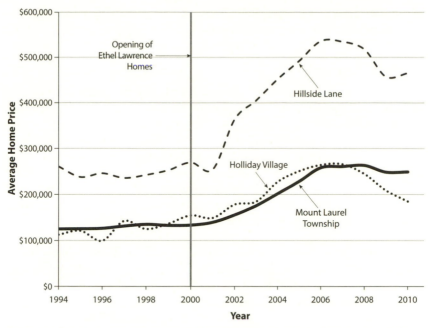

Figure 5.3. Trends in property values in Mount Laurel and neighborhoods adjacent to the Ethel Lawrence Homes (*Source*: Asbury Park Press Property Records 1994–2010)

$260,000 in 1994, considerably above the Mount Laurel average, the average home value in Holiday Village was around $112,000, slightly below the Mount Laurel average. Home values remained flat through the late 1990s and even stagnated somewhat in Hillside Lane, but then increased beginning around 2000. Whereas the trend in Holiday Village closely followed that of the township, property values increased more rapidly in the upscale Hillside Lane neighborhood, peaking at $534,000 in 2006. After 2008 prices declined in Hillside Land and Holiday village, but not in Mount Laurel Township as a whole.

The statistical tests performed in the bottom panel of table 5.2 indicate that the price increase after 2000 in Hillside Lane was significantly greater than price increases either in the township as a whole, or in Holiday Village. In addition, the difference in slopes between 1994–2000 and 2001–2010 was much greater. Although the difference in the Holiday Village slopes between 1994–2000 and 2001–2010 is negative (-$601) compared with the positive differences in the township as a whole and in Hillside Lane, Wald tests of the hypothesis that the Holiday Village slopes are equal demonstrate that the pre- and post-2001 difference is not statistically significant. In other words, there is no statistical evidence of a discontinuity in Holiday Village property values before and after the opening of the Ethel Lawrence Homes.

Effects on Taxes

Finally, in figure 5.4 we show trends in effective property tax rates in Mount Laurel and the three comparison townships from 1997 through 2010. Effective tax rates are adjusted by state tax authorities to allow comparisons across municipalities based on the assumption that all municipalities are at 100 percent valuation. Although the New Jersey Division of Taxation did not publish data on effective tax rates before 2000, we were able to use published data on the general tax rate for the years 1997 through 1999 to compute the adjusted rates for those years as well, giving us a before-and-after sequence.

Looking at the figure, we see that in all four townships the effective tax rate declined somewhat from 1997 to 2000 then rose again between 2000 and 2005 and then declined steadily between 2005 and 2008 before tax reassessments pushed the rates back upward a bit, with the largest increase observed in Cinnaminson. Despite the reassessments, however, in all townships, effective tax rates in 2010 remained below those in

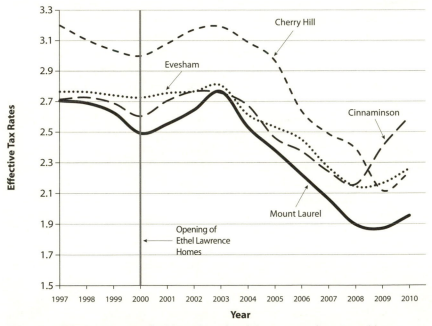

Figure 5.4. Effective tax rates for Mount Laurel and three comparison townships (*Source*: NJ Division of Taxation)

prevailing in 2000 when the Ethel Lawrence Homes opened, and the effective rate was the lowest of all in Mount Laurel. Clearly, then, the opening of ELH did not generate higher tax rates for Mount Laurel residents, a conclusion confirmed by the statistical tests presented in table 5.3. As can be seen, the change in tax rates after 2000 was no different in Mount Laurel than in any of the other townships, and within Mount Laurel itself, there was no change in rate of change before or after the project's opening.

In sum, we find no evidence that the opening of Ethel Lawrence Homes caused an increase in crime rates, a decline in property values, or an increase in property tax rates in Mount Laurel after the project was opened in 2000. Indeed, crime rates dropped and property values rose in Mount Laurel after this date, and formal tests did not detect even a slowing of the decline in crime rates or increase in property values relative to other comparable townships nearby. Even in neighborhoods adjacent to ELH we detected no effect on property values. Indeed, in one neighborhood, home values rose more rapidly than in the township generally. Overall, tax rates fell in all townships between 2000 and 2010 despite upward bumps in 2003 and after 2008, but the effect tax rate was lowest in Mount Laurel, and overall trends were not statistically different from the comparison townships,

The lack of a direct economic cost to the taxpayers of Mount Laurel reflects two agreements reached between Fair Share Housing Development and township authorities, one for an annual Payment in Lieu of Taxes and another to provide the township a percentage of the rental income from ELH to offset the costs of municipal services such as police,

Table 5.3. OLS regressions of property taxes on time (year) in Mount Laurel and comparison townships

Township	Pre-ELH (1997–2000)		Post-ELH (2001–2010)		Pre v. Post
	β	$\beta{\neq}\beta_{\text{Mt. Laurel}}$	β	$\beta{\neq}\beta_{\text{Mt. Laurel}}$	$\beta_{1997-2000}{\neq}\beta_{2001-19}$
Comparison Townships					
Mount Laurel	−0.07	---	−0.10	---	No
Cherry Hill	−0.07	No	−0.09	No	Yes***
Cinnaminson	−0.04	Yes*	−0.08	No	No
Evesham	−0.01	Yes***	−0.08	No	Yes***
No. of Observations	4		10		

*p <. 0.01; ** p < 0 .05; ***p < 0.01. Based on Wald Test of hypothesis that slopes are equal.

Source: New Jersey Division of Taxation 2011

fire, and trash collection. There is one potential cost to taxpayers that is real but indirect: the added costs involved in educating the children of EHL residents. Given that our survey identified just thirty school-age children scattered across different primary-, middle-, and secondary schools, however, their effect on class sizes, school composition, and district budgets was necessarily small. Moreover, in the broader scheme of things, educating poor children in Mount Laurel is more cost effective, given that the per-pupil cost of education is much lower in suburban districts such as Mount Laurel than in the disadvantaged urban districts where most students originated. Thus, as demonstrated in chapter 8, the move produced better educational outcomes for children at a lower cost to the state as a whole.

Managing Social Disorder

Given the logic of social disorganization theory and the history of public housing in the United States, we might have expected the opening of the Ethel Lawrence Homes to contribute to higher crime rates, lower property values, and a greater tax burden on township residents. We attribute the absence of this outcome not to the inherent benignity of affordable housing projects, but to specific design features of the project's architecture, the managerial policies of ELH staff, and the social practices of ELH residents. Specific features of planning, management, and social organization worked to mitigate potential threats to disorder that are latent in a 100 percent affordable housing project. Rather than producing social disorganization, these features generated a high degree of social organization within the project, a high degree of participation by residents in community organizations, and generally high levels of satisfaction and social cohesion among tenants despite their common background of material hardship.

Preventing Crime

The ELH management team runs what both residents and staff call a "tight ship." As noted earlier, applicant screening is thorough and includes credit checks, criminal background checks, income verification, and a home visit. Of the population seeking affordable housing in New Jersey, then, the residents of Ethel Lawrence are a screened subset of people who are probably less likely than poor people in general to have the proclivity, knowledge, and ability to engage in criminal or delinquent activities.

In addition, once tenants have entered the project, ELH managers are very closely involved in their daily lives. The management office is located at the front of the complex and it houses a property manager, a leasing agent, and a social-service coordinator. A maintenance worker also lives on-site in one of the 140 units and the entire staff works to solve problems quickly. Staff members also seek to resolve lease infractions quickly and do not hesitate to employ eviction against troublesome tenants. Most residents say they like the management's heavy hand and believe that it contributes to maintaining a desirable community. Residents regularly share information with management during casual conversations that occur when they drop off their monthly rent or bring children to homework club. These conversations provide regular check-ins during which good and bad feelings about neighbors, management, or the complex may be voiced.

In general, residents see the ELH management style as intrusive but ultimately positive for the complex and its inhabitants. As one resident put it in an in-depth interview, "they're not so much in your business; like they let you live, but they tell you what you can and can't do. As far as, like, in the place, you can't have a whole lot of problems, you can't have people coming in and out of your house, can't be causing trouble, which makes sense because you don't want your neighborhood torn up. So it makes sense." Another resident added that "the reason I feel safe is all credit due to management. I think that if they find anybody who causes too much trouble, it's my opinion that they're thrown out of here. So, I think that parents are on top of their children because of that."

As noted in prior chapters, ELH staff members have organized a Neighborhood Watch group that meets monthly and is affiliated with the township's Neighborhood Watch program, which in fact trained several of the group's members. At meetings, residents discuss their observations about the neighborhood. Based on our reading of minutes for Neighborhood Watch meetings held between 2006 and 2010, residents displayed values congruent with those typical in surrounding suburban neighborhoods. The most common issues discussed focused on the improper disposal of trash and litter, the irregular parking of cars, threats to private property, quality-of-life issues such as loud noises and pets, and the monitoring of strangers. Special attention was paid to events and behaviors that seemed out of place. These meetings also offered a chance for residents to learn from management about any police actions or criminal activity in the wider area. Other topics commonly discussed at Watch meetings included community events, suggestions for improvements, access to social-welfare resources, job opportunities, and school information.

Township police run regular patrols through the development's cul-de-sacs, and officers maintain close contact with the ELH managers, seeking and sharing information pertaining to ongoing criminal investigations. Indeed, from the project's inception, the police worked closely with developers and provided valuable input into the design of the Ethel Lawrence Homes in an effort to build social control into its physical structure. As a result of police input, for example, the construction of high fences was prohibited so as not to impede the ability of residents to monitor public spaces, and plans to build a handball court were scrapped to prevent the wall becoming a magnet for graffiti. Although residents are somewhat ambivalent about the heavy police presence, they are generally supportive. In the words of one resident, "[T]hey stay on top of it, I'll give them that. You know, I feel safe down here, but just don't have nothing to do with me." Residents regularly report suspicious or threatening incidents to property managers and police, although management feels they are too often called to intervene in situations when police should be called, such as when residents hear or observe domestic disputes or arguments between neighbors.

In addition to the Neighborhood Watch, ELH management also runs an on-site after school "homework club" for students. Hosted in a trailer near the entrance to the development, children are given daily time and space to do homework as well as the opportunity to receive any assistance with it they might need. The center has a computer lab that is open for leisure use as well as instruction. In addition, there are snacks and other regular activities such as soccer, guest speakers, educational programs, and development activities. Among younger children in the complex, attending the homework club is considered "cool," and children are eager to participate. Beyond providing educational enrichment for ELH children, the club also provides children with an adult-supervised place to congregate after school, which reduces the potential for conflict and delinquency. Figure 5.5 is a picture of students currently attending the homework club, which was recently christened the Margaret Donnelly O'Connor Education Center at Ethel R. Lawrence Homes, along with Peter J. O'Connor, the founder and executive director of Fair Share Housing Development and the Fair Share Housing Center.

Beyond these formal control mechanisms, residents have evolved a variety of informal means of social control, such as the active sharing of information and the ongoing monitoring of people's behavior in and around the complex. Key components of information come from parents' ongoing monitoring of their children, and neighbors keeping an eye out for one another. The shared information focuses mostly on the activities of other residents: who they are, where they work, what they are up to, who is coming in, who is leaving, problems in the home, and so forth. Particularly important in the flow of information are children, who serve both as active collectors and distributors of data. As one mother describes it, "Oh yeah, I feel safe here. There really isn't any crime here. No. I think it's pretty much because it is a small complex; people are always looking

Figure 5.5. Students from the Margaret Donnelly O'Connor Education Center at Ethel R. Lawrence Homes with Peter J. O'Connor, founder and executive director of Fair Share Housing Development (*Source*: Fair Share Housing Development)

out and checking out what's going on. And the kids know everything, you know. I mean I can get the whole story from my son, what I'll do is ask him what's going on in the neighborhood."

Another indicator of the high level of collective efficacy that residents have achieved in the project is the close attention paid to outsiders—people who do not live in Ethel Lawrence but may be staying in or visiting the complex (Freeman and Botein 2002). Members of the Neighborhood Watch group regularly comment on suspicious vehicles and people in the neighborhood, and informants emphasize that everyone is on the lookout for people who do not live in the neighborhood. Indeed, much of the gossip and most complaints in the complex involve allegations of nonregistered adults living in ELH units. Despite their overall approval of management practices, some residents feel that staff members pay too much attention residents' behavior inside their own homes. As one resident stated, "They worry about who's coming in and out of your house instead of what need to be done in your house, you know what I mean?" Another resident put it this way:

> It's supposed to be crime watch out here, but I don't really believe people know what crime watch is. You know what I mean? It's just like, people

just watch you. Out here I feel like I'm in a halfway house or something—like I'm trying to get rehabilitated for society or something. That's how it feels out here because you don't have enough privacy. Anything you do it goes back to the office, or somebody going to say to the office this that and the third, it's a whole bunch of nonsense.

Despite the existence of such complaints, our in-depth interviews suggest that most residents see formal and informal monitoring as essential to security in the complex. Our findings echo those of Miller (1998), whose study of a mixed-income development in Illinois found a similar trade-off between domestic control and public safety. Interestingly, despite frequent gripes about intrusive monitoring, Ethel Lawrence residents regularly complain to the management about what they perceive as insufficient screening of rental applicants, and regularly ask for stricter screening policies, paradoxically echoing calls made by the project's critics in earlier hearings.

In the end, the latent tendencies toward disorder that stem from the physical concentration of poor people within a compact project are overcome by a combination of efficacious physical design, careful management practices, and informal social control. As a result, the project is anything but disorganized, and very little crime is reported in or around the Ethel Lawrence Homes. Reports of crimes are largely confined to domestic disturbances. Minor crimes do occur in Ethel Lawrence, but management and residents count on reliable and well-developed formal and informal communication channels and social-control mechanisms to keep crime rates down and maintain order. The constant monitoring of residents and visitors reduces the potential that people with criminal intentions will find safe harbor in Ethel Lawrence.

Preventing Social Isolation

During a planning hearing before the construction of Ethel Lawrence Homes, one of our interviewees heard a local resident allege that the project would become a "ghetto in a field." Aside from the obvious racist undertone, this comment also reflects the community's initial concern that the project would move people from the inner city to a suburban housing complex where they would know not know anyone, would have little or nothing to do, and would remain isolated from the surrounding community. ELH residents themselves also reported worries about social isolation, mostly following from a total dependence on automobiles for transport in Mount Laurel and surrounding suburbs. According to the 2000 Census, 86 percent of the township's workers commuted to work alone in an automobile, compared to 3 percent who used public transportation and 0.3 percent who walked (U.S. Bureau of the Census 2009). The nearest bus stop is 2.25 miles from the Ethel Lawrence Homes, and given the spatial scale and car-based transportation infrastructure in the region, walking to a shopping center, school, or workplace is impractical. Indeed, it can often be dangerous, given the lack of sidewalks.

As a result, in their in-depth interviews, residents frequently complained about the lack of amenities within walking distance of ELH. As one resident described the situation,

> We're in an enclosed development, and there's nothing around here. When we were in Pine Hill, there was a recreational center, basically within walking distance. There was a bus that went right outside the development, so if the kids wanted to take a bus to the mall, they could do that. There's absolutely nothing to do in Mount Laurel. At least nothing we can walk to. So, as far as, socially, there's really nothing available.

Nonetheless, although most residents come from a low-income background, our survey revealed that 87 percent of ELH households had managed to acquire a car by the time of the survey. Maintaining and insuring an automobile is expensive, however, and when asked for their biggest criticism of the project, residents repeatedly mentioned the lack of access to public transportation. Only 2 percent of survey respondents said they depended on public transit for their daily needs. A recurring theme in interviews was the lack of access to a transportation "safety net" when cars broke down. Many residents voiced frustration about how the lack of public transportation access sometimes made it difficult for friends and family to visit, particularly from urban areas.

Despite the lack of access to public transit, on the survey residents nonetheless reported strong ongoing connections with friends and family. Indeed, as we show later, in chapter 7, we observed no drop in the frequency of social contact with relatives and peers among residents after they moved into the project. In terms of services and amenities, some ELH residents continued to maintain ties to previous places of residence in terms of doctors, dentists, and shopping. Other residents, however, quickly found new service providers within Mount Laurel. In any event, whether they connected with people and resources in Mount Laurel or elsewhere, ELH residents reported getting access to the resources and supports they needed.

In sum, although ELH residents complain somewhat about being physically isolated, owing largely to the project's location away from bus lines on open land distant from stores, schools, and businesses, this has not translated into very much social isolation, mainly because the vast majority of families have come to own a car and the ELH community is itself well integrated socially. The biggest problem is for young people, who lack playgrounds and other amenities on or near the site, and teen-agers. They often complain about having "nothing to do and nowhere to go"; but these are complaints made by teenagers everywhere.

Minimizing Threats to Property Values

Previous research has found that the design and density of affordable family-housing projects, and their aesthetic compatibility with surrounding structures, are key in determining effects on local property values. One of the central concerns raised by local residents about the project was that it would be unattractive and easily identified as "public housing." In addition, many feared that poor management would quickly lead to the project's becoming dilapidated and unsightly, thereby "bringing down" the surrounding neighborhood aesthetically and materially. In addition to implementing policies and encouraging informal actions to prevent social disorder and social isolation, therefore, management paid considerable attention to the aesthetics of the housing complex.

Being well aware of the neighbors' concerns about ugliness and di-lapidation, ELH developers sought to create and maintain housing that was physically attractive and aesthetically similar to that in surrounding neighborhoods. Rather than erecting a traditional public-housing com-plex of brick and concrete buildings densely packed into a square, de-velopers erected framed town houses on cul-de-sacs using materials and designs that were similar to those used in nearby suburban homes. As already noted, the plan for Ethel Lawrence was carefully crafted only after an in-depth study of housing elsewhere in the township, and the resulting architecture generally matches that in surrounding neighbor-hoods. The dominant spatial organization of housing in Mount Laurel is the residential subdivision. Subdivisions are, in turn, organized into enclaves, and although detached homes predominate, a quarter of the township's dwellings are single family town houses such as those found in ELH. Landscaping is outsourced to a professional and modeled after properties in the upscale suburbs of Haddonfield and Moorestown. Thus management's concern for aesthetics has worked to minimize the stigma of the project within Mount Laurel and contributed to its low profile in the community.

Indeed, when asked their perception of the housing, a common re-sponse from neighbors is to assess its aesthetics and to conclude it doesn't really look like affordable housing. In a letter to the school district, one resident of Mount Laurel living outside of Ethel Lawrence stated in 2006 that "I recently drove through Ethel Lawrence and it looked so nice you would have no clue that it's affordable housing." A resident in a nearby subdivision told us that "Ethel Lawrence fits in to Mount

Laurel. It doesn't look cheap and the landscaping is nice. If I were new to the area, I wouldn't know it was affordable housing." So nondescript was the project that in response to our survey of neighboring residents, described in the next chapter, a majority said they were aware that there was affordable housing in the township but a sizable share were unsure about where it was located.

Of those who did know that Ethel Lawrence Homes was an affordable development, however, including the residents of ELH themselves, there is one element of aesthetics that management seemed to have gotten wrong from the residents' perspective, and that is nomenclature. Within Mount Laurel, subdivisions tend to have names, most of which connote bucolic splendor. Some reflect the town's recent rural past (Larchmont Farms, Countryside Farms, Saratoga Farms), whereas others are suggestive of nature (The Lakes, Laurel Creek, Tricia Meadows, Wildflowers, Fox Run, Rancocas Pointe), and still others have names that connote British high culture (Canterbury, Devonshire, Cambridge Estates).

Residents generally agree with the township critic who, at one of the hearings, predicted that "the majority of the citizenry will look upon a development with the name Ethel R. Lawrence Homes as a low-income housing project, and it will be like painting a bold 'P' for poverty on the tenants' foreheads." In our in-depth interviews, many residents reported that the moniker "Ethel Lawrence Homes" offered a clear and unambiguous signal to others that the development is indeed subsidized. The perceived stigma stemming from the name of the development is exacerbated by the names given to the project's cul-de-sacs, which diverge sharply from the pastoral labels common to surrounding neighborhoods. One resident described his feelings as follows:

> The names of the courts are Faith, Tolerance, Hope, and Equality. That makes me self-conscious. When I say I live on Equality Court people automatically think it is affordable housing. Why couldn't they have just named it Green Tree Lane to make it fit in with the town? People ask me where I live and I say, in Mt Laurel. If they press, I tell them I live off of Moorestown Mt Laurel Road. I don't come out and say the Ethel Lawrence Homes.

It is ironic that after paying so much attention to the project's design, architecture, and aesthetics to avoid stigmatizing residents, the developer ended up conferring stigma upon residents through their naming choices. To be sure, Ethel Lawrence is a local saint, widely known as the Rosa Parks of affordable housing. Indeed, the Mount Laurel school-district offices have a mural of Ethel Lawrence in the lobby citing her as one the township's greatest citizens. Naming the development in her honor is entirely fitting; but stigma might have been mitigated by calling it the Ethel Lawrence Estates rather than the Ethel Lawrence Homes, which is more in keeping with suburban conventions. The naming of the cul-de-sacs, however, could have been more discreet, though in the end, the naming issue is a minor complaint among residents considering the other benefits they readily acknowledge.

Conclusion

In this chapter we have systematically evaluated the effect of low-income housing on property values, crime rates, and tax burdens in the suburban community of Mount Laurel, New Jersey, accompanied by an analysis of the attributes, mechanisms, and managerial practices thought to influence these outcomes. We believe our findings offer a novel contribution to the research literature on affordable housing, being based on a multiple control-group time-series design with multiple outcome measures that are supplemented by qualitative fieldwork and interviews done within the project and surrounding community.

Our data strongly suggest that the Ethel Lawrence Homes did not increase crime, decrease property values, or raise property taxes either in the township or in adjacent neighborhoods. We attribute this null outcome to particular features of the Mount Laurel project—its aesthetics, spatial design, social controls, and management practices. All these factors help to account for the lack of significant effects on the surrounding community, and appear to produce emergent values among project residents that are congruent with those expressed by people in surrounding suburban neighborhoods.

Our findings have important policy implications in suggesting that affordable housing can indeed be developed in affluent suburban areas without increasing social disorganization or producing negative externalities. We find that widely expressed fears of a negative influence on the community did not come to fruition even after ten years. However, our findings also point to certain critical mitigating mechanisms that must be considered in understanding this benign outcome. The aesthetic and spatial consistency between affordable housing and surrounding developments, including items seemingly as trivial as the name of the complex, are important in lessening effects on crime rates and property values. In addition, we argue that high levels of informal and formal social control in the complex reduce the potential for criminality and social disorder. Specifically, the presence of an on-site property manager, the existence of a Neighborhood Watch program, and well-networked neighbors all contribute to feelings of safety and self-efficacy among residents and, in turn, the prevention and monitoring of potential criminal activity.

In short, our analysis clearly shows that poor people can be integrated into middle-class suburban communities without increasing levels of social disorganization. Poverty-dispersal programs therefore can be a useful policy tool in attempting to ameliorate existing patterns of racial and class segregation, and suburban communities can integrate poor tenants into their neighborhoods more effectively than many residents of those communities expect. To the extent that moving into a safe, quiet, affluent suburb provides project residents with new access to benefits and resources with which they can make their way out of poverty, affordable housing may constitute an important social mobility program capable of breaking the cycle of disadvantage they left behind in poor urban neighborhoods. We consider the efficacy of the Ethel Lawrence Homes in a later chapter, but first we take a closer look at community perceptions of the project ten years after its controversial origins.

CHAPTER 6

All Things Considered

NEIGHBORS' PERCEPTIONS A DECADE LATER

As prior chapters have clearly demonstrated, the path from the earliest efforts to bring affordable housing into Mount Laurel to the final opening of the Ethel Lawrence Homes was anything but smooth (as reflected in figure 2.1). The intervening decades were filled with multiple lawsuits, endless rounds of litigation, raucous media debates, emotional public hearings, protests, threats, and even acts of vandalism. Much of the opposition seems to have been grounded in the widely expressed fear that the opening of an affordable housing development would create a "ghetto in the field," and thus bring a host of unwanted urban problems into a tranquil suburban environment, ultimately raising crime rates, lowering property values, and increasing tax burdens. The prior chapter revealed, however, that these feared outcomes never came close to realization. Indeed, life in the township went on more or less as it had before.

Although the previous chapter presented quantitative data to support the conclusion that there were few, if any, negative effects associated with the project's opening, in human affairs, there is often a gap between what the facts indicate and what people believe. In this chapter, we consider not what actual data and statistics tell us about the project's consequences for the community, but focus instead on what those who live in surrounding neighborhoods believe the consequences to have been. In chapter 4 we described a representative survey of neighbors undertaken in the adjacent retirement community of Holiday Village and the upscale subdivision we call Hillside Lane. Here we analyze what respondents from those neighborhoods told us about the Ethel Lawrence Homes and explore their perceptions of its inhabitants, but before doing so we first we document the contrasting social backgrounds of community residents and ELH tenants.

A Study in Contrasts

The fears and apprehensions that Mount Laurel residents expressed about affordable housing in the township were ultimately grounded in perceptions of difference between themselves and their potential new neighbors. The comments made by township residents in the media and public hearings before 2001 clearly indicated that they expected tenants be quite different from them on a variety of social dimensions—notably race, class, and family composition—factors that historically have been laden with considerable suspicion and prejudice in American culture. The data in table 6.1 come from the surveys we conducted of ELH residents and neighbors in adjacent subdivisions and confirm the contrasting social backgrounds of tenants and their nearest neighbors. Respondents were adults, typically the household head (in the case of ELH residents) but sometimes the spouse of the head in surveys of households in adjacent

Table 6.1. The comparative social backgrounds of ELH residents and their nearby neighbors

Characteristic	ELH Residents	ELH Neighbors	Significance of Difference
Mean Age	43.1	68.9	**
Gender	91.4	58.3	**
Years in Mount Laurel	6.0	10.6	*
Marital Status			
Married or Cohabiting	16.4	52.6	**
Divorced or Separated	23.3	16.3	**
Widowed	10.3	28.4	**
Never Married	50.0	2.0	**
Race-Ethnicity			
White	9.5	94.4	**
Black	58.6	1.7	**
Asian	0.9	3.3	
Hispanic	29.3	0.6	**
Other	8.6	0.3	*
Education			
< High School	12.9	1.4	*
High School Graduate	25.9	20.0	**
Some College	50.0	28.4	**
College Graduate	11.2	50.2	**
Labor Force Status			
Working Full Time	55.2	20.1	**
Working Part Time	37.1	20.5	*
Not Working	7.8	59.4	**
Average Income ($000)	26.3	75.9	**

**p < 0.01; *p < 0.05

neighborhoods). As can be seen, on virtually all indicators, the two groups differ significantly from each other.

ELH residents are younger, for example, than the residents of adjacent neighborhoods (with an average age of forty-three versus sixty-nine among nearby neighbors). They are also much less likely to be currently married or cohabiting (16 percent versus 53 percent), less likely to be widowed (10 percent versus 28 percent), and much more likely to be never married (50 percent versus 2 percent). At the same time, ELH residents are, as expected, much more likely to be minority group members (58 percent black and 29 percent Hispanic) than those living in adjacent subdivisions (94 percent white). At the same time, compared with ELH residents, the residents of surrounding neighborhoods are more likely to be college graduates (50 percent versus 11 percent), more likely to be not working (59 percent versus 7.8 percent—mostly owing to the large number of retirees in Holiday Village), and displayed much higher annual household incomes (around $75,000 versus around $26,000). In sum, if fears and anxieties take root in social difference, there would be ample soil for apprehensions to grow in the wide expanse of social terrain between ELH residents and their immediate neighbors.

Perceptions and Interactions

Despite all the negative emotions expressed about affordable housing in Mount Laurel in the run-up to the project's construction, and irrespective of the yawning socioeconomic gap between project tenants and township residents, the actual opening of the Ethel Lawrence Homes and its occupation by poor minority families was greeted less with a bang than with a whimper. As table 6.2 shows, even simple awareness of the project's existence is surprisingly limited, and actual interaction with tenants is even more restricted. Although 80 percent of the neighbors living in adjacent communities were aware that affordable housing existed somewhere in Mount Laurel, and 69 percent knew a project was located in the immediate area, these figures imply that a fifth of all respondents in adjacent areas didn't know the township contained affordable housing and nearly a third didn't know it was present in their neighborhood. Moreover, among those neighbors who did know that an affordable housing existed nearby, only around 40 percent could successfully name the project, representing just 27.5 percent of all respondents. Most said they knew about the project from the controversy during the proposed building phase in 1997. As one neighbor put it in an in-depth interview, "I know that it's Ethel Lawrence only because I lived here when there was the fight over it. But, I mean, if I wasn't here then I'd have no clue.

Table 6.2. Level of awareness about Ethel Lawrence Homes and degree of contact with tenants among residents of adjoining neighborhoods

Indicator of Awareness or Interaction	Percentage
Level of Awareness of ELH	
Aware of Affordable Housing in Township	80.1
Aware of Affordable Housing in Neighborhood	68.8
Knows Name of Project	27.5
Degree of Interaction with ELH Residents	
Has Interacted with ELH Residents	12.9
Knows ELH Residents	7.3
Children Know Children from ELH	6.6

Driving past there, you'd have no clue it's affordable housing. It looks like any other development."

Beyond simple awareness, personal contact with project residents was even rarer. Only 13 percent of all respondents had ever interacted with an ELH resident; just 7 percent said they personally knew a tenant; and just 7 percent reported that a child of theirs knew someone from the project. Given that a sizable number of neighbors don't even know about the existence of ELH, and that the vast majority have no contact with its residents, we would not expect the project to loom very large in framing the perceptions of respondents, and this is generally what we find. Table 6.3 examines neighbors' perceptions of change in their personal circumstances. The first panel focuses on property values, a key concern of project opponents from the very beginning.

Despite all the rhetoric about the seeming inevitability of falling home values in the wake of the project's opening, 45 percent of the residents in neighboring areas perceived the value of their home to have increased since 2001. At the same time, 43 percent felt its value had fared better than other homes in the township, and 33 percent felt their home value had fared better than other homes in the county. In contrast, only 7 percent said their home value had fared worse than others in the township and just 2 percent said it fared worse than others in the county. These views are not consistent with a widely shared perception of property decline in adjoining neighborhoods. Instead, neighbors generally hold accurate perceptions very much in keeping with the overall rise in property values we observed in the previous chapter.

The project's lack of salience in the social cognition of neighbors is further underscored by their perception of racial and ethnic change in the area. Despite the fact that the opening of the Ethel Lawrence Homes

Table 6.3. Perceptions of trends in personal and local circumstances among residents of neighborhoods adjoining the Ethel Lawrence Homes

Indicator of Perception	Percentage
Perceptions of Property Values	
Home Value Has Increased	45.2
Home Value Has Fared Better Than Others in Township	42.9
Home Value Has Fared Worse Than Others in Township	7.0
Home Value Has Fared Better Than Others in County	32.5
Home Value Has Fared Worse Than Others in County	2.3
Perceptions of Racial-Ethnic Change	
Racial-Ethnic Diversity Has Increased	42.2
Racial-Ethnic Diversity Has Decreased	50.0
Increased Racial-Ethnic Diversity Is a Good Thing	36.6
Increased Racial-Ethnic Diversity Is a Bad Thing	7.0
Perception of Local Services	
Quality of Public Schooling Is Improving	44.6
Quality of Public Schooling Is Declining	10.6
Quality of Public Transportation Is Good or Very Good	9.7
Quality of Public Transportation Is Poor or Very Poor	36.5
Supports Additional Public Transportation Close to Home	64.4

in 2001 and its expansion in 2004 obviously increased racial-ethnic diversity within the locality, in the second panel of table 6.3 we see that 50 percent of those living in adjacent neighborhoods believed diversity had declined in recent years, compared to 42 percent who (accurately) perceived an increase. Despite the relative lack of awareness about the direction of change in racial-ethnic diversity, some 37 percent nonetheless stated that increasing racial diversity was a good thing as opposed to just 7 percent who saw it as a bad thing. In one interview, for example, a neighbor said:

> I am happy with the development of Ethel Lawrence in the town, because I want more diversity in the town. I think diversity is good. It's good for opening up the minds of our children. But I am also concerned about the impact of the children on our schools. I don't want the children to bring down the quality of the schools. I want all of the children to be striving for high achievement and have positive aspirations. I worry that some of these children are not striving and working hard and that will rub off on my children. The diversity is good, I just want to know that all of the children

are working hard. So as long as school quality does not go down, then I think the increase in diversity is a positive thing.

In sum, fewer than half of all respondents even registered the recent shift in racial-ethnic composition in their cognitive maps, and only a tiny minority thought that increasing racial diversity was a bad thing in any event. In general, we also found that perceptions of increased diversity, and diversity as a bad thing, were unrelated. The last panel of table 6.3 examines perceptions about changes in the quality of local services, the most important of which is education. Despite widespread concern expressed about potential declines in school quality prior to the project's construction, 45 percent of the neighbors felt the quality of local public schooling was, in fact, improving, whereas just 11 percent said it was declining.

The one area where neighbors were critical of services was public transit, 37 percent of whom rated it as poor or very poor compared with just 10 percent who said it was good or very good. As already noted, this perception is an accurate appraisal of the current situation, as the nearest bus stop is more than two miles away, and to reach it, a pedestrian must walk along busy Moorestown–Mount Laurel Road, which in most segments lacks sidewalks. The absence of accessible public transportation constitutes a hardship not only for low-income families living in the Ethel Lawrence Homes, but also for elderly residents of Holiday Village, many of whom are unable to drive. As a result, nearly two-thirds of the neighbors surveyed offered their support for bringing additional public transportation closer to home.

Rather than examining neighbors' perceptions of their personal circumstances, table 6.4 focuses on their views about conditions in the neighborhood and the township generally, where "neighborhood" was defined explicitly for respondents as "roughly a two block radius around your home." The top panel reports perceptions of the direction of change with respect to three fundamental concerns of suburbanites everywhere: property values, crime rates, and school test scores. Respondents were asked to compare current circumstances with circumstances before 2000 (if they moved in before that date) or relative to those at the time they moved in (if they arrived afterward).

Despite neighbors' generally favorable views about trends in the value of their own homes, they were more pessimistic about trends in property values for the township and the neighborhood in general. Around 47 percent saw property values as somewhat or much worse in the neighborhood, and 46 percent perceived worsening property values for the township. In contrast, only a third saw property values as somewhat or much better in the neighborhood, and 35 percent expressed this perception for the township. The greater prevalence of pessimism here likely reflects the

Table 6.4. Percentage of respondents to neighbor survey who feel that selected conditions are getting somewhat worse or much worse in the neighborhood and the township after 2000

Condition	Condition Seen as Somewhat Worse or Much Worse		Condition Seen as Somewhat Better or Much Better	
	Neighborhood	Township	Neighborhood	Township
Principal Concerns				
Property Values	46.5	46.3	33.2	35.3
Crime Rates	13.7	29.9	5.1	3.3
School Test Scores	6.5	9.5	31.4	25.6
Quality of Life Indicators				
Garbage Pick-Up	25.7	27.1	1.7	2.3
Recycling	2.6	4.8	4.8	2.8
Graffiti	5.3	7.7	1.1	2.9
Loitering	5.4	5.6	0.3	0.0
Traffic	25.9	60.5	0.0	0.0
Noise	4.1	17.6	0.0	0.0
Air Pollution	4.6	10.8	0.0	0.0
Overall Quality of Life	0.0	4.6	20.8	25.4

effect of the bursting of the national housing bubble and the onset of recession just before we began data collection, events that indeed did flatten and reduce home values after 2008.

In keeping with this interpretation, the level of pessimism is not nearly as accentuated with respect to crime rates, which in fact did not move upward with the onset of the recession. Only 14 percent viewed crime as somewhat or much worse in the neighborhood and just 30 percent reported this perception for the township. In fact, as noted in chapter 5, crime rates continued to head downward at the time of the survey, though at a slower pace than before the recession. Compared with property values and crime, neighbors were even more optimistic about educational trends. Whereas just 7 percent saw student test scores as getting somewhat or much worse in the neighborhood and 10 percent in the township, 31 percent perceived test scores as getting somewhat or much better, and 26 percent perceived these outcomes in the township.

Thus neighborly perceptions about trends in property values, crime rates, and school performance do not suggest that most residents believe fears about the consequences of the project have come true. The large majority of respondents saw crime rates as being the same or better than before, consistent with the fact that crime rates were indeed trending downward; and public school performance was generally seen most favorably, with substantial majorities seeing no change or an increase in school test scores. Property values did decline after the housing bubble burst, of course, and respondents accurately perceived this event to have affected home prices in their neighborhood and in the township as a whole, even though most remained personally sanguine about the value of their own homes. Many residents perceive the Mount Laurel Doctrine itself as a factor mitigating potential effects on property values. As one interviewee put it, "I don't think it (ELH) impacted our home value because every town in the state has to have affordable housing. So this stuff is happening everywhere. So it's not just our town that has affordable housing, so the local impact is less when it's built."

We also asked neighbors about other issues connected to the quality of suburban life and found little variation on most indicators. With respect to recycling, graffiti, loitering, noise, and air pollution, most people perceived no significant change since 2000 or when they moved into the neighborhood. The major exceptions were garbage collection and traffic. No one saw traffic getting better. Indeed, 26 percent perceived it getting worse in the neighborhood and 61 percent saw it getting worse in the township. Likewise, whereas only 2 percent saw garbage pick-ups as getting better in the neighborhood or township, 26 percent perceived garbage collection as getting somewhat or much worse. In more detailed analyses not shown here, however, we found these to be general complaints that were disconnected with feelings and perceptions about the housing project or its residents.

In order to probe neighborly perceptions more closely and to employ a more unstructured and less intrusive approach to assess their sentiments, toward the end of the survey, we asked those respondents who knew about the affordable housing project in their neighborhood to state "the first five words that come to mind to describe the residents of this development." Of the eighty-eight persons who knew the project existed, seventy-eight offered at least one word to describe it, forty-eight offered two words, twenty-eight offered three, sixteen offered four, and eight offered five. In table 6.5, we code these responses into content categories, undertaking one coding for the first word mentioned and a separate coding for all later words combined.

We found that responses could be grouped into seven basic categories, which we array vertically in the table along with frequencies and examples of the words typically employed by respondents. Some 19 percent said they did not know any residents and offered no further comment. Aside from this null response, the two most commonly mentioned kinds

Table 6.5. Words that came to mind to describe the Ethel Lawrence Homes among neighbors interviewed in neighborhood survey

Category of Response and Examples	First Word	Later Words
Income of Residents	19.2	10.1
"low income," "lower income," "affordable," "unfortunate," "low-to-moderate income," "moderate income," "poverty," "less expensive housing," "single income," "affluent"		
Positive Traits of Residents	19.2	34.3
"friendly," "happy," "hard working," "normal," "ambitious," "good people," "helpful," "no problem," "opportunity," "pretty good," "quiet," "seem OK," "very good," "social," "stable," "caring," "family oriented," "good neighbors," "great dancers," "no problems," "pleasant," "better their lives," "respectful," "hard working," "funny," "active," "deserving," "good people who don't make enough money," "ambitious," "good kids," "don't create problems," "want nice homes"		
Race of Residents	16.7	13.1
"black," "diverse," "African American," "all ethnic backgrounds" "African American majority," "mixture," "predominantly black," "Hispanic." "people of color," "ethnic group," "white people"		
Architecture or Design of Project	11.5	14.1
"well kept," "beautiful," "decent," "neat," "nice," "attractive," "clean," "town houses," "spacious," "cute"		
Negative Traits of Residents	10.2	18.2
"noisy," "aggressive kids," "clannish," "keep to themselves," "separate," "sloppy," "tons of kids," "undisciplined," "dangerous," "fights on school bus," "unstable families," "no pride," "transient," "messy," "increased graffiti," "crime," "won't come to parties"		
Other Impressions	3.8	7.7
"renters," "young," "part of Mount Laurel decisions," "not all drive," "haven't been affected," "community not affected," "named after activist in housing," "they don't bother me and I don't bother them," "no effect on community," "right to live where they want to"		
Don't Know Any Residents	19.2	2.0
Total Responses	78	99

of words focused on the income or economic status of project residents, or else listed some positive trait or characteristic to describe the tenants, with roughly 19 percent in each category. The high frequency of references to income or economic status is only to be expected given that ELH is an affordable housing development, and this fact was widely discussed in public hearings and media debates. Beyond the first word used to describe the project, however, the use of income-related words drops to 10 percent whereas the mentioning of positive traits about respondents increases to 34 percent among later words. Positive words used to describe tenants ranged from generic terms such as "friendly," "happy," and "hard working" to other words that perhaps damned with faint praise such as "normal," "pretty good," and "no problem" to surprising entries such as "funny," "active," and, perhaps stereotypically, "great dancers."

After income references and positive trait descriptors, the next most common content category involved some reference to the race or ethnicity of tenants. Indeed, around 17 percent of all respondents referred to the race or ethnicity of tenants as the first word that came to mind, underscoring the continued salience of race in the United States and its central if unspoken role in the Mount Laurel controversy. Another 13 percent referred to race or ethnicity in a later word. The most common racial reference was simply to note that most residents were black or African American. Others mentioned Hispanics, and a few were surprised to note that some whites lived in the project as well.

Next in order of frequency, accounting for 12 percent of first words and 14 percent of later words, was a reference to the design, architecture, or physical character of the project itself, suggesting that, in accordance with developers' wishes, ELH indeed succeeded in overcoming stereotypical negative views about public housing in the United States. Many neighbors seemed surprised and rather pleased that the project was composed of "well-kept," "beautiful," "nice," "clean," "spacious," and "cute" town houses, and that the development itself was "decent," "neat," and "attractive."

It was not all sweetness and light, though. One neighbor we interviewed perceived ELH residents as freeloaders, telling us, "I get ticked off because the people living there are renters. I am paying taxes for their kids to go to school, and they aren't paying property taxes. That ticks me off." Around 10 percent of the neighbors we surveyed mentioned a negative trait to describe residents in their first word, and another 18 percent did so in a later word. Traits commonly referred to included "noisy," "aggressive," "clannish," "messy," "sloppy," "unstable," "no pride," and "undisciplined," and some respondents explicitly mentioned "crime" and "fights on the school bus" and labeled project residents as "dangerous."

The final category consisted of a grab bag of diverse references that together accounted for just 4 percent of first words mentioned and 8 percent of later words mentioned.

Explaining the Perceptions

In order to limit the burden to respondents, minimize refusals, and mitigate potentially negative reactions to the survey, our questionnaire did not go into great detail in assessing the social, economic, political, and psychological background of interviewees. As table 6.1 suggests, however, we did gather basic social and demographic information from the people we spoke to, and here we use these data to explore the individual determinants of perceptions about the project and its residents. A key variable in all models is potential exposure to information about the project and its residents. First we consider the degree to which neighbors were exposed to the acrimonious debate leading up to the project's construction by defining a dummy variable that equaled 1 if the respondent lived in Mount Laurel prior to 2001, and 0 otherwise. Second, we assessed the overall potential for exposure to the project by computing total years lived in Mount Laurel, assuming that the longer a neighbor lived in the area, the more likely he or she was to have had contact with the development or its tenants.

We begin by considering respondents' awareness of racial-ethnic differences between themselves and township residents, as evidenced by the realization that diversity had increased in the township since 2001. The left-hand columns of table 6.6 show a logistic regression model estimated to predict the odds that a respondent perceived diversity to be increasing in response to a direct question on the topic, expressed as a function of basic demographic and socioeconomic characteristics and potential exposure. As can be seen, only two factors influence the perception of rising racial and ethnic diversity—age and years spent in Mount Laurel. In general, older residents were less likely to be aware of rising diversity, with the relative odds of perceiving greater diversity falling by around 5.3 percent with each additional year of age (given the negative coefficient of −0.054 for age, the relative odds are computed as $1 - \exp [-0.054] = 0.053$). Holding age constant, however, those neighbors who spent more years in Mount Laurel were significantly more likely to be aware that racial and ethnic diversity had increased, with the relative odds rising about 15 percent per year of residence (given the positive coefficient of 0.143, the odds are determined as $\exp [0.143] = 1.154$). Thus older people, most commonly residents of the retirement community of Holiday Village, appear to be more isolated and less aware of the growing racial-ethnic

Table 6.6. Logistic regression models estimated to predict neighbors' perceptions about racial and ethnic diversity within in Mount Laurel Township

Independent Variables	Diversity is Increasing		Diversity a Bad Thing	
	Regression Coefficient	Standard Error	Regression Coefficient	Standard Error
Demographic Background				
Female	−0.267	0.494	0.087	0.683
Age	−0.054*	0.025	−0.026	0.026
Married	−0.640	0.602	−1.363	0.922
Nonwhite	0.243	0.734	1.897*	0.793
Socioeconomic Background				
College Educated	0.089	0.701	1.928	1.233
In Labor Force	−1.058	0.719	−0.580	0.756
Income $100,000+	−0.876	0.670	1.311	0.945
Exposure				
Present Before 2001	0.666	0.856	−0.269	0.919
Total Years in Mount Laurel	0.143*	0.065	0.030	0.062
Intercept	2.426	2.006	−2.437	2.542
Log Likelihood	−66.91	−22.59		
Pseudo R^2		0.23		0.25
Number of Cases	127		127	

*$p < 0.05$

diversity in their midst, unless of course they were long-term residents of Mount Laurel.

The right-hand columns show the results of a model estimated to predict whether respondents perceived greater racial and ethnic diversity as a bad thing. Here the only significant variable is the race of the respondent. Contrary to what some might expect, nonwhite respondents were more likely than whites to see growing diversity in a negative light, with the odds of perceiving such change as bad being 6.7 times greater (exp [1.897] = 65.666). Although nonwhite status significantly predicted the perception of diversity as bad, only four of the fourteen respondents who had this perception were nonwhite. All earned high incomes well in excess of $100,000 per year; all were college graduates and three held graduate degrees; and two were black with one Asian and one Hispanic. Thus the effect of nonwhite status on the perception of diversity as bad was driven by four high-earning, well-educated people who are not at all typical minority group members.

We can make sense of these facts in the context of the history of residential segregation in the United States. Historically, aspiring minority families found it difficult to escape the confines of segregation, and those who did manage to relocate into integrated areas generally found that the neighborhood subsequently turned over to become a segregated minority community once again (Massey and Denton 1993). The resegregation was not the fault of entering minority families, but stemmed instead from discriminatory practices in the real estate and lending industries and prejudicial choices made by white renters and home buyers. Nonetheless, minority residents of integrated middle-class neighborhoods (quite accurately) came to see the arrival of more minorities as a harbinger of decline and a threat to their longer-term interests. Thus nonwhite survey respondents may perceive rising racial and ethnic diversity as a sign that resegregation and neighborhood decline are under way.

In table 6.7 we move on to explore the determinants of contact or familiarity with the ELH project and its residents. To measure the degree of contact, we created a simple additive index that summed responses to six items from the survey indicating whether the respondent was: (1) aware of affordable housing in the township, (2) aware of affordable housing in the neighborhood, (3) could correctly name the project, (4) had personally interacted with an ELH resident, (5) personally knew an ELH resident, and (6) had children who knew children from ELH (see appendix A6). With each response coded 1 if yes and 0 if no, summation yielded a 0–6 scale of contact with a relatively high reliability ($\alpha = 0.778$).

The fact that the resulting scale has a mean value of just 2.03 out of a possible 6 indicates the relatively low level of contact and awareness of ELH among residents of neighboring subdivisions. When it is regressed on indicators of demographic background, socioeconomic status, and potential exposure, we again see that only two factors are significant: age and years lived in Mount Laurel. With each additional year of age, the degree of contact with project residents drops by 0.033 points on the 0–6 scale ($p < 0.05$); but holding age constant, each additional year of residence in Mount Laurel increases contact by 0.045 points ($p < 0.10$). In other words, contact with the project is greatest among those respondents who were relatively young but have lived in Mount Laurel for some time—for example, someone who grew up in Mount Laurel and perhaps entered adulthood after the project opened.

Prior to the project's opening, township residents expressed very clear and explicit fears about what the consequences of its construction might be, and the right-hand columns show the effects of selected variables on an index we created to measure the degree to which respondents perceived these fears to have come true, this time summing responses are across nine items coded 1 if yes and 0 otherwise, specifically: (1) whether

Table 6.7. OLS regression models estimated to predict neighbors' index of contact with ELH residents and index of degree to which neighbors' fears were realized

Independent Variables	Degree of Contact with ELH		Degree Fears Realized	
	Regression Coefficient	Standard Error	Regression Coefficient	Standard Error
Demographic Background				
Female	−0.151	0.262	−0.290	0.376
Age	−0.033*	0.014	0.003	0.107
Married	0.155	0.292	−0.125	0.396
Nonwhite	−0.226	0.448	−0.522	0.587
Socioeconomic Background				
College Educated	0.099	0.344	−0.603+	0.321
In Labor Force	0.116	0.415	0.697+	0.364
Income $100,000+	−0.112	0.373	−0.335	0.461
Exposure				
Present Before 2001	0.557	0.412	−0.428	0.452
Total Years in Mount Laurel	0.045+	0.024	−0.021	0.029
Degree of Contact with ELH	----	----	0.013	0.111
Perceptions				
Racial Diversity Increased	----	----	−0.245	0.330
Racial Diversity a Bad Thing	----	----	0.827	0.696
Intercept	3.516**	1.257	−2.437	2.542
R^2		0.22		0.25
Number of Cases	127		127	

**p < 0.01; *p < 0.05; +p < 0.10

the respondent's own home value has decreased, (2) whether respondent's home value has fared worse than others' in the township, (3) whether the respondent's home value has fared worse than others in the county, (4) whether property values are worse in the neighborhood, (5) whether property values are worse in the township, (6) whether crime is worse in the neighborhood, (7) whether crime is worse in the township, (8) whether the quality of public schools is declining, and (9) whether school test scores are getting worse.

Simple summation yields a 0–9 index of acceptable reliability (α = 0.641) to measure the degree to which the a priori fears of local residents were realized after the opening of ELH (see appendix A6). When we regressed this measure on indicators of socioeconomic status, demographic background, and exposure, we found only two significant relationships, both of which were relatively weak (p < 0.10). This is consistent with the fact that most people did not see commonly feared outcomes as having come true (indeed the mean value of the scale was just 2.06 out of a possible 9). In general, those who were college educated were less likely to feel that commonly held fears had been realized, whereas those in the labor force were more likely to express such a realization. In the context of our survey data, these results imply that college-educated retirees are least likely to perceive that fears about the neighborhood had come true, whereas less educated workers were more likely to express such fears.

The foregoing indices were constructed from responses to explicit, structured questions and therefore carry some risk that responses were shaped and guided by the questionnaire and the interview process itself. Earlier we saw that simply asking respondents to state the first word that came to mind when thinking about the project yielded responses that appeared more spontaneous and less filtered. In table 6.8, we regress the likelihood of using words falling into three content categories on indicators of demographic background, socioeconomic status, exposure, and perceptions about racial-ethnic diversity. The three content categories are those pertaining to income or economic status, race or ethnicity, and design or architecture, and all models refer to classifications of the first word offered by respondents.

As shown in the left-hand columns of the table, the likelihood of using a first word related to income or economic status is much greater among men than women and rises sharply with a person's degree of contact with the project and its residents. Compared to males, the odds that a female used an income-related term were 89 percent lower $(1 - \exp [-2.226] = 0.892)$; and each unit on the six-point contact scale increased the odds of using an income-related word by a factor of 2.3 $(\exp [0.828] = 2.289)$. Thus the perceptual framing of Ethel Lawrence Homes in terms of the income of its residents is greatest among men who have had considerable contact with the project and its residents.

As shown in the middle columns, the odds of using a race-related word to describe the project are greatly increased by perceiving racial diversity as a bad thing and by greater exposure to ELH and its residents. Each point on the contact scale increases the odds of uttering a race-related word by 51 percent $(\exp [0.415] = 1.514)$ while each additional year spent in Mount Laurel increases the odds of such an utterance by around 9 percent $(\exp [0.085] = 1.089)$. In other words, the longer one has lived in the township and the more contact and awareness one has about ELH and its residents, the greater the likelihood of perceiving the project in terms of the race or ethnicity of residents.

Table 6.8. Logistic regression models estimated to predict neighbors' likelihood of using a first word related to income, race, or architecture to describe the ELH project or its residents

Independent Variables	Used Income-Related Word		Used Race-Related Word		Mentioned Design/Architecture	
	Regression Coefficient	Standard Error	Regression Coefficient	Standard Error	Regression Coefficient	Standard Error
Demographic Background						
Female	-2.226**	0.769	1.410	1.067	2.098+	1.273
Age	0.049	0.040	0.011	0.042	-0.127*	0.057
Married	0.740	0.833	1.678	1.215	-0.148	1.158
Nonwhite	0.548	0.983	-0.252	1.382	0.632	1.389
Socioeconomic Background						
College Educated	-0.797	0.793	0.674	0.753	-3.397+	1.950
In Labor Force	0.893	1.272	-1.462+	0.845	-1.588	1.103
Income $100,000+	1.620	1.122	-1.015	1.143	2.247	1.853
Exposure						
Present Before 2001	-0.920	1.132	-0.539	0.997	4.425*	1.850
Total Years in Mount Laurel	-0.024	0.078	0.085+	0.046	-0.113	0.099
Contact with ELH	0.828**	0.263	0.415*	0.197	0.231	0.390
Perceptions						
Racial Diversity Increased	0.142	0.842	-0.012	0.932	-1.599	1.497
Racial Diversity a Bad Thing	0.860	0.896	2.440*	1.135	-0.406	1.495
Intercept	-7.367*	3.670	-6.815+	4.013	2.608	4.760
Log Likelihood	-25.91**		-27.76*		-12.77**	
Pseudo R²	0.39		0.23		0.40	
Number of Cases	127		127		127	

+p < .10; * p< .05; **p < .01

Holding these significant effects constant, the odds of using a race-related word to describe the project are most strongly increased by perceiving racial diversity as a bad thing. Indeed, those who saw diversity as bad were 11.5 times more likely to use a racial term than others (exp [2.440] = 11.473)! Of course, given the cross-sectional nature of the data, we cannot say whether people who perceive racial diversity as bad are more likely see the project in racial terms, or whether people who see the project in racial terms are more likely to see diversity as bad. Suffice it to say that race is intimately involved the cognitive framing of the project and its residents for some (14 of 127) people living in adjacent neighborhoods, most of whom are white (10 of 14).

Finally, the right-hand columns of table 6.8 show that the odds of mentioning some feature of the architecture or design of the project as the first word are significantly predicted by four variables: age and presence in Mount Laurel before 2001 (both $p < 0.05$) and being female and college educated (both $p < 0.10$). Compared to men, women were 8.1 times more likely to mention design features in their first utterance about the project (exp [2.098] = 8.149), and those living in the township before 2001 were 83.5 times more likely to do so (exp [4.425] = 83.513). In contrast, the likelihood of mentioning architecture or design fell by 12percent with each year of age (1 – exp [–0.127] = 0.119), and the odds were 97 percent lower among those with a college education (1 – exp [–3.397] = 0.967). In some, those most likely to be pleasantly surprised by the project's suburban aesthetics and compatible design were younger, non–college educated women who had lived in Mount Laurel since before the project's opening.

Finally, in table 6.9 we estimate two logistic regression models to predict the odds that the first word used to describe the project referred first to a positive characteristic and then to a negative characteristic of tenants. As can be seen, those in the labor force were less likely to mention a negative trait, whereas contact with the project and its residents and perceiving that racial diversity had increased both quite strongly and positively predicted the use of a negative attribute to describe the project. For example, each unit of contact with the project raised the odds of describing the project using a negative trait by a factor of 2.9 (exp [1.059] = 2.883), and seeing racial diversity as a bad thing raises the odds of doing so by a massive factor of 116.4 (exp [4.757] = 116.396)! In contrast, being in the labor force reduced the odds of using a negative descriptor by around 98 percent (1 – exp [–3.797] = 0.978).

A negative framing of the project is thus most likely to be made by neighbors who are out of the labor force, have considerable contact with ELH residents, and believe rising racial diversity is a bad thing. The likelihood of using a positive trait as the first word to describe the project was

Table 6.9. Logistic regression models estimated to predict neighbors' index of contact with ELH residents and index of degree to which neighbors' fears were realized

Independent Variables	Mentioned Negative Trait		Mentioned Positive Trait	
	Regression Coefficient	Standard Error	Regression Coefficient	Standard Error
Demographic Background				
Female	−1.020	1.619	1.600+	0.921
Age	−0.035	0.056	0.025	0.030
Married	−1.859	1.362	0.658	0.923
Nonwhite	1.952	1.356	−0.049	1.298
Socioeconomic Background				
College Educated	−0.977	1.265	3.150**	1.007
In Labor Force	−3.797*	1.865	0.356	1.120
Income $100,000+	1.894	2.350	−2.654*	1.185
Exposure				
Present Before 2001	−1.204	1.921	4.835**	1.655
Total Years in Mount Laurel	−0.175	0.152	−0.198*	0.097
Contact with ELH	1.059**	0.392	0.921**	0.275
Perceptions				
Racial Diversity Increased	4.757**	1.366	0.386	0.890
Racial Diversity a Bad Thing	0.313	1.555	----	----
Intercept	−2.254	4.858	−10.102**	3.703
Log Likelihood	−12.77**		−25.68**	
Pseudo R²	0.46		0.41	
Number of Cases	127		127	

+p < .10; *p < .05; **p <. 01

also strongly related to the perception of racial diversity as a bad thing, but the effect could not be estimated because it perfectly predicted the outcome. Not one person who saw racial-ethnic diversity as bad used a positive word to describe the project or its tenants! Beyond this large but inestimable effect, the likelihood of using a positive descriptor fell with rising income and with more time spent in Mount Laurel, dropping by 18 percent with each year lived in the township (1 − exp [−0.198] = 0.180) and being 93 percent lower among those with household incomes above $100,000 (1 − exp [−2.654] = 0.930).

Holding constant total years lived in the township, however, being present before 2001 increased the odds of describing the project in positive terms, as did the degree of contact with the project and its residents and having a college education. The odds of using a positive descriptor were thus 23.3 times greater among the college educated (exp [3.150] = 23.34) and almost 126 times greater among those who were present before 2001 (exp [4.853] = 125.84). As in the prior model, the relatively high pseudo R-squared indicates a relatively strong set of effects. All in all, the type of respondent least likely to frame the project in positive terms was a less educated male with a high income who had moved into the township after 2001 but had nonetheless accumulated significant time in the community without having much contact with the project or its residents.

Conclusion

Despite all of the sturm und drang leading up to the project's opening in 2001, after the dust settled in the ensuing years, reactions from immediate neighbors were surprisingly muted. Although the social backgrounds of tenants and neighbors were indeed a study in contrasts—economically, socially, and racially—these apparent differences were not enough to put Ethel Lawrence Homes on the cognitive maps of a surprising number of people living in adjacent neighborhoods. Around a fifth of all the respondents we interviewed didn't know that the township contained an affordable housing development and nearly a third did not know that a project existed right next door. Only 13 percent said they had ever interacted with a project resident and just 7 percent said they personally knew an ELH tenant.

Eight years after the first tenants arrived, in other words, awareness of and contact with the project and its residents were quite limited. On our 0–6 scale of contact, the average neighborhood respondent achieved a value of around 2.0. This finding underscores a pragmatic limitation of theories of neighborhood change that posit myriad positive effects as arising naturally from social interaction between residents of different socioeconomic classes when affordable housing is made available in suburbs. If neighbors of different classes have limited contact or aren't even aware of one another's existence, then the assumptions underlying those theories are not met, and positive effects such as social capital formation, positive role modeling, productive norm reinforcement are unlikely to follow.

Perhaps not surprisingly given the limited level of awareness and contact with ELH, most respondents did not perceive dire consequences for their well-being as a result of the project's opening. On the 0–9 scale measuring the degree to which feared consequences had indeed come true, the average score was again just 2.0. Among the neighbors surveyed, 54 percent perceived property values in the township as stable or increasing,

70 percent saw crime rates as stable or decreasing, and 90 percent saw school test scores as stable or improving. In terms of their personal circumstances, few saw themselves as harmed, with 93 percent saying their home value had fared equal to or better than others in the township and 98 percent seeing their home value faring equal to or better than others in the county. Even in terms of the most obvious traits of race and ethnicity, 58 percent perceived diversity as stable or decreasing (when it in fact had increased) and 36 percent opined the greater racial and ethnic diversity was a good thing.

This sanguine perception of local conditions in the wake of the opening and expansion of the Ethel Lawrence Homes emerged in response to explicit questions about the project and its people. In another exercise, however, we asked those who were aware of the project's existence to report the first five words that came to mind in thinking about it; and in this unstructured, unobtrusive, and less scripted task a distinct racial undercurrent emerged, albeit among a minority of respondents. Among17 percent of respondents, a racial or ethnic descriptor was the first word that popped to mind in thinking about the project, and among 10 percent a negative adjective came to mind. Among words beyond the first one, 13 percent mentioned race and 18 percent reported a negative characteristic of respondents. The use of a race-related first word was strongly predicted by the perception of racial and ethnic diversity as a bad thing, raising the odds of reporting such a word by a factor of 11.5. Likewise, perceiving diversity as bad raised the odds of reporting a negative trait as the first word a remarkable 116 times and perfectly predicted the likelihood of not using a positive term.

A few (29 percent) of those who saw greater diversity as bad were themselves nonwhite, but all were well educated and affluent and likely saw greater diversity as a potential harbinger of neighborhood decline and resegregation, in keeping with historical precedent. The remaining white respondents who saw diversity as bad likely harbored racial stereotypes and resentments, with race being the first thing that came to mind in thinking about the project and strongly favoring negative terms and avoiding positive terms to describe project residents. Thus race remains a potent if unacknowledged element in how neighbors perceive the Ethel Lawrence Homes and those who live there.

Generalizing to the broader controversy about affordable housing in Mount Laurel and elsewhere, these results suggest, first, that the expression of strong negative emotions in media exchanges, public hearings, and demonstrations was strongly conditioned by underlying racial hostility but, second, that the controversy may have been a tempest in a teapot stirred by a small number of highly motivated, racially antagonistic individuals who mobilized themselves to vociferously oppose the project in a context where most others were indifferent or positive, but did not feel that strongly about the issue of affordable housing. Despite the angry threat of one citizen who vowed after the approval of plans for ELH that "you're history!" (referring to elected officials then present), in the next election, the mayor and most township council members retained their seats. As usual, those who show up at public hearings and express their views to the media are not a random sample of the community at large.

CHAPTER 7

Greener Pastures

MOVING TO TRANQUILITY

When the struggle to bring affordable housing to Mount Laurel began in the late 1960s, it was merely a local effort to guarantee a place in the community for longtime residents who were being priced out of a booming real estate market. As the battle lines hardened and litigation mounted, however, the struggle became much more than a local zoning dispute. It became part of a larger debate about the role of race, class, and place in perpetuating socioeconomic inequality in the United States. Over time "Mount Laurel" became shorthand for how class exclusion preserved the privileges of the suburban few at the expense of the urban many, trapping poor minority families in deteriorating neighborhoods characterized by rising concentrations of poverty and declining opportunities. The larger moral and political struggle came to be seen as one in which "suburbs under siege" were pitted against outside activists and "audacious judges" (Haar 1996) who sought to circumvent the will of local residents by dismantling class barriers to suburban residence and thus change the nature of suburban life. From a local zoning dispute, the Mount Laurel case grew into a state and then a national battle for "the soul of suburbia" (Kirp, Dwyer, and Rosenthal 1995).

By the time the Ethel Lawrence Homes finally opened in 2000, it was no longer a test case about the rights of longtime residents not to be forced out of their hometown. Instead, it became a test case for whether affordable housing developments could provide a path out of poverty for the urban poor, and what kinds of costs such programs might impose on suburban residents. By the time the Ethel Lawrence Homes began accepting residents, other projects—the Gautreaux Demonstration Project and Moving to Opportunity Experiment—had been launched to test, with varying degrees of success, the hypothesis that housing mobility programs constituted not just a feasible way to moderate widespread racial and class segregation in the United States, but a practical policy to ameliorate entrenched urban poverty.

To this point, the data we have adduced from our study of the Ethel Lawrence Homes indicate that few, if any, costs were imposed on residents either of Mount Laurel generally or adjacent neighborhoods particularly, as a result of its opening. Project developers took explicit account of prevailing fears about the project's aesthetics and potential effects, and through careful architectural design and judicious planning sought to prevent the feared outcomes from happening. As a result, contrary to fears expressed before the fact, crime rates did not rise, property values did not fall, and tax burdens did not increase after the project opened. In the end, many of the neighbors were not even aware that they lived adjacent to an affordable housing development, and the vast majority had little or no contact with its tenants. If the opening of Ethel Lawrence homes had few negative consequences for the township or its residents, the central question then becomes: what effect did the project have on those who moved in? Did ELH residence, in fact, improve their lives and provide a path out of poverty? In addressing these questions, we hope to improve on the earlier evaluations done in association with the Gautreaux and MTO programs to shed new light on the viability of housing mobility programs as social policy.

The Context of Mount Laurel

In order to understand the character and quality of life in the Ethel Lawrence Homes, it is helpful first to situate the project geographically. Ethel Lawrence Homes is located on the Moorestown–Mount Laurel Road, a two-lane road that primarily carries local automobile traffic traveling to destinations within the township. The road leads directly to major state highways—to the west Route 38 and to the east Route 70. The municipal heart of the township lies two miles west of ELH where the library, post office, police station, and township offices are located. As the town lacks an official "Main Street" this municipal cluster constitutes the de facto center of town. Following the road east from ELH one encounters the township's middle school, a church, and a Friends meeting house.

Route 38 runs westward to Camden and into Philadelphia, and eastward to Fort Dix and McGuire Air Force Base. It has an interchange that provides access to Interstate 295, a main north-south artery in the region. Owing to this interchange, Route 38 has become one of the major employment and service hubs in South Jersey, crowded with shopping centers, office parks, and a branch of the county college. Mount Laurel has two other interchanges allowing access to Interstate 295 as well as an interchange for the NJ Turnpike. At each interchange, there is a cluster of the usual amenities: gas stations, convenience stores, and fast food outlets. Mount Laurel's basic layout is thus one of densely developed highways that provide a regional draw, bracketing networks of smaller local roads thick with residential subdivisions.

Given its proximity to Route 38, residents of ELH have relative access to a wide variety of services and amenities. The nearest grocery store is 1.3 miles away, and five grocery stores are located within a five-mile radius. The elementary schools lie within two miles of the development, and the high school within three miles. Interstate 295 is three miles away and recreational amenities such as the YMCA and a large park also lie within a distance of three miles. Office complexes and light industrial parks along Route 38 house some of Mount Laurel's largest employers, including a defense contractor, mortgage and finance companies, and computer and technology service firms. Two large indoor shopping malls are also located nearby: the Moorestown Mall is around four miles from the project, and the Cherry Hill Mall is around six miles away.

As noted in chapter 3, the housing stock in Mount Laurel Township is relatively young, mostly built since 1970. Single-family detached homes are the most prevalent type of housing in the township, comprising just under half of the total housing stock. Attached single-family town homes are the second most common type of housing, making up about 24 percent of the stock. Multifamily complexes, such as apartments and condominiums, make up another 23 percent of the municipality's housing. Most housing in Mount Laurel is owner occupied. According to the 2010 census, of 16,570 occupied housing units, approximately 84 percent are owner occupied, and 16 percent renter occupied.

The dominant spatial organization of housing in Mount Laurel is the residential subdivision, a contained residential enclave most often built by a single real estate developer. Within each subdivision, there is a selection of homes based on standardized home designs modeled at different price points. The subdivisions typically have one or two entrances with a sign advertising a bucolic name. The township also has three large age-restricted 55+ communities, and, as in much of the United States, the late 1990s witnessed a boom in the development of large, luxurious single-family homes. In addition to residential subdivisions, Mount Laurel also has a number of stand-alone homes located on secondary roads. Sidewalks are common within the subdivisions, but not on the secondary roads.

Beyond residences, the town is sprinkled with preserved open space and forested green acres. In addition to large retail centers located along the main highways, there are also numerous small commercial complexes throughout the town, which typically contain a dry cleaner, pizza or Chinese food restaurant, and a convenience store. The town contains one substantial park known as Laurel Acres, whose amenities include soccer fields, baseball diamonds, a fishing pond, a sledding hill, nature trails, fitness paths, and children's playgrounds. Laurel Acres hosts an annual Fall

Festival and a five-kilometer fun run. There are numerous other small recreational parks around the township that contain basketball courts and recreation fields, as well as local playgrounds in many subdivisions. Residents of Mount Laurel have expressed concern about the lack of a town center or main street, which adjacent towns such as Mount Holly and Moorestown both have. In its 2003 strategic plan, the Mount Laurel library proclaimed its vision: "The Mount Laurel library will be the community's Main Street."

Neighborhoods Transformed

In addition to wanting better and more affordable housing, a common motive for moving to Mount Laurel for ELH tenants is to gain access to better neighborhoods and schools. Some 21 percent of those who applied to ELH mentioned improved safety or greater economic opportunity as the primary reason for submitting an application. In a statewide survey of low-income households that also moved in response to the Mount Laurel Doctrine, 23 percent said they hoped to find a safer neighborhood, and 22 percent said they sought better schools for their children (Bush-Baskette, Robinson, and Simmons (2011). In our in-depth interviews, one ELH resident told us that she "moved to Mt. Laurel because I thought the schools were even better." Another mother stated that "my big concern was about safety in schools. In [my child's former school], somebody walking in with like a gun, or things, even though you have to worry about that anywhere you go, but I feel more comfortable over here than I would, say, in the area we were actually at."

One female ELH resident from New York City learned about ELH while visiting a friend who was a tenant and immediately decided to apply herself, telling us that "this was like a dream for me. Coming from New York to here, this is like a dream for me to come to live here, because New York, I lived in a big building, housing, with drugs, fights, and seen this all. I didn't really want my kids to grow up over there." Another woman escaped similar circumstances in nearby Camden:

> Where I was at people was getting killed in front of my door, like my kids wasn't allowed to go outside and play, like they had to go to my mom's house to go outside and play. There was no going outside, here they can go outside and play and I don't have to sit outside, you know, I can be in the house, whatever I need to do. One point, my youngest child, was scared to death to go outside. I want my kids to have a better childhood than what I had. So, I was born and raised in Camden all my life, and I saw I was going to get the opportunity to get my kids out of Camden, that's what it was going to be.

One resident described a series of moves she had made to escape neighborhood disorder and violence before finally arriving in Mount Laurel:

> There's a lot more areas, like in Lindenwold and Blackwood, or stuff, that you actually have to worry about. As far as, people standing on the corner selling drugs, and things like that. Like when we first met before, like when we first had our son, we were in an area in a development that was really bad. And we moved from there into the place we were at before here. And, so it was like, and then I got pregnant with my daughter, my second child, so like, we need to keep going.

Another woman similarly told us how long she had waited for the opportunity to get into the project:

> I saw a big ad in the paper. And I thought, wow I would love to live back in—I was always wanted to raise her in Mount Laurel. Just because the area was so much better. And there's so much, there would be more for her to do out there. And I was like, I would love to move back to Mount Laurel. And so when I saw the ad, I applied. But they said it was a long waiting list. And I mean, it took me, like I said, five years.

Data from our survey of ELH residents and nonresident applicants allow us to assess rather precisely the degree to which neighborhood circumstances improved as a result of people gaining access to affordable housing in an affluent suburb. In order to establish a baseline, we asked both sets of respondents to think "back to the specific area where you lived in 1999" and asked, "When you lived in this neighborhood in 1999, how often do you recall seeing the following circumstances during that calendar year?" The question was followed by a list that included "homeless people on the street," "prostitutes on the street," "gang members hanging out on the street," "drug paraphernalia on the street," "people selling illegal drugs in public," "people using illegal drugs in public," "people drinking or drunk in public," "physical violence in public," and "the sound of gunshots." Respondents answered in terms of a six-category response continuum consisting of the words "never," rarely," "sometimes," "often," "very often," and "every day." After going through this exercise, we changed the temporal focus to the current day and asked, "Thinking of your current place of residence, within the past twelve months, how often do you recall seeing" the same set of circumstances.

The answers to these questions allow a before-and-after comparison for ELH residents and nonresidents as well as a direct comparison of current neighborhood conditions experienced by a treatment group of people who moved into the project relative to a control group of people who had applied but not yet secured entry. Table 7.1 summarizes the data by reporting the percentage of respondents who reported ever witnessing

Table 7.1. Whether ELH residents and nonresidents reported witnessing signs of disorder and violence within their neighborhoods in 1999 and 2009

Sign of Disorder	Ethel Lawrence Nonresidents		Ethel Lawrence Residents	
	1999	2009	1999	2009
Homeless People	58.0	50.4	50.5	13.3
Prostitutes	38.7	31.5	32.4	4.4
Gangs	44.7	42.8	39.4	12.4
Drug Paraphernalia	61.7	52.2	47.8	15.2
Selling of Drugs	57.6	48.8	48.7	13.3
Use of Drugs	51.3	42.0	42.0	19.8
Public Drinking	72.9	57.1	62.5	16.9
Physical Violence	56.4	55.4	54.5	23.0
Gunshots	40.5	37.3	34.6	5.4
Average	53.5	46.4	45.8	13.7

selected instances of disorder and violence in 1999 and 2009. If moving into ELH brought about an improvement in neighborhood conditions, we would expect to see a drop in the frequency of negative incidents witnessed between the two dates among residents but not among nonresidents; and in 2009 we would expect to observe a significant gap between residents and nonresidents with respect to current levels of exposure to disorder and violence.

The results summarized in the table generally conform to these expectations. Across all neighborhood circumstances considered, the average percentage witnessing a negative event stood at 53.5 percent for nonresident applicants in 1999 and 46.4 percent in 2009, a small and insignificant decline over the decade. In contrast, the average percentage of negative events witnessed by ELH residents plummeted from 45.6 percent in 1999, before they entered the project, to just 13.7 percent in 2009, afterward. Thus the before-after contrast for residents yields basically the same result as the resident versus nonresident comparison, a drop of about 32 points in exposure to instances of violence and social disorder emanating from the neighborhood.

In addition, the largest contrasts are generally observed for the most violent events. Among project residents, for example, the percentage witnessing gang activity dropped from 39.4 percent to 12.4 percent between 1999 and 2009, while the share witnessing physical violence dropped from 54.5 percent to 23.0 percent and the share hearing gunshots fell from 34.6 percent to 13.7 percent In contrast, among nonresident applicants, the corresponding declines were small and insignificant, with the frequencies going from 44.7 to 42.8 percent for gangs, 56.4 to 55.4 percent for physical violence, and 40.5 to 37.3 percent for gunshots. Although tests of statistical significance are not strictly appropriate here since we do not have random samples but a population of residents matched with a purposive sample of nonresidents, all comparisons between treatment and control are nonetheless significant at the 1 percent level.

As noted above, respondents rated their exposure to negative neighborhood circumstances on a six-point continuum, thereby enabling the construction of an index of exposure to violence and disorder through summation. However, simple summation weighs each incident equally whereas there are very clearly large differences in the severity of the negative event witnessed by respondents. Seeing physical violence and hearing gunshots are obviously more threatening and consequential than seeing homeless people or prostitutes on the street. Following Massey et al. (2003), therefore, we constructed a Weighted Disorder Scale, weighting each negative event with its corresponding score on Wolfgang-Sellin Crime Severity Index (Wolfgang et al. 1985) and then multiplying by frequency coded on a 0–5 scale before summing up, thereby yielding an index that reflects not only the frequency with which different transgressions were witnessed but also the severity of the transgression itself. The resulting scale ranges from 0–209 and has a very high reliability ($\alpha = 0.962$). Details about the computation of the disorder index are provided in appendix A.6.

Figure 7.1 shows average scale values for residents and nonresidents in 1999 and 2009. As can be seen, the severity-weighted violence-and-disorder scale was higher for nonresidents than residents at both dates, and a decline was observed in both groups, likely reflecting a drop in the rate of violent crime over the decade in the community generally (see chapter 5). Of course all applicants demonstrated a desire to improve their neighborhood circumstances, and even those not yet admitted into ELH may have succeeded in moving somewhere better in the interim. Nevertheless, the drop in exposure to disorder and violence was much sharper for those who moved into ELH between the two dates, with the average weighted scale value for residents falling from 52.5 to 9.2 compared with a drop of 63.5 to 48.1 among nonresidents. The difference in scores between residents and nonresidents in 2009 is highly significant ($p < 0.01$), and over the time, the gap between the two groups widened from 11 points to 39 points, also a statistically significant shift ($p < 0.01$).

The foregoing results strongly suggest that ELH residents did, in fact, achieve a dramatic improvement in neighborhood circumstances as a result of moving into the project. Whether we compare the conditions that residents experienced before and after entering the project, or contrast

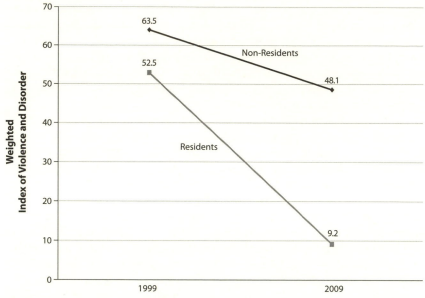

Figure 7.1. Exposure to violence and disorder in neighborhoods of ELH residents and nonresidents in 1999 and 2009

the circumstances experienced by residents and nonresidents in 2009, it is clear that moving into the Ethel Lawrence Homes brought about a marked decrease in exposure to social disorder and violence for project residents. These quantitative results are generally consistent with qualitative comments made by project residents during in-depth interviews. The large majority of respondents described the Ethel Lawrence Homes as "quiet and peaceful."

It is but a short drive from Camden to the Ethel Lawrence Homes, but the route takes one from a bleak setting of dense row houses, abandoned buildings, and trash-strewn lots in a city cross-cut by freeways, then along a road lined with strip malls, shopping centers, and liquor stores, finally to arrive at a scene of rolling green hills with forests and fields punctuated by attractive housing developments. A common locution used by many residents was to refer to the project and its surroundings as "out here" in stark contrast to "back there," the dense urban environment whence most people originated.

When asked what they like the most about ELH, a common first response is a feeling of connection to nature. One woman said that during her first week of living in her new apartment, she marveled at the variety of nature outside her door. She said she had never seen frogs before, and called her mother to tell her about one that hopped up to her front door.

Residents describe seeing deer, raccoons, rabbits, and squirrels, and say that these sights of nature are calming. The ELH property manager told us that most of the calls she received when the project first opened were from residents who were concerned, scared, or just interested in the animals they saw around the development.

Implicit in the notion of "out here" is also the notion that ELH is a place where residents can be free from fear of endemic public violence. As noted at the outset of this chapter, many residents described past residential environments in which crime and violence were regular occurrences. Thus, when resident's use the term "out here," it also means they are in a safe place. As one project resident put it,

> We like it here. It's a little far from Camden, but you know. It's, you know, you don't have to worry about anything. Everything, it's nice in here. That's the way I like to live, I like to live nice and quiet. You know. Some of the people are friendly, and everything is nice and quiet. You know, because I go over to my aunt's house, every other week in Camden. She's eighty-eight. My uncle is eighty-six. And we go there and play bingo and stuff. It's like, the whole day we were there it was like, fire engines, and police sirens, and, I said oh I can't take this.

Another woman told us about how she had lost her fear of leaving her home unoccupied, and for the first time felt free to leave for extended periods of recreation. As one resident describes it,

> I am a big beach person. Every weekend I head down to the beach. But when I was living in Camden I wouldn't leave on weekends because people would know I would be away and I didn't want them breaking in. Now I can go down to the beach and totally relax and not have to worry about what is going on back at home. Cause I've done that. I've gone to the beach, and come back, and the house is broken into, or stuff has been vandalized, and it's not a good feeling, because it makes you think, well, was I stupid for leaving? Or who wants to stay cooped up in the house? I'm a prisoner? And you're staring out the window watching, making sure everything's ok. That's no way to live. Too much. So I like the fact, like I said, out here I can breathe.

In order to assess the effect of project residence more formally, we estimated a series of multivariate regression models to compare the neighborhood circumstances of ELH residents and nonresidents during 2009. Our analytic strategy involves the successive estimation of three statistical models using Ordinary Least Squares. First, we regress the weighted exposure index on a simple dummy variable indicating project residence (1 if yes and 0 if no). Second, we repeat the analysis adding controls for individual and family characteristics (age of head, gender, percent of household members who are female, race, marital status, and education). As explained in chapter 4, a critical failing in most cross-sectional comparisons is that entry into the treatment group (here project residents) is selective, thus rendering their unobserved motivations for seeking entry as uncontrolled and possibly confounding variables. In the present case, however, members of both the treatment and control groups (nonresident applicants) have selected themselves into the set of people wanting to move into an affluent white suburb, thus holding roughly constant the confounding influence of unmeasured motivations.

In order to add an additional level of control for preexisting differences, in the second model we used data from the application form to estimate propensity scores that capture the relative likelihood of actually gaining entry to the project. As outlined in chapter 4, variables coded from the application form included position on waiting list, number of bedrooms desired, current living situation, gender, age, relationship status, presence of children, income, neighborhood racial composition, neighborhood poverty rate, neighborhood vacancy rate, percentage of renters in neighborhood, and stated reason for applying to ELH. Using these variables, we estimated an equation to predict residence in ELH and used it to generate the predicted probability of entry for each person (i.e., the propensity score), which we then include as a covariate in the second equation to provide additional control for preexisting differences on these variables and factors correlated with them.

Finally, in the third model we use the aforementioned propensity scores to create a matched sample of residents and nonresidents. Specifically, based on the propensity scores, we match the 116 residents in the sample to a corresponding set of nonresidents with similar propensity scores using nearest-neighbor matching with a caliper of 0.05. We chose to match with replacement (following Dehejia & Wahba 2002) because the distribution of propensity scores differed between the two groups, with nonresidents having fewer cases at the upper end of the score distribution. In other words, after each match, we put nonresidents back into the pool of cases potentially eligible for the next match. This method yielded a final sample of 51 nonresidents, weighted such that each of the 116 residents in the sample has one non-unique match. The mean propensity score for the sample of residents is identical to that of the weighted sample of nonresidents at 0.59. We then re-estimated the full multivariate model for the matched sample, absent the propensity score control, of course.

Coefficients and standard errors for the three regression models are presented in appendix A7, and the coefficients associated with ELH residence in each of the three models are graphed in figure 7.2. All the

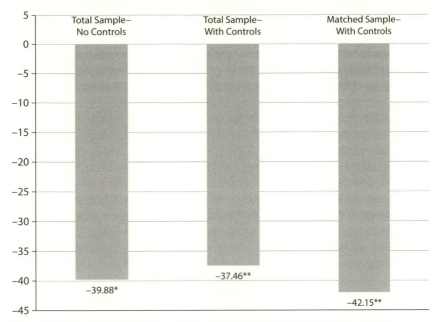

Figure 7.2. Effect of ELH residence on exposure to disorder and violence within neighborhoods

coefficients were negative, indicating that project residence was associated with a significant *reduction* in exposure to disorder and violence. The left-hand bar shows the raw effect of project residence estimated without any controls. On average, ELH residents experienced a reduction of 40 points in exposure to disorder and violence compared to their nonresident counterparts, a large effect on the 0–209 scale. Adding in controls for background characteristics and the propensity score reduces the value of the coefficient slightly, to a value around –37.5 as indicated by the middle bar graph. The effect of project residence, however, remains strong and highly significant, and the reduction in value is not itself statistically meaningful. Finally, the most rigorous test of the neighborhood-effects hypothesis comes from the multivariate comparison of residents and nonresidents using cases equalized by propensity score mating, and results of this exercise are graphed in the right-hand bar. In this specification of the model, the effect of project residence actually *increases* slightly to –42.2. Although the increase is not itself significant, the effect of project residence in reducing exposure to disorder and violence remains strong and significant in each of the models ($p < 0.01$). In short, the move into ELH clearly appears to have reduced residents' exposure to neighborhood disorder and violence.

Stress from Negative Life Events

With lower levels of exposure to disorder and violence emanating from the surrounding neighborhood, we would naturally expect ELH residents to experience fewer negative life events than their nonresident counterparts. To put it bluntly, if project residents are exposed to fewer drug deals, less physical violence, and fewer gunshots by virtue of living in Mount Laurel, we expect them less frequently to experience negative events such as robbery, burglary, injury, or death. In our interviews with ELH residents and nonresident applicants we asked, "Within the past twelve months, how many times have the following events happened to you or someone who lives with you?" The events we asked about are listed down the side of table 7.2 and include everything from illness to death. We then went on to ask how many times the same set of events happened "to a relative or friend of yours."

If moving into Ethel Lawrence Homes conferred protection from the vicissitudes of neighborhood violence and disorder on project residents, then we would expect them to display lower frequencies of negative life events compared with nonresidents. We would not, however, expect to see a difference in the frequency of negative life experiences among the network of friends and relatives of residents versus nonresidents. A

Table 7.2. Number of times negative life events were experienced by Ethel Lawrence residents and nonresidents in the past year within the respondent's household and among the respondent's friends and relatives

| | Members of Sample Households | | Friends and Relatives of Sample | |
| | ELH | ELH | ELH | ELH |
Negative Life Event	Nonresidents	Residents	Nonresidents	Residents
Serious Illness	0.95	0.89	1.08	1.11
Serious Injury	0.36	0.34	0.48	0.54
Death	0.37	0.26	1.40	1.20
Unexpected Pregnancy	0.18	0.19	0.29	0.58
Arrest	0.20	0.10*	0.41	0.51
Incarceration	0.13	0.09*	0.34	0.35
Expelled from School	0.21	0.10*	0.29	0.25
Loss of Job	0.61	0.35*	1.24	1.26
Loss of Home	0.21	0.19	0.39	0.49
Robbery	0.14	0.10*	0.27	0.34
Burglary	0.38	0.19**	0.37	0.39
Total Negative Events	3.74	2.80+	6.56	7.02

*$p < 0.05$; +$p < 0.10$

priori, we have no reason to presume that members of residents' social networks are any more likely to experience improved neighborhood circumstances than the friends and relatives of nonresidents. In other words, the network of friends and relatives here constitutes a kind of control comparison group for the contrast between residents and nonresidents.

Table 7.2 systematically compares the frequency of negative life events experienced by project residents and nonresidents and their respective sets of friends and neighbors. As expected, the frequency of negative events is generally lower for ELH residents than nonresidents. Whereas the average project resident experienced 2.8 negative life events during 2009, the average nonresident experienced 3.7 such events. Although once again statistical tests are not strictly appropriate given that we have a population of ELH residents and a matched sample of nonresidents rather than two random samples, the difference between ELH residents and nonresidents is nonetheless significant at the 10 percent level. Other significant differences include the frequency of arrest (0.20 events among nonresidents versus 0.10 among residents), incarceration (0.13 versus 0.09), expulsion from school (0.21 versus 0.10), loss of job (0.61 versus 0.35), robbery (0.14 versus 0.10), and burglary (0.38 versus 0.19). Although it was not itself significant, the contrast in the risk of death was also rather large at 0.37 versus 0.26.

Turning to the friends and relatives of residents and nonresidents we find no significant differences between the two groups. Since the total number of friends and relatives is generally expected to be greater than the total number of household members, the absolute number of negative events experienced is much greater within friendship and kinship networks than households, with values of 6.6 and 7.0 for nonresidents and residents, respectively. The difference between the two numbers is not significant, however. Indeed, if anything, the friends and relatives of ELH residents seem to report slightly more negative events happening to them during the prior year than nonresidents.

Thus moving into the Ethel Lawrence Homes seems to have brought about a reduction in negative life events experienced by project residents compared with a similarly self-selected set of nonresidents. Once again, however, the sum of negative events reported at the bottom of table 7.2 weights all events equally, when very clearly some events (death, injury, robbery) are far more serious and stressful than others (illness, job loss, burglary). Following Massey and Fischer (2006) and Charles et al. (2009), therefore, we used the Holmes-Rahe Stress Scale (Holmes and Rahe 1967; Holmes and Masuda 1974) to construct a Stress-Weighted Life Events Scale. Specifically, as discussed in appendix A6, we multiplied the frequency of each event coded 0–4 by the severity of the stress associated with the event (from the Holmes-Rahe Scale) and then summed the

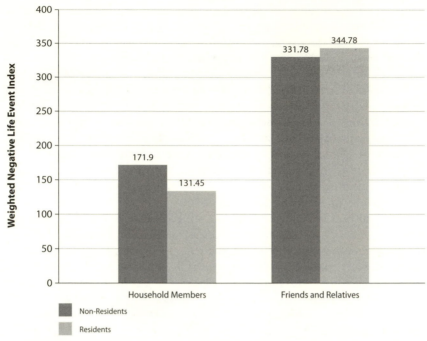

Figure 7.3. Exposure to negative life events among ELH residents and nonresidents and their family members during past year

products to yield a weighted index of life stress that ranged from 0–4,790 with considerable reliability ($\alpha = 0.874$).

Figure 7.3 shows the resulting stress-weighted negative life event index for resident and nonresident households as well as the friends and relatives of both groups. Once again, the degree of stress experienced by friends and relatives of ELH residents and nonresidents does not differ significantly, and, if anything, the friends and relatives of project residents experience a slightly higher stress score (344.8) than those of nonresidents (331.8). In contrast, project residents experienced a life event stress score (131.5) that was 24 percent below that of nonresidents (171.9), a statistically significant difference ($p < 0.10$).

In order to test systematically the effect of project residence on exposure to negative life events, we repeated the three-equation analysis described in the prior section, estimating one model that predicted the stress-weighted life event index from a dummy variable indicating project residence with no controls, another model containing the dummy variable plus individual background characteristics and propensity scores, and another model containing the dummy variable and controls for

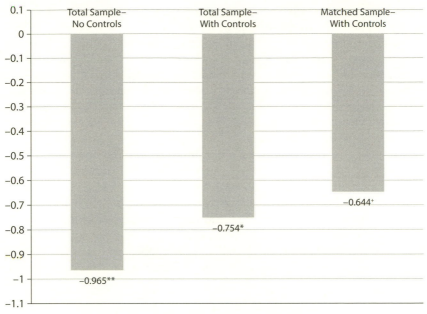

Figure 7.4. Effect of ELH residence on exposure to negative life events

residents and nonresidents matched using propensity scores. Because the distribution of the stress-weighted life event index was highly skewed, we took the natural log of the index before estimating the regressions. The full equations are included in appendix A7, and the coefficients indicating the effect of project residence on exposure to negative life events are summarized in figure 7.4.

Across all models the effect of project residence is negative and statistically significant, indicating that moving into the project did indeed bring about a clear reduction in exposure to negative life events for project residents. In the figure, we graph the effects as positive, thereby indicating the extent of the reduction in exposure to stressful life events brought about by moving into the Ethel Lawrence Homes. Given the logarithmic transformation of the dependent variable, the coefficients can be interpreted as indicating the percentage reduction in negative life events achieved by project residence. With no controls the estimated effect is −0.965, meaning that moving into the project was associated with a 97 percent decrease in exposure to negative life events. The addition of controls in the second model reduces the effect to a 75 percent decrease, and the estimated coefficient from the propensity-matched data suggests a decrease of 64 percent, all substantial improvements in substantive terms.

So far, we have been assuming that the frequency of negative life events experienced by project residents will fall because they are exposed to less dangerous and disorganized neighborhood environments. In order to conduct a formal test of this assumption, we included the severity-weighted index of disorder and violence as an additional control in the matched and unmatched analyses. If improved neighborhood circumstances are indeed responsible for the effect of project residence, then we would expect the size of the associated coefficient to fall significantly once the controls is introduced.

The full equations for this test are again presented in appendix A7, and the effect of adding the control for neighborhood disorder and violence is summarized in figure 7.5. As can be seen, our hypothesis is sustained. In the unmatched model with controls for background characteristics and the propensity score, the addition of the disorder-violence index reduces the coefficient to insignificance, whereas in the matched sample the addition of the index essentially reduces the coefficient to zero. Not only did moving into Ethel Lawrence Homes reduce the frequency of negative

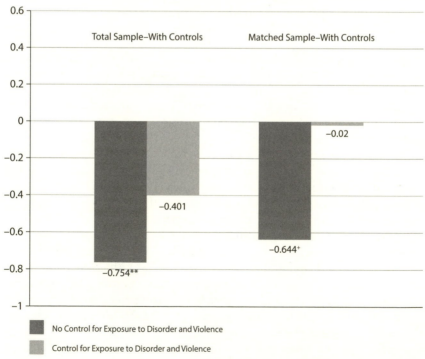

Figure 7.5. Effect of ELH residence on frequency of negative life events before and after controlling for exposure to disorder and violence

life events for project residents, but this outcome appears to have been brought about by a lower exposure to neighborhood violence and social disorder in ELH compared with the neighborhoods they would otherwise have inhabited.

Social Support

Data from demonstration projects associated with the Moving to Opportunity, Greautreax, and Hope VI programs also documented significant improvements in neighborhood circumstances arising from their respective housing mobility interventions, but these studies also revealed clear costs to program participants in terms of access to daily needs, basic services, and social supports (Ludwig et al., 2008; Clampet-Lundquist 2004a., 2004b, 2007, 2010). Although public-housing projects are, in essence, segregated enclaves of concentrated poverty, most inhabitants have grown up in them, and many are indeed descendants of others who have grown up in them. As a result, they are embedded within extensive networks of kinship, friendship, and acquaintance, which provide a significant social buffer against the ups and downs of life at the lower end of the socioeconomic spectrum (see Stack 1974; Lomnitz 1977; Edin and Lein 1997), yielding what social scientists have come to call social capital (Putnam 2000; Small 2004). Housing projects also tend to be centrally located near public transit stops and social service centers; and even though they are dangerous and lack many resources, at least they constitute familiar territory with known risks (Suttles 1968).

Moving to a new neighborhood necessarily disrupts social networks, separates people from familiar points of service provision, and plunges them into an unknown and unfamiliar social geography. Despite the improvement of neighborhood conditions, therefore, the most immediate effect of a relocation on individual well-being might very well be negative, as people are cut off from supportive social ties, alienated from familiar neighborhood environments, and distanced from service providers they had come to know (Clampet-Lundquist 2004a, 2007; Murphy and Wallace 2010). It naturally takes time to reconstruct new social networks, build new mental maps, and establish new connections with service agencies and vendors, and only gradually will the benefits of the new residence be fully expressed (Clampet-Lundquist 2004b, 2010).

Research designs based on a one-time allocation of housing vouchers to bring about mobility, such as Gauteaux, Moving to Opportunity, and Hope VI, are hampered by the fact that the potentially beneficial effects of the treatment (moving to an advantaged neighborhood) are confounded with a variety of negative side effects (fragmented support networks, disrupted mental maps, and loss of local knowledge). As a result, in immediate post-treatment assessments of well-being, the negative effects predominate and the expected benefits may fail to materialize. Moreover, if program participants all move at roughly the same time, everyone will spend the same amount of time in the advantaged neighborhood, yielding little variance in neighborhood exposure to disentangle the contrasting effects.

In the current study, however, tenants moved into the Ethel Lawrence Homes at different times, entering in a staggered, first-come, first-served order that unfolded in two major waves, one following the initial opening in 2000 and another following the project's expansion in 2004. In addition, over time families came and went, yielding new entrants to the project as well as a set of former project residents with truncated experience in the neighborhood. These features of the project design yield a variety of exposures to the beneficial effects of living in an advantaged suburban neighborhood as well as a variety of times since the disruptive effects of moving occurred. In this section, we take advantage of this variation to consider the potential costs to project residents of disruptions in their systems of social support as a result of entering the Ethel Lawrence Homes.

In order to assess the potentially negative effects of residential mobility on social support provided by family and nonfamily members, we asked both ELH residents and nonresidents to report on the frequency of their interactions with selected categories of relatives and nonrelatives before and after the move. Specifically, we asked respondents to think about where they lived in 1999 and how often they recalled interacting with their grandparents, parents, siblings, other family members, neighbors, and friends. The possible responses were "never," "rarely," "sometimes," "often," "very often," and "every day." We then repeated the question referring instead to interactions with the same people "in the past twelve months."

Table 7.3 summarizes the results of these queries by presenting the percentage of ELH residents and nonresidents who said they interacted with various social actors often, very often, or every day in 1999 and 2009. The bottom line of the table presents a summary index created by assigning the frequency ratings numeric values from 0 (never) to 5 (every day) and averaging across items, which yields a relatively reliable index of social interaction ($\alpha = 0.709$). Details of index construction are again included in appendix A6. The table offers two opportunities to measure the potentially disruptive effects on social support of moving into ELH. First, we can compare the frequency of social interaction reported by project residents in 1999 versus 2009, before and after the move; and second, we can compare the frequency of social interaction between residents and nonresidents in 2009.

Table 7.3. Percentage of respondents who said they interacted often with selected social actors

Target of Interaction	Ethel Lawrence Nonresidents		Ethel Lawrence Residents	
	1999	2009	1999	2009
Family Members				
Grandparent	56.0	58.9	53.3	51.3
Mother	92.1	81.7	76.7	81.9
Father	61.3	56.9	67.2	61.5
Siblings	83.2	72.6	77.3	75.3
Other family	53.7	61.0	61.5	64.5
Nonfamily Members				
Neighbors	52.8	35.1	43.2	47.9
Friends	78.2	64.3	81.9	72.6
Total Interaction Scale (0–5)	3.22	3.00	3.12	3.06

Neither comparison indicates that ELH residents paid a significant cost in terms of social disruption associated with their move into the project. Considering the summary index of social interaction, we see that both residents and nonresidents experienced a slight but nonsignificant decrease over time, with the nonresident index going from 2.27 to 1.97 and the resident index going from 2.20 to 2.03. Although overall levels of social interaction did not differ between residents and nonresidents, either in 1999 or 2009, when we consider family and nonfamily interactions separately, we find some differences. In terms of family, whether we consider grandparents, mothers, fathers, or other family members, we see few differences in the frequency of interaction across time or between groups. Among neighbors, however, we see a sharp decline in the frequency of interaction among nonresidents (with 53 percent saying they interacted often, very often, or every day in 1999, but only 35 percent in 2009), whereas among residents, the frequency of neighboring actually increased slightly (going from 43 percent in 1999 to 48 percent in 2009). Likewise, whereas interaction with friends fell for both groups, the decline in the frequency of interaction was much smaller for residents (who went from 82 percent in 1999 to 73 percent in 2009) than for nonresidents (from 78 to 64 percent).

In sum, whereas family interactions remain fairly constant between groups and over time, nonfamily interactions seem to display significant divergences. In order to consider this possibility, we broke the social

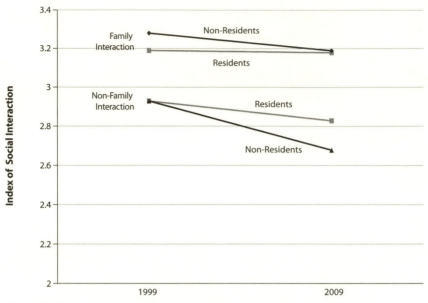

Figure 7.6. Family and nonfamily interaction reported by ELH residents and non-residents in 1999 and 2009

interaction index into two separate components: interactions with relatives and interactions with nonrelatives (see appendix A6). Figure 7.6 compares indices of family and nonfamily social interaction in 1999 and 2009 for ELH residents and nonresidents. As can clearly be seen, the frequency of family interaction was quite similar for both groups in 1999 and became identical by 2009, owing mainly to a slight decline in the frequency of family interaction among nonresidents. In contrast, whereas the frequency of nonfamily interaction was identical in 1999, by 2009 a gap had emerged in which ELH residents evinced a higher frequency of interaction with nonfamily members than nonresidents.

In order to test statistically for the effect of project residence on nonfamily social interaction we once gain estimated our three statistical models (included in appendix A7), and we summarize the results in figure 7.7. The left-hand bar shows that the raw, uncontrolled effect of project residence on the frequency of nonfamily interaction is positive but insignificant, with a coefficient of 0.155. Adding controls for background variables and propensity scores increases the coefficient slightly, to 0.222, but the effect remains insignificant. In the comparison of ELH residents and nonresidents using the propensity-matched data, however, we find a very strong and significant effect with a coefficient of 0.532 ($p < 0.01$), which suggests that ELH did provide an environment more conducive

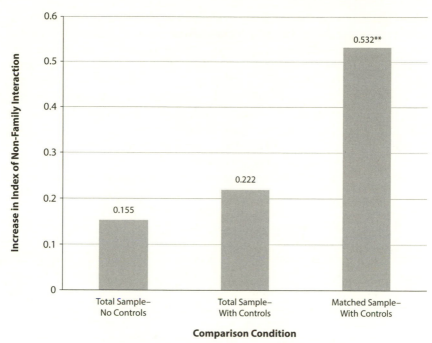

Figure 7.7. Effect of ELH residence on frequency of nonfamily interactions

to social interaction among friends and neighbors than residents would have otherwise experienced.

In analysis not shown here, we added the indicator of disorder and violence to the last model, but it had no effect in reducing the size of the coefficient associated with project residence. Thus the apparent effect of greater interaction with nonfamily members has nothing to do with the lower levels of violence and disorder generally experienced in the Ethel Lawrence Homes, but stems from other conditions in the project, most likely the deliberate efforts of project administrators to build internal cohesion through architectural design (the location of town houses around common circles and greens) and social organization (by holding regular formal meetings, sponsoring a Neighborhood Watch, and offering services such as child care on-site).

Meeting Daily Needs

The foregoing results provide little evidence that project residents paid a cost in terms of social support for improving their neighborhood circumstances, and there is some evidence that it actually brought about an increase in networking and social-capital formation among nonrelatives such as friends and neighbors. Another potential cost of moving, however, is the disruption of daily routines. Anyone who lives in a particular residential area for any period of time learns how to most efficiently meet life's daily needs, gradually working out the fastest way to work, the best places to shop, and the closest outlets for services such as medical care, filling prescriptions, child care, and education.

We sought to assess, in two ways, the efficacy with which ELH residents and nonresidents were able to meet their daily needs—first by asking how difficult ELH residents and nonresidents found it to get to a grocery store, drug store, workplace, school, day care center, and doctor's office in 1999 and 2009, and then by asking them to estimate the travel time it took them to reach each setting. The latter was measured in minutes and the former in terms of a five-point response continuum of difficulty: very easy, somewhat easy, neither easy nor hard, somewhat hard, very hard.

The resulting data are summarized in table 7.4, which presents in the upper panel the percentage of respondents saying it was hard or very hard to access various services, and in the bottom panel the reported travel time required to access the same set of services. Information in the top panel is summarized using a scale created by assigning values of 0 (very easy) to 4 (very hard) to categories on the response continuum and averaging ratings across the six services listed, yielding a very reliable scale ($\alpha = 0.893$) whose computation is described in greater detail in appendix A6. The lower panel shows the travel times required to access the same services in 1999 and 2009, and the average travel time is shown at the bottom.

Once again, the data suggest that ELH residents sacrificed little by moving into the project. Among project residents, the average difficulty rating for accessing services was 0.54 in 1999, before moving into the project, and 0.54 in 2009, afterward. The corresponding figures for nonresidents were likewise equal at both dates, with a value of 0.69. In neither 1999 nor 2009 was the difference between ELH residents and nonresidents significant. Among residents, the percentage saying it was hard to access the service in question changed relatively little except for child care, where the percentage dropped from 11 to 0 percent reflecting the existence of a child care center on-site at the Ethel Lawrence Homes. The travel times tell essentially the same story: little change between 1999 and 2009 for both residents and nonresidents, and no difference between them in either year. Likewise, when we undertook our three-equation analysis, we found no significant difference between residents and nonresidents in any of the models.

Table 7.4. Relative access to routine resources reported by project residents and nonresidents

Resources	Ethel Lawrence Nonresidents		Ethel Lawrence Residents	
	1999	2009	1999	2009
Percent saying it is hard to access:				
Grocery Store	9.0	16.1	9.7	5.3
Drug Store	7.3	9.0	6.3	8.0
Place of Work	11.6	10.2	14.5	8.8
Child's School	3.5	14.1	8.0	4.7
Child Care	13.2	7.1	11.4	0.0
Doctor	7.2	16.4	10.8	11.7
Difficulty of Life Scale (0–4)	0.69	0.69	0.54	0.54
Average minutes travel to:				
Grocery Store	11.8	11.1	11.5	7.2
Drug Store	10.7	8.6	10.4	10.2
Place of Work	24.6	23.0	23.7	21.6
Child's School	11.8	12.6	10.5	9.0
Child Care	17.5	17.2	13.2	12.9
Doctor	16.0	16.6	17.4	20.2
Average	15.1	13.9	14.9	13.5

The one arena in which we found significant differences between residents and nonresidents was with respect to transportation. Table 7.5 summarizes data we collected about access to transportation among ELH residents and nonresidents. On the 0–4 scale measuring ease of access to public transit (with higher numbers indicating greater access), nonresidents gave an average rating of 2.8 compared with just 1.3 among residents. Likewise, 68 percent of ELH residents rated public transit as poor or very poor compared with just 22 percent of nonresidents. In order to make up for the lack of access to public transit, project residents, like everyone else in the suburbs, turned to automobiles. Whereas 69 percent of nonresidents said they presently owned a motor vehicle, the figure was 87 percent among project residents.

Although owning a car provides greater freedom of movement, it also entails greater costs and responsibilities. One point on which both project residents and their township neighbors concur is that local public transit could really stand to be improved. In one of our in-depth interviews, an ELH resident told us about "teenagers who are able to get a job, if,

Table 7.5. Transportation situation of residents and nonresidents of Ethel Lawrence Homes in 2009

Transportation Indicator	Ethel Lawrence Nonresidents	Ethel Lawrence Residents
Presently Owns Motor Vehicle	68.8%	86.7%
Uses Public Transportation	29.7	1.8
Rates Public Transit Service as Poor	21.6	68.1
Access to Public Transit (0–4)	2.8	1.3

let's say you're working. I can't get you to work on time. If there was a bus stop, I'd be able to—here's the token or money or whatever they do now—and you know they're getting on the bus taking them to [Route] 38 or whichever way they're going, they could switch buses to their job. But it's hard for them to get that first job, or job out here, they don't have transportation."

Onward and Upward

No matter how we analyze the data marshaled in this chapter, we come to the same conclusion: moving into the Ethel Lawrence Homes significantly improved the residential environment experienced by project residents, dramatically reducing their exposure to social disorder and violence within neighborhoods and consequently reducing the number of negative life events they experience. These conclusions hold whether we compare the experiences of project residents before and after they entered the project, or whether we compare the experiences of project residents and nonresidents during the survey year. The latter finding persists when we control for background characteristics and entry propensities and when we compare residents and nonresidents statistically after propensity score matching.

We also showed that these improved neighborhood and personal circumstances did not come at the expense of social support, the ease of daily living, or access to needed services. Among project residents, the frequency of social interaction with family members was about the same after the move as before, and we detected no difference in family interaction frequency between residents and nonresidents at any point in time. Moreover, with respect to interactions with nonrelatives such as friends and neighbors, we found some evidence that the frequency of interaction actually increased to yield a significant difference between residents and nonresidents at the time of the survey.

Likewise, we found no change over time or difference between residents and nonresidents in the difficulty of daily living or the travel time required to access needed services. Our findings parallel those of Bush-Baskette, Robinson, and Simmons (2011), whose survey of households that moved into units certified by the Council on Affordable Housing revealed that the vast majority reported access to services and amenities that equaled or exceeded what they had experienced before moving. As with ELH residents, the notable exception was public transportation. In the present case, however, the latent potential for social isolation and alienation from services owing to a lack of access to public transit was overcome by motor-vehicle ownership, which was almost universal among project residents. In contrast, nonresidents relied on public transit to a much greater extent.

Although reactions to the Ethel Lawrence Homes among project residents were overwhelmingly positive, the in-depth interviews did reveal a few sources of tension. The downside of the project's bucolic location was its relative isolation. Although adults could use cars to overcome barriers of distance to access the services and amenities they needed, the burden of social isolation fell more heavily on teenagers who could not yet drive or did not have access to a car. As one resident noted in chapter 5, "We in an enclosed development and there's nothing around here. . . . There's absolutely nothing to do in Mount Laurel. At least nothing [kids] can walk to."

The other source of tension stemmed from the fact that most tenants were racial minorities in an overwhelmingly white suburban environment. Few respondents reported experiencing overt prejudice or discrimination. More often it was a subtle feeling of discomfort, of being out of place and looked at suspiciously by white townspeople who were unaccustomed to dealing with blacks or Hispanics on a routine basis. One woman told us how she felt when she first moved into Mount Laurel from the nearby black enclave of Willingboro:

> Well, I felt that, when I moved to Mount Laurel from Willingboro. When I first went into the grocery story there was just so few blacks there. I just felt uneasy, you know. And, I can't say that it was what people did to me, as much as what I felt like I know what they were thinking. You know, it's not easy being black out here, trust me, it really isn't, because everywhere you go, you've never felt it, you don't know what it's like to, everywhere you go, think that everybody hates you. And you didn't even do anything. You walk into a room, it's just being black, it's horrible. This one, if you're sensitive. If me and you go to a restaurant, any restaurant in Cherry Hill, I'm thinking everybody hates me. How do you like to live like that?

Another young African American woman described her discomfort in feeling that she was constantly on display and was under pressure to uphold the dignity of the race:

> In Mt. Laurel I can't go into the store like this, you know (pointing to ca-
> sual clothes). But if I'm in Willingboro, I can throw on my shoes and my
> little jacket and go shopping and not have to worry. Out here, they tend to
> watch you more. If I go in there like this, they tend to watch me more. But
> then when I get dressed and go grocery shopping, they're not watching.

Nonetheless, despite the feeling that commercial places and public space were frequently sites for invidious judgment and evaluation,
some residents were able to relate instances in which they felt like public
encounters produced positive outcomes and improved interracial sentiments, as in the case of one resident who told us:

> I know myself, a couple of times, a friend of mine, lives down the block
> here, have been in the grocery store, and we see an elderly white person,
> and you see them reaching for something on the shelf, and it's like impossi-
> ble for them to reach it, and we ask, can we help you? And they don't turn
> around and say like "I didn't know black people were like that. You know
> what I mean, so people do have some stereotypes, and I think with us being
> here, we have broken some of 'em for some people. Because, you know,
> people aren't bad, you know. So, I think in a way we have helped.

Despite the inevitable problems emanating from the racial and class
divides that separate ELH residents from their neighbors in Mount Laurel, and despite certain criticisms of the project's location and management practices, the balance of pros and cons was decidedly positive for
all residents and they were more than willing to put up with uncomfort-
able racial and class undercurrents in return for access to a high-quality
home in a safe and secure neighborhood that, despite its pastoral location, nonetheless provided access to resources for their daily needs and
enabled social interactions with friends and relatives. The issue to which
we turn in the next chapter is whether residents have been able to use
the safe setting of the Ethel Lawrence Homes as a platform for broader
success in life—whether inhabiting a secure, nonthreatening environment
indeed provided residents with a springboard to move onward and upward on the socioeconomic ladder.

CHAPTER 8

Tenant Transitions

FROM GEOGRAPHIC TO SOCIAL MOBILITY

Like earlier studies, to this point we have documented a significant improvement in neighborhood conditions for low-income households as a result of their participation in a housing mobility program. Specifically, by moving into the Ethel Lawrence Homes in Mount Laurel, Jersey, low- and moderate-income families from throughout the region were able to trade inferior housing in high-poverty, predominantly minority, city neighborhoods for well-appointed town houses located in an affluent white suburb. In doing so, they dramatically lowered their exposure to social disorder and violence and reduced the frequency with which they experienced negative life events; and these benefits did not come at the cost of social interactions with family members or access to essential services. As a bonus, evidence suggests that residents may even have experienced an increase in interaction with neighbors as a result of the move.

The obvious question at this point, then, is whether these improved neighborhood circumstances had any influence on the broader life trajectories of program participants, providing them with a pathway out of poverty and a means to advance toward economic self-sufficiency. On the issue of economic independence, prior work has produced a decidedly mixed set of results. As noted earlier, studies emanating from the Gautreaux Demonstration Project generally found improvements in mental health, economic self-sufficiency, and children's educational outcomes as a result of moving into a low-poverty, suburban neighborhood. In contrast, although evaluations from the Moving to Opportunity Demonstration Project did find improvements in mental health as a result of moving to low-poverty neighborhoods, MTO investigators did not find strong, significant, or even positive effects on adult economic independence or children's educational outcomes.

It has been difficult for scholars to adjudicate between these conflicting findings because both studies had methodological problems that complicated interpretation of the results (cf., Clampet-Lundquist and Massey 2008; Ludwig et al., 2008; Sampson 2008). The Gautreaux Program, for example, did not randomly assign subjects to suburban versus city neighborhoods and was thus subject to charges of selection bias. Although the MTO program did begin with random assignment, it suffered from problems of design and implementation that likely introduced other sources of selectivity into the study—for example, a large fraction of those randomly assigned a mobility voucher did not use it to move; most of those who moved went to another segregated minority area rather than to a white suburb; and many of those who did move into better neighborhoods quickly returned to high-poverty neighborhoods (Clampet-Lundquist and Massey 2008).

Although the Monitoring Mount Laurel Study by no means eliminates all threats to internal validity stemming from selection biases, it does hold constant self-selection into the pool of people seeking access to better housing in an affluent white suburb. In addition, propensity score matching offers additional controls for selectivity, at least with respect to factors included on the application form and unmeasured characteristics associated with them. Although our ability to eliminate potential confounding variables may not be perfect, the design of the Mount Laurel study offers strengths and weaknesses complementing those of prior studies and thus provides a fresh lens with which to consider the influence of residential mobility on people's lives.

As in earlier studies, we begin our consideration with a look at the health of project residents and nonresidents, for without health, achievements in other domains of life become difficult. Although we find no differences in physical health between ELH residents and nonresidents, we do find modest improvement in mental health among residents as a result of their moving into the project, and largely attributable to residents' lower level of exposure to disorder and violence within neighborhoods and lower frequencies of experiencing negative life events. We also find greater economic independence among ELH residents than nonresidents, with higher levels of employment and earnings, lower levels of welfare dependency, and a higher fraction of income earned from work. Among the children of ELH residents, we document greater access to a quiet study space, more academically supportive parental behavior, and more time spent studying as a result of moving into the project. ELH residence also brought children greater access to high-quality schools and lower levels of exposure to school disorder and violence. Although the effect of ELH residence on grades earned was positive, the effect was small and not statistically significant. In sum, both the adult ELH residents and the children who accompanied them appear to be much better off in social and economic terms than they would have been if they had remained in their former neighborhoods.

Moving to Mental Health

It is difficult, intrusive, and quite expensive to work a physician's exam into a social survey; but in most populations, a simple question asking respondents to state whether their health is excellent, very good, good, fair, or poor has been found to provide a valid and reliable assessment of a person's overall health (Lundberg and Manderbacka 1996; Idler and Benyamini 1997; Haddock et al., 2006). Figure 8.1 summarizes responses to this question by whites, blacks, and Hispanics in the U.S. population generally (Wolf et al., 2008) and among ELH residents and nonresidents interviewed in the Monitoring Mount Laurel Study. In the general population, around 59 percent of whites, 44 percent of blacks, and 34 percent of Hispanics rate their health as very good or excellent, whereas 13 percent of whites, 21 percent of blacks, and 31 percent of Hispanics rate it as fair or poor. In our survey of ELH residents, however, only 36 percent rated their health as very good or excellent, compared

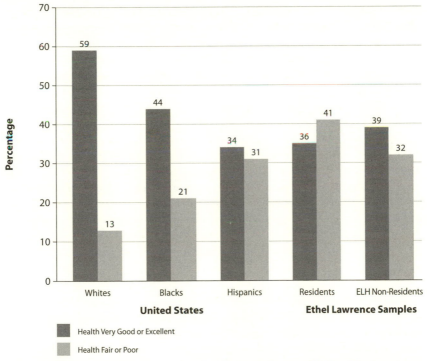

Figure 8.1. Self-reported health in the United States and among ELH residents and nonresidents

with 39 percent of nonresidents, whereas 41 percent and 32 percent of these two groups rated their health as fair or poor, respectively. Thus the physical health of both ELH residents and nonresidents appears to be much worse than whites in the general population and slightly worse than blacks and Hispanics generally. However, we found no significant differences in the physical health of ELH residents and nonresidents. At the time of the survey, in other words, members of both groups appear to be drawn from the same population of disadvantaged, predominately minority, health-compromised people.

This finding generally replicates findings from the early rounds of the MTO study (Ludwig et al., 2008), though more recent analyses do indicate that moving into low-poverty neighborhoods did modestly lower rates of obesity and diabetes among program participants (Ludwig et al., 2011). Nonetheless, both the MTO and Gautreaux demonstration projects found clearer and more consistent effects of program participation on mental than physical health. In order to assess psychological well-being, our survey asked respondents to estimate the frequency with which they experienced various symptoms of anxiety and mental distress, such as "trouble falling asleep," "trouble relaxing," "frequent crying," "fearfulness," "being very tired for no reason," and "waking up tired." Each person was asked to rate the frequency with which they experienced these specific symptoms in the past twelve months using the response categories "never," "a few times," "once a week," "almost every day," and "every day."

In table 8.1 we show the percentage of ELH residents and nonresidents who reported experiencing each symptom at least once a week, and at the bottom of the table we summarize the data by computing a mental distress index that averages frequency ratings across all six symptoms after assigning numerical values from 0 (never) to 4 (every day) to the response categories ($\alpha = 0.764$, see appendix A6). As earlier studies of residential mobility have found, the summary index of mental distress indicates that program participants experienced better mental health, on average, than nonparticipants. Whereas the average index of mental distress for nonresidents was 1.15, indicating an average frequency of symptoms somewhere between a few times and once a week (more toward the former), the average index for ELH residents was 0.88, indicating a response between never and a few times, an admittedly modest but nonetheless statistically significant difference ($p < 0.05$). Considering the six symptoms separately, the frequency of distress was less for residents than nonresidents in all cases, and the gap was statistically significant in three instances: "trouble falling asleep," "fearfulness," and "waking up tired."

In order to test more systematically whether moving into the Ethel Lawrence Homes improved the mental health of project residents, we

Table 8.1. Selected symptoms of anxiety and poor mental health reported occurring at least once a week among ELH residents and nonresidents

	Percent Reporting Symptom At Least Once a Week	
Symptom	Nonresidents	Residents
Trouble Falling Asleep	40.2	27.0 *
Trouble Relaxing	33.0	24.3
Frequent Crying	11.3	8.8
Fearfulness	28.7	5.2 **
Very Tired for No Reason	25.9	19.0
Wake Up Tired	38.8	28.1+
Mental Distress Index	1.15	0.88 *

$**p < 0.01$; $*p < 0.05$; $+p < 0.10$

followed procedures used in the previous chapter and estimated three regression models: one that pooled residents and nonresidents together and regressed the index of mental distress on a dichotomous variable for ELH residence; another that used the same pooled set of data but also included controls for personal characteristics and the individual propensity score; and a final equation estimated using individual-level controls with samples of residents and nonresidents matched using propensity scores. The estimated equations are presented in appendix A7, and the effects of ELH residence derived from the models are summarized in figure 8.2.

In the absence of controls, the estimated effect of ELH residence on mental health is to reduce mental distress by around −0.22 points, a significant reduction that is equal roughly to a quarter of a standard deviation on the distress scale. Adding in controls for individual characteristics and the propensity score does not significantly change the size of the estimated effect, but when it is estimated using the matched sample of residents and nonresidents, the coefficient drops to -0.13 and is no longer statistically significant. Despite this reduction, however, the shift in the size of the coefficient is not itself statistically significant, and the net effect remains in the expected direction.

On balance, therefore, the evidence seems to indicate that moving into ELH produced a slight improvement in mental health among project residents, though the improvement is modest under any scenario. Another way to test the validity of this conclusion is to add controls for exposure to disorder and violence and the frequency of negative life events, under the theory that the greater mental distress experienced among nonresidents reflects their elevated exposure to deleterious neighborhood circumstances. If this is true, then one or both of the control indices should

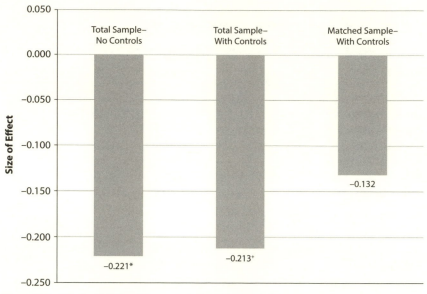

Figure 8.2. Effect of ELH residence on index of mental distress

prove to be significant in regression equations and carry a positive sign, while the effect of ELH residence should be reduced or disappear entirely.

As shown in figure 8.3, this is precisely the scenario that plays out when the additional controls are added. After the effects of exposure to neighborhood disorder and negative life events are held constant, the estimated effect of ELH residence not only drops to statistical insignificance in both the unmatched and matched comparisons, but the sign of the coefficient turns from negative to positive. In the full equations (see appendix A7), both the disorder-violence scale and negative life-event index prove to be positive and highly significant in predicting mental health. These results imply that moving into ELH lowered residents' exposure to disorder and violence, which in turn lowered the incidence of negative life events, and that both these developments combined to reduce the mental distress experienced by ELH residents versus nonresidents.

This statistical evidence rings true given what ELH residents said in the personal interviews we conducted. For example, one woman told us:

> I find that living in the city, in the inner city, to me, personally, there seems to be a lot of negativity; and out here, you can read. You have a feeling, you can hear the birds singing; and you can just go out the door and work in your yard a little bit. All that worrying and negativity in the city takes up a lot of your energy. So, definitely yes, living here has made me feel less stressed. And that's not saying that you don't have other pressures and

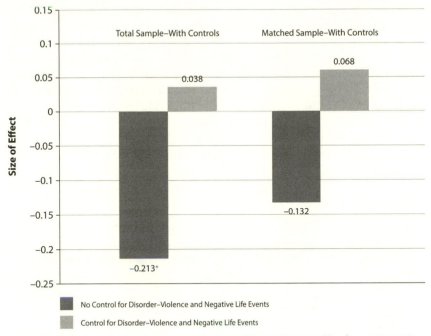

Figure 8.3. Effect of ELH residence on mental distress after controlling for exposure to disorder and violence and experience of negative life events

stresses in your life; that stuff is normal. But that's at least something I don't have to worry about, one less thing.

Another resident, a mother of two, said she felt more at peace in her new environment, telling us:

> You're not worrying, if your kids go to—not that there is a corner store they could go to here—but, if they were to leave, and say they wanted to go to the store, you were like, wondering every minute, "It's been five minutes, you're not back yet, did something happen? Or do I need to go look for you?" It definitely gives me a sense of peacefulness.

A second example is from a woman in her seventies who explained that the opportunity to baby-sit local children and to garden outside gave her a more positive mental outlook:

> If they need me, I am here for them, and I like that. And I feel kids help you a lot. Because I don't have time to dwell on my problems and I am far from being bored. They keep me going. Even after I don't watch them anymore, in the summer when I have my plants outside, they will come by and be interested, and want to be involved, the girls do, and I help them with that.

Although it may not be captured well in our quantitative analyses, qualitative data suggest that exposure to lower levels of social disorder and violence provided benefits to residents that went beyond mental health. One resident in his early fifties explained how moving to Mount Laurel had improved his physical health as well. At the time he applied to the project, he was living in a week-to-week rental located in a boarding house in rural New Jersey. The first floor had been divided into four single-room apartments, each containing a hot plate for cooking. Residents shared an old refrigerator in the hallway, turnover in the apartments was very high, and his food and medicine were regularly pilfered. In addition, the walls were covered in mold, and the interior paint and wallboards were deteriorating, exacerbating his already tenuous medical condition. In his interview he recalled:

> I was diabetic all of my life, and I lost my vision in my right eye, so I've had a lot of medical issues over the years. So, I'm happy to be in this situation, in this environment. Because, like my immune system is like turned off; the doctor has it at like 10 percent, because of the transplants. So that's a foreign entity in your body and, you know when you rent rooms and stuff, you never know who you're in contact with, lots of turnover. And my mother is only a mile away so I'm close back this way because she's elderly, and you know, I'm very happy where I'm at—very, very happy.

One final test of the validity of the conclusion that project residence improves mental health is to consider the effect on mental distress of time spent in ELH. If moving out of a neighborhood with high levels of social disorder and violence and a high risk of experiencing negative life events into a safer and more secure residential area indeed improves mental health, then logically we would assume that the longer a person lives in the more tranquil surroundings, and the farther away from disorder and violence he or she gets in space and time, the greater the reduction in symptoms of mental distress. To test this hypothesis, we substituted the number of years spent in ELH for the dichotomous indicator of residence in EHL in the three regression models and assigned nonresidents a value of 0 for years spent in the project. The results of this operation are summarized in figure 8.4, which uses equations estimated from matched and unmatched samples of residents and nonresidents to predict the mental-distress index exhibited at different durations of project residence, assuming mean values for all independent variables except time lived in ELH. Again the full equations are shown in the appendix A7.

As can clearly be seen, mental distress declines steadily with years lived in ELH. In the unmatched equation, the index for persons with no project experience stands at 1.05 whereas after ten years it is predicted to drop to around 0.86, roughly a rate of 0.025 points for each year of

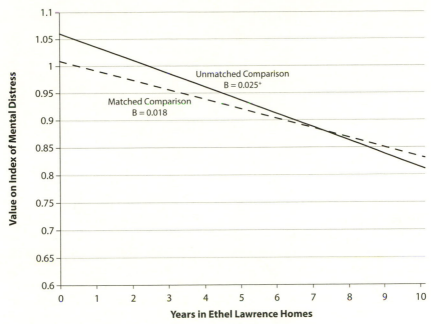

Figure 8.4. Effect of years lived in ELH on mental distress

project residence (p < 0.10). Although the estimate from the matched comparison is slightly lower (a decline of 0.018 points per year), it is not significantly different from the unmatched comparison, and in practical terms, duration of residence has much the same effect. We thus conclude that moving to ELH appears to improve the mental health of project residents by lowering their exposure to neighborhood disorder and violence, and by reducing the frequency with which they experience negative life events, the longer they live in the project, the lower the level of mental distress they suffer.

Climbing the Economic Ladder

As noted earlier, prior evaluations of residential mobility programs have also documented mental-health improvements among participants. The principal discrepancy in research done to date is the general failure of MTO to find significant effects on indicators of economic independence, compared with Gautreaux's finding of improvements in employment and wages and declines in welfare use among suburban movers relative to city movers. In order to assess the economic effects of ELH residence,

Table 8.2. Indicators of employment and earnings reported by ELH residents and nonresidents

Economic Indicator	Nonresidents	Residents
Percent Working for Pay	55.2	67.2+
Income from Work	$12,912	$19,687 **
Total Income	$21,022	$26,271 *
Percentage of Income from Work	42.2	60.3 **
Index of Economic Independence	–0.110	0.162 **

**p < 0.01; *p < 0.05; +p < 0.10

we asked respondents to report whether they were currently working for pay and ascertained the current income they earned from work as well as their total household income. From answers to these queries we also computed the share of income derived from work, and the resulting statistics are summarized in table 8.2 for ELH residents and nonresidents.

As in the Gautreaux study but unlike the MTO analysis, we find significant differences between residents and nonresidents on all economic outcomes. Specifically, compared with nonresidents, ELH residents were more likely to be working for pay at the time of the survey (67.2 percent versus 55.2 percent, p < 0.10) and earned significantly more annual income from work ($19,687 versus $12,912, p < 0.01). Although we do not show it in the table, a significantly smaller percentage of ELH residents (4.2 percent) also said they received welfare payments than nonresidents (12.9 percent, p < 0.05), which implies that although ELH residents received more income from work, they also got less money from welfare. The balance of these gains and losses is indicated by total income, which was much higher (p < 0.05) for ELH households ($26,271) than nonresident households ($21,022). Thus the income gained from work was greater than the income lost from state transfers by moving from welfare to work, yielding a clear financial incentive for work attributable to the move. Not surprisingly, ELH residents received a significantly greater share of their total income from work (60.3 percent) than nonresidents (42.2 percent, p < 0.01).

In order to summarize differences between residents and nonresidents with respect to economic independence, we factor analyzed the variables shown in table 8.2 and used the resulting loadings as weights, which we then applied to each variable's z-score to create a factor index of economic self-sufficiency (α = 0.924, see appendix A6). Average factor scores are shown at the bottom of table 8.2 and clearly indicate a significant difference in the degree of economic independence between ELH residents and nonresidents, with a mean value of –0.110 for the latter

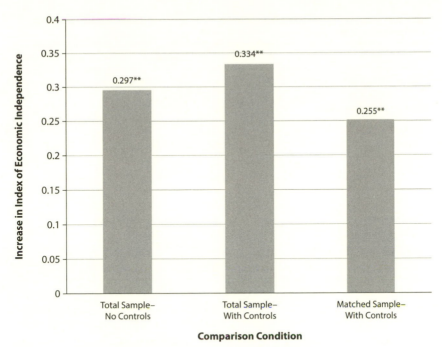

Figure 8.5. Effect of ELH residence on economic independence

compared with an average of 0.162 for the former (p < 0.01). Entry into the project thus appears clearly to increase the economic independence of tenants.

Figure 8.5 formally tests this hypothesis by showing coefficients for ELH residence derived from our standard three-equation analysis (see equations in appendix A7). The left-hand bar indicates that in the absence of any controls or matching, the factor scale of economic independence is 0.297 units greater for ELH residents than nonresidents, roughly 30 percent of a standard deviation. However, when individual characteristics are held constant and selectivity is controlled by including propensity scores as controls, the estimated effect of project residence on economic independence *increases* to 0.330, or about a third of a standard deviation. When selectivity is controlled by propensity score matching, the value is only 0.255, but this is still significant statistically. In table 8.3, we move on to summarize the results of the three-equation analysis for each of the separate components of the economic independence scale. Specifically, we show the estimated effects of ELH residence on the likelihood of employment, income from work, total income, and percentage of income from work. As can be seen, across all comparisons, living in ELH

Table 8.3. Effect of ELH residence and years spent in ELH on selected indicators of economic independence

Independent Variable	Total Sample		Matched Sample
	No Controls	With Controls	With Controls
Effect of ELH Residence			
Employment	0.571*	0.844*	0.637+
Income from Work	$5,629**	$7,423**	$7,255**
Total Income	$3,317**	$5,025**	$5,291**
% of Income from Work	19.6**	22.8**	21.0**
Effect of Years in ELH			
Employment	0.069+	0.101*	0.090+
Income from Work	$909**	$1,101**	$1,129**
Total Income	$696**	$821**	$875**
% of Income from Work	2.6**	2.9**	2.8**

$**p < 0.01$; $*p < 0.05$; $+p < 0.10$

has a strong and significant positive effect on economic status, serving to raise levels of both income and employment.

The empirical evidence adduced to this point is thus consistent in showing that movement into ELH enables project residents to improve their economic status relative to what they would have achieved had they not made the move. In an effort to determine why this effect occurs we re-estimated the equations predicting economic independence after adding controls for indicators of disorder-violence, negative life events, and mental distress. The full equations are shown in appendix A7, and the effect of adding these controls is summarized in figure 8.6, which presents coefficients for ELH residence estimated before and after adding the new indicators to the matched and unmatched comparisons. Again, if improved neighborhood circumstances are responsible for the improvement associated with project residence, then the addition of the indicators should reduce or eliminate the effect of ELH residence.

In both the matched and unmatched equations, the negative life scale has a strong and significant negative effect ($p < 0.01$) on economic independence, whereas exposure to disorder and violence and the frequency of mental distress have no apparent effect (see equations in appendix A7). Economic independence thus appears to be improved at least partially by reducing the frequency of negative life events experienced by project residents, suggesting that the negative events accumulate to detract from work effort and employability. Despite the fact that the effect of

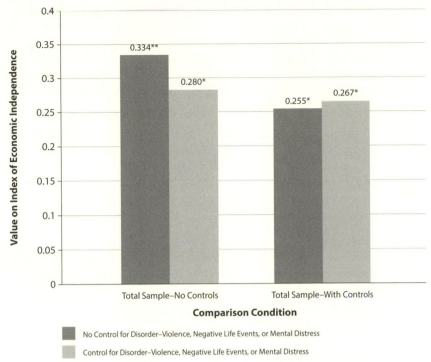

Figure 8.6. Effect of ELH residence on economic independence before and after controlling for exposure to disorder-violence, negative life events, and mental distress

ELH residence is somewhat reduced by the inclusion of the negative life events index (going from 0.321 to 0.265) in the unmatched comparison, the effect is slightly increased in the matched comparison, and in each case, the effect of ELH residence is by no means eliminated and remains significant. In other words, even though moving into the Ethel Lawrence Homes may have improved the economic prospects of residents by reducing the frequency of negative life events they experienced, the move also appears to have brought about other positive benefits not captured in the measures at our disposal, perhaps placing residents closer to jobs, giving them better access to information about employment opportunities, and reducing place-based stigma and discrimination (as when employers refuse to hire residents of Camden).

Some sense of the mechanisms by which ELH residence enhances economic independence comes from our in-depth interviews. For example, one single mother of two made a direct connection between her sense of safety for herself and her children and her desire to improve her life, telling us:

You can think clearer out here. Like I said, this goes back to the security, and the worrying thing. And children are my main concern. So as long as they are feeling comfortable, it gives me time to concentrate on other things. This is a place I want to stay until I find a home that is mine. I would say that moving here has made me feel less stuck, makes me know that I can do better. And to me, this is a place that is good now, but it makes me want to do more.

Another single mother told us that before moving to Mount Laurel she had been living in a public housing complex in New York City in which a mother of four had been shot and killed right in front of the building. She described to us how her desire to create a better life for her children had led her to look for employment so she could meet the minimum income requirement for admission into the Ethel Lawrence Homes. She told us:

My life has changed completely. In New York, I wasn't happy there, and I don't have nowhere to go that I can afford. I can't pay. I can't go and rent in another nice neighborhood, because I don't have the money. I'm by myself with the kids, so was hard for me, and I was worried. You know, the neighborhood wasn't good. So I decide to move down here. And some of my friend, they told me, "Are you crazy? How you going to move there, it's not city, it's boring, it's quiet down here, and you don't have a job?" Because I didn't have a job. But you know what? I feel it, I say no, I know I'm going to find a job, and at the time I was on unemployment, I was collecting, so I have income. Not too much but I have a income, so I say, well, I'm doing because my kids. I know I'm going to find a job and I know they going to grow up. And I moved here and in one week I found two jobs, one cleaning and one helping with the school buses. So I know my sacrifice is going to work, is working. It takes me time and sacrifice in that. I suffer, because, everything different, I always think of my kids. And my children are happy now. So that's why. I don't care what my friends tell me.

Whatever the precise combination of mechanisms, moving into ELH clearly raised income and employment and increased the economic independence of project residents. In figure 8.7 we consider the effect of time spent in ELH to assess whether ELH residence offers a static, one-time benefit or a cumulative advantage that builds over time. To generate this figure we substituted years spent in ELH for the dichotomous indicator of ELH residence into the regression equations and used the result to generate predicted values (in this and all other duration regressions we tested for nonlinearities in the effect of time and found none). The equation estimates revealed a strong and significant ($p < 0.05$) effect of time spent in ELH on economic self-sufficiency (see equations in appendix A7). In the unmatched regression, the scale of economic independence was estimated

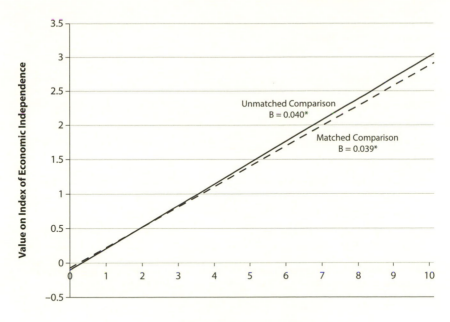

Years in Ethel Lawrence Homes

Figure 8.7. Effect of years lived in ELH on economic independence

to increase by 0.040 units per year, compared with 0.039 units per year in the matched regression, a trivial difference. In the course of ten years of residence, therefore, the predicted value on the scale of independence went from below zero to around 3.0, a remarkable improvement of around three standard deviations. In conclusion, not only does project residence enhance economic independence, but the longer the duration of time spent in the project, the greater the boost to self-sufficiency.

Educational Resources at Home

Given their greater access to household income, we might expect the children of ELH residents to fare better educationally than those of nonresidents by reason of their greater access to material resources. In addition, ELH adult residents are also exposed to less neighborhood violence and experience fewer negative life events than nonresidents, while displaying better mental health and incurring no additional time burden to satisfy daily needs, so we might also expect parents to have more emotional and psychic energy to support their children's learning, thus yielding better educational outcomes. In table 8.4 we assess a variety of additional

Table 8.4. Educational resources available to children within the households of of ELH residents and nonresidents

Educational Resources	Nonresident Parents	Resident Parents
Residential Resources		
Has Own Room	65.7	85.7+
Has Place for Undisturbed Study	68.6	91.4 *
Parental Resources		
Check Homework Often or Very Often	44.2	61.8+
Help with Homework Often or Very Often	29.4	40.0
Participate in PTA Often or Very Often	25.7	25.7
Talk to Other Parents Often or Very Often	28.6	37.1
Take Child to Library Often or Very Often	5.8	45.8 **
Index of Supportive Parenting	1.58	2.14**
Number of Students	30	28

**p < 0.01; *p < 0.05; +p < 0.10

educational resources potentially available to the children of residents and nonresidents, beginning with simple access to personal space.

The top panel shows the percentage of resident and nonresident children who have access to their own bedroom and a quiet location for undisturbed study. Housing constraints were a major motivation for moving into ELH in the first place, with 41 percent of nonresidents and 53 percent of residents listing housing problems as the main reason for applying, compared with 38 percent among people moving into affordable units generally throughout New Jersey (Bush-Baskette, Robinson, and Simmons 2011). It is perhaps not surprising, therefore, that children living in the Ethel Lawrence Homes do better when it comes to having access to quiet study space. Whereas 86 percent of the ELH children enjoyed a private bedroom, the figure was only 66 percent for nonresident children; and whereas 91 percent of ELH children said they had access to a quiet place for study, only 69 percent of nonresident children did so. Having a bedroom obviously has a big effect in providing a quiet study space.

Figure 8.8 formally tests the hypothesis that ELH increased access to study space by showing the estimated effect of ELH residence on the probability of having a quiet study space, once again estimated using logistic equations specified in our usual three ways: no controls, controls for individual characteristics and propensity scores, and controls for individual

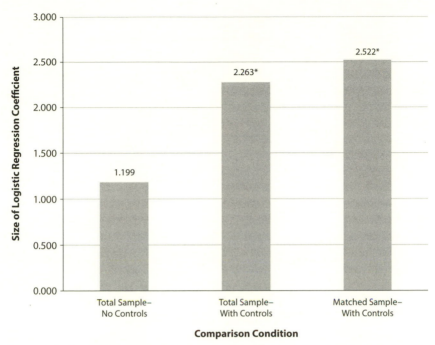

Figure 8.8. Effect of ELH residence on the likelihood that child has a quiet place to study

characteristics with resident and nonresident children matched using propensity scores. Because of the scarcity of degrees of freedom (just thirty resident children and twenty-eight nonresident children), we simplified the equations using a two-stage procedure. First, we estimated the equation using all variables, and then after determining which controls were significant, we retained only those in estimating the final equation, yielding a model that contained controls for the child's age, the child's gender, parent's age, parent a college graduate, parent married or cohabiting, parent employed, and household income (shown in appendix A7).

As seen in figure 8.8, in the absence of controls, the effect of ELH residence is positive, but not significant. Once controls are added, however, the estimated effect *rises* substantially and achieves significance in both the unmatched and matched specifications, increasing the odds of having a quiet study space by a factor of almost 10 in the former case (exp [2.263] = 9.612) and more than twelve times in the latter (exp [2.522] = 12.453). Moreover, when we substituted time spent in ELH for the dichotomous indicator of simple ELH residence, we found a significant positive effect, indicating that the longer a family lived in the project, the greater the likelihood that a child reported having a quiet place to study.

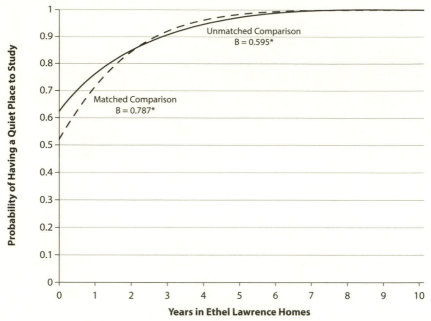

Figure 8.9. Effect of years lived in ELH on likelihood of having a quiet place to study

Figure 8.9 graphs the probability of having a quiet study space by years spent in ELH predicted using the unmatched and matched equations while holding control variables constant at their means. As can be seen, although the duration of time spent in the project is statistically significant, the positive effect of ELH residence is expressed quite quickly after entry. Within three years of entry, the probability of having a quite study space goes from around 52 to 90 percent in the matched comparison and from 63 to 90 percent in the unmatched comparison, with only an asymptotic rise toward 100 percent being predicted for years three to ten. Thus moving into ELH brings about a quick—if not entirely instantaneous—improvement in the household study environment for the children of project residents, compared to what they would have had if their parents had not moved.

Probably the most important scholarly resource for any child is the human capital that parents bring to the task of instruction, and the time and attention they have available to put into mentoring (Lareau 1989, 2003). Coming from similarly disadvantaged backgrounds, neither ELH residents nor nonresidents have large endowments of human capital to help their children succeed in school. Only 12 percent of each group of parents had graduated from college, whereas around 13 percent were high school dropouts and another 26 percent had completed no more than a high school education or its equivalent. Given the lack of a significant difference in educational attainment between ELH residents and nonresidents, parental human capital is not likely to emerge as significant in differentiating the academic performance of resident and nonresident children, and this is indeed what we found.

The second panel of table 8.4 therefore focuses on other parental input into the educational process by asking how often parents checked homework, helped with homework, participated in PTA, interacted with other parents, and took children to the library. The response categories were "never," "rarely," "sometimes," "often," "very often," and "always." We hypothesized that in a more tranquil neighborhood environment where they were beset by fewer negative life events, ELH parents would have more time and energy for educationally supportive actions, and this is generally what we find when we look at the percentage of students who said their parents engaged in pro-educational behaviors at least often.

On four of the five parental actions considered, the children of ELH residents reported parents to be more active than nonresident parents; and in two cases the differences were statistically significant. ELH parents were significantly more likely to check their children's homework, with 62 percent doing so often or more frequently compared with just 44 percent of nonresident parents (p < 0.10). Likewise ELH parents were also far more likely to take their children to the library than nonresident parents (46 percent versus 6 percent, p < 0.01). In two other instances intergroup differences were sizable though not statistically significant. Whereas 40 percent of ELH children said their parents helped with homework often or more frequently, the figure was 29 percent among nonresident children. Likewise, whereas 37 percent of resident children said their parents communicated with other parents, again only 29 percent of nonresident children did so. The only dimensions on which the two groups of children reported the same frequency of parental behavior was with respect to participation in the PTA, with 26 percent of parents participating often, very often, or always.

When we coded the response categories 0–5 in order of increasing frequency and averaged across the five items, we obtained a reliable index of parental academic support, with average values shown for ELH residents and nonresidents at the bottom of the panel ($\alpha = 0.763$, see appendix A6). The differences in frequency of support yield an overall index of parental academic support of 2.14 for ELH children and 1.58 for non-ELH children, a 35 percent differential that is highly significant (p < 0.01). Thus moving into ELH appears to bring about an increase in the frequency of pro-educational behavior among parents, an effect we also tested using the three-equation approach. Figure 8.10 shows the effect of

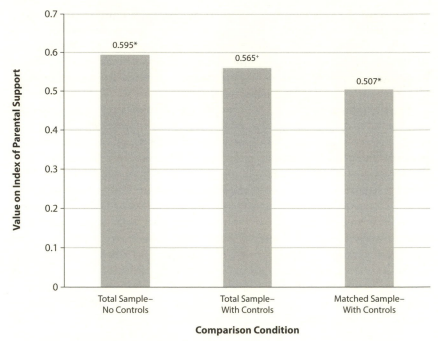

Figure 8.10. Effect of ELH residence on index of parental support

ELH residence on parental support for academics estimated using OLS regressions with no controls, individual and propensity controls on all respondents, and individual controls for matched resident and nonresident children (equations in appendix A7).

In all three cases the estimated effect lies between 0.5 and 0.6 and is statistically significant, meaning that ELH residence increased the frequency of pro-educational parenting between 55 percent and 66 percent of a standard deviation. When we re-estimated the equations after replacing the ELH dummy variable with time spent in ELH, we also found a significant positive coefficient of 0.08 in both the matched and unmatched models. As shown in figure 8.11, this value implies that for the average child, the frequency of receiving academic support from parents rose from an index value around 1.6 initially to 2.5 after ten years of residence, slightly less than one standard deviation.

In qualitative interviews with parents, many cited the high-quality school system as a contributing factor in their ability to assist their children with schoolwork. Parents who used the school district's online software found it a particularly valuable resource. In the words of one mother, "If I want to find out where or what class she is in, I can go right

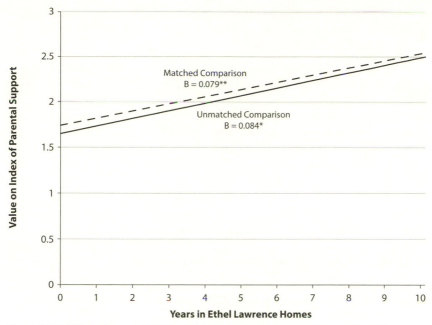

Figure 8.11. Effect of years of ELH residence on parental support for academics

on the computer and it will tell me exactly where she's at within the day, and also any comments the teachers have. A lot of times where they can't talk to somebody's student they'll leave notes on the computer, and if you want to call them after school hours, they're accessible. It is very, very convenient and very good."

Another mother described the experience she had with her son, who initially was having trouble making the adjustment to the new school system. She attributed his difficulties, in part, to the new school having higher academic standards than his previous school. Working with school officials and the resources they offered, however, she felt her son was able to make strides forward:

> Well, you know in New York City, I think, education is poor over there. So when he came he worked hard, because in that school, they want you to work a lot. But he was slow. He wasn't at the same level, that's what the teacher told me. Yeah, so he cries. He loves school here, but in New York he doesn't like it. But when we came here, yes, he loves to go to school. But the problem is that he can't do right things in school. He's confused. It's different, New York and here. I think right here is a better, much better education. So the teacher called me, and he work hard. They send me work,

extra work. I have to work with him every day. There is a homework club right here, so they help me too. Everybody, we work together. And then finally, at the end, he did good.

Apart from residential and parental resources, educational outcomes obviously depend critically on the effort that children expend at home on school-related activities such as reading and studying, especially in comparison to other activities such as work or recreation. The child questionnaire asked students to estimate "during a typical seven-day week during the school year" the number of hours they spent in a series of different activities, including watching TV, playing video games, listening to music, socializing, using the internet, doing household chores, looking after siblings, working for pay, studying, and reading. The average number of hours devoted to each activity by children living in resident and nonresident households is shown in table 8.5.

These data reveal no significant difference between the two groups in hours devoted to recreational activities, with time devoted to all five

Table 8.5. Estimated time that ELH resident and nonresident children spent pursuing selected activities in the household

Activity	Nonresident Children	Resident Children
Recreation		
Watching TV	11.6	13.6
Playing video games	6.7	5.2
Listening to Music	15.6	16.7
Socializing	13.3	12.7
Using the internet	13.6	12.7
Total	60.5	60.6
Work		
Doing chores	9.1	8.4
Looking after younger sibling	6.7	2.0 +
Working	4.6	4.6
Total	20.5	14.9
Academic		
Studying	5.3	10.7 **
Reading	3.1	5.2
Total	8.4	15.9 **
Number of Students	30	28

**$p < 0.01$; *$p < 0.05$; +$p < 0.10$

recreational pastimes totaling around sixty-one hours for both resident and nonresident children. We also found few differences in time devoted to work activities, although nonresident children did report spending 6.7 hours, on average, watching younger siblings, compared with just 2 hours among project residents ($p < 0.10$), likely reflecting the access parents have to on-site day care services at Ethel Lawrence Homes. As noted in earlier chapters, the project also offers an after-school "homework club" for resident children, and reflecting the existence of this structured venue for the completion of schoolwork, ELH children reported spending twice as much time studying as non-ELH children, an average of 10.7 hours compared with just 5.3 hours for children from nonresident households ($p < 0.01$). ELH children were also somewhat more likely to report time reading (5.2 hours versus 3.1 hours), and the combination of time devoted to the two activities yielded a significant difference in total hours devoted to academic pursuits (15.9 versus 8.4 hours, $p < 0.01$).

In terms of the academic effort expended outside of school, therefore, moving into ELH appears to have provided the children of residents with two clear advantages—more time devoted to studying and less time devoted to taking care of younger siblings. When we did systematic tests of differences between resident and nonresident children with respect to looking after siblings, however, we found no significant differences between the two groups and dropped the variable form further consideration. In contrast, when we examined differences between ELH and nonresident children with respect to hours studied, we not only found significant differences, but the estimated advantage accruing to ELH children actually increased when controls were introduced. As shown in figure 8.12, in a simple OLS regression with no controls, resident children were estimated to study 4.5 more hours per week than nonresident children, but when controls were added, the premium associated with ELH residence rises to around 6.4 hours per week in both the unmatched and matched regressions. Finally, as shown in figure 8.13, when time spent in ELH is used to predict study time instead of the dichotomous indicator of project residence, we find that time spent studying rises by around 0.8 to 0.9 hours per year of residence, going from around 5 hours per week initially to around 14 hours per week after ten years of residence. This effect is after controlling for age, so it is not simply a matter of children getting older and more mature and studying more.

During in-depth interviews, parents often described the on-site homework club as a particularly useful resource, not only in getting homework done, but in providing after-school day care and tutoring assistance as well as offering information and contact with school administrators and teachers. In the words of one grateful parent:

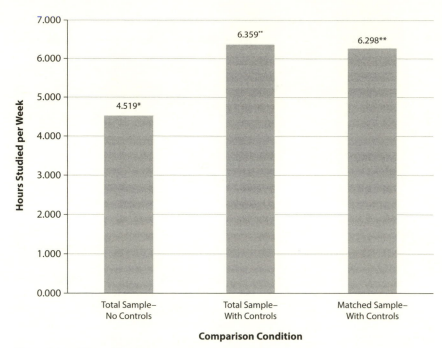

Figure 8.12. Effect of ELH residence on hours studied per week

You come in with any homework you have and, they're available to go back and research it for you, and to help you out with your homework; and it's like I said, they're hands on, right there helping you, and giving you more information as far as the parent coming up and working with them. A lot of parents aren't up to speed, they need it, with the new math and the new history. You know, that's available and all. But having that there, like I said, the information, you can come in, you can talk, you can chat. That makes people a lot more comfortable. Plus it helps to know what's going on with the schools, because, like I said, making that changeover, a lot of people are shy because they don't know the math or the homework the kids are bringing home. But they make you feel comfortable, saying like, "Come on, we're going to show you! This is how this is done. Let's go with this." So it's more the parent and your kids working together, as a team, with this development.

In short, moving into the Ethel Lawrence Homes appears to have provided students with an abundance of new resources to support academic achievement. Compared to what they would have experienced in the absence of the move, ELH children appear more likely to have

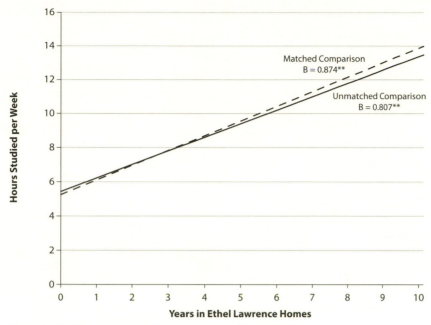

Figure 8.13. Effect of years in ELH on hours studied per week

access to a quiet place to study, to receive greater parental support for academics, and to study more hours per week. In addition, these benefits appear to cumulate over time. With each year of ELH residence, the likelihood of having a quiet study space rises (at least for the first three years), the frequency of parental support increases, and hours studied per week rise.

Educational Resources at School

As part of the survey, students were also asked which school they attended, and using this information, we were able to access New Jersey's 2009 School Report Card File (New Jersey Department of Education 2011) and employ the database to compute average characteristics of the schools attended by project residents and nonresidents, which are summarized in table 8.6. On most indicators of school quality, ELH resident children show dramatically better educational circumstances compared with nonresident children. Although the average class size of 23.3 students for project residents is slightly larger than the average size of 17.4 for nonresidents, all of the other measures favor ELH children.

Table 8.6. School quality indicators and educational outcomes reported for children in ELH resident and nonresident households

Educational Indicator	Nonresident Children	Resident Children
Middle School or High School		
Average Class Size	17.4	23.3 **
Student Mobility Rate	14.4	5.4 **
Percent of Students Proficient on State Language Exam	69.7	89.0 **
Percent of Students Proficient on State Math Exam	56.9	81.2 **
High School Only		
Average High School SAT Score	1292	1515 **
Percent Scoring 3+ on at Least AP Exam	29.8	88.8 **
Attendance Rate	89.4	94.4 **
Dropout Rate	4.3	0.6 **
Graduation rate	79.3	96.2*
School Quality Index		
Middle School Quality	−0.159	0.207 **
High School Quality	−0.369	0.308 **
Number of Middle School Students	6	12
Number of High School Students	22	22

Source: NJ Department of Education 2011
**p < 0.01; *p < 0.05; +p < 0.10

Whereas the student mobility rate was 14.4 for nonresidents, for example, it was just 5.4 for residents, indicating a more stable learning environment with fewer students coming and going. Likewise, although only 70 percent of students in schools attended by nonresident children passed the state language arts test with proficiency, and just 57 percent passed the state math test, among project residents the figures were 89 percent and 82 percent respectively. The average SAT score of 1515 in schools attended by resident children was 17 percent greater than the value of 1292 in schools attended by nonresident children, and whereas 89 percent of students in the schools of resident children scored three or higher on at least one Advanced Placement exam, the share was just 30 percent in the schools attended by nonresident children. The schools of resident children also had a higher attendance rate (94 percent versus 89 percent), a lower dropout rate (0.6 percent versus 4.3 percent), and a higher graduation rate (96 percent versus 79 percent) than the schools of nonresident children.

In short, by moving into the Ethel Lawrence Homes, resident children very clearly acquired the opportunity to attend markedly better schools. To demonstrate this outcome more succinctly, we factor analyzed the various indicators in table 8.6 and used the factor loadings to weight the z-score for each indicator to create an additive scale of school quality (see appendix A6). Averages are shown separately for middle school students ($\alpha = 0.902$) and high school students ($\alpha = 0.976$) at the bottom of the table. Both measures reveal a huge gap in school quality between resident and nonresident children. On the factor scale of middle school quality, children in ELH households display a value of 0.207, compared with a value of –0.159 for those in non-ELH households. Likewise, among high school students the average school quality is –0.369 for nonresident children but 0.308 for resident children. Both contrasts are highly significant (p < 0.010), despite the rather limited degrees of freedom.

This finding holds up well in formal tests. As figure 8.14 shows, although the effect of project residence on school quality is reduced when controls are added in the matched and unmatched comparisons, project residence nonetheless remains strong, positive, and highly significant. In the uncontrolled model, project residence is associated with nearly a

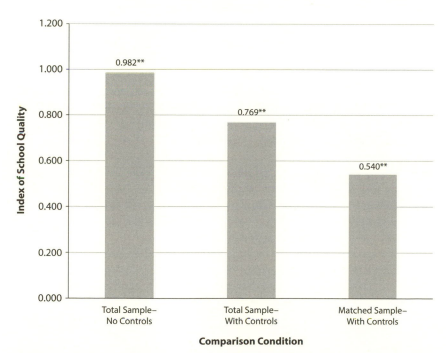

Figure 8.14. Quality of schools attended by children of residents and nonresidents of ELH

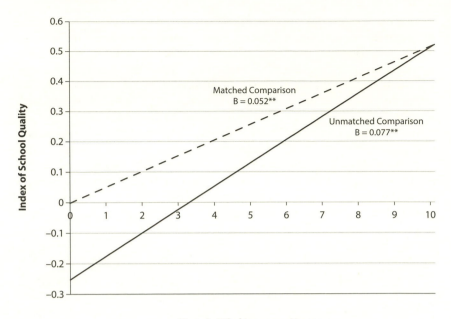

Years in Ethel Lawrence Homes

Figure 8.15. Effect of years in ELH on school quality

one-unit increase in school quality whereas in the unmatched comparison with controls it falls to 0.78 and in the matched comparison with controls it is further reduced to 0.55. Nonetheless, even the latter is significant at the 1 percent level and corresponds to an improvement in school quality of around 60 percent of a standard deviation, a rather large effect.

When the regressions are estimated using time spent in ELH rather than simple residence, the matched model with controls suggests that school quality grows by 0.05 units per year, going from an index value of 0 initially to 0.5 after ten years, as shown in figure 8.15. The mechanism by which school quality improves with time is not clear from the data, however. It may be that parents learn more about schools and school quality the longer they live in the Mount Laurel School district and learn to work the school system better to achieve better educational environments for their children; or perhaps the longer parents live in Mount Laurel, the more likely they are to send their children to the Mount Laurel public schools rather than to a public or parochial school in their former community.

Again some insights into the benefits provided by the Mount Laurel Schools come from the in-depth interviews, in which ELH parents report that the quality of education their children receive there is invariably superior to that available at their previous place of residence. As one mother described it:

I am super happy with my kids' education. They're straight A and B students. They love to read, and [when] I compare them with my family members who still are in Camden, there's no comparison. Like, my daughter knows as much, and she's in 7th grade, she knows what a 12th grade student is probably learning now. Like that's how bad. Like I have a niece who's 19, and she's still at the second grade level; and it's like, whoa. So moving here was an awesome blessing, for my kids because they got the right education; that I was praying that they would get.

One of the strengths that parents most often cited in interviews was the communication practices of teachers in Mount Laurel. According to one mother, "the teachers, they always call you [to tell you] how he's doing. If he's doing bad, they call you, they let you know. I think it's communication. The teachers before? She wouldn't. There is no communication there; but right here yes, they worry. Here, they take care, they good take care." Parents also described the teachers as being receptive to their efforts at being proactive in support of their children's education. One mother relayed to us her appreciation for the regular two-way communication she experienced with various members of the school community:

And the office—the secretary, the principal and the nurse, and all of—you know, they all know, even down to the extended day care people who, actually, one of them was my Brownie troop leader, but yeah—they're all—they know that I want them to come to me, good bad or indifferent. And they do. And they have in the past, like it's always been someone did something or said something that they felt, you know, we need to kind of just touch base. They've not hesitated.

Another respondent, a father who had moved in from the historically black suburb of Willingboro, described his progressive connection with the school and its teachers and administrators in this way:

Well, when we first came in, I looked around and I was really lost because I didn't know how the school system was operating, and how things was going. But the people here in Mount Laurel are so friendly. They were reaching out, Hillside School, Hartford, Harrington, now Lenape—they all reached out when I went to the meetings. I had PTA meetings, I tried to keep involved with everything I possibly could. For the blessing that I had here as far as the house. But the education, like they [are] just hands-on with the kids. It was like, any little thing they had a discrepancy with, a problem with as far as reading, math, academics, they were right there. To say, okay let's make some adjustments here to make you feel more comfortable. And that one-on-one was great. The teachers would call my house and say can we talk?

In addition to culling objective characteristics about schools from publicly available data and interviewing parents, we also asked the children themselves to offer their subjective assessments of conditions in the school they attended. Specifically, adapting items developed by Massey et al. (2003) for the National Longitudinal Survey of Freshmen, we asked students to estimate the frequency with which they witnessed various signs of social disorder and violence "on school property during school hours" during the past three months. The various instances of disorder and violence are listed down the side of table 8.7, which also shows the percentage of ELH resident and nonresident children who reported witnessing the events often or very often. As in other tables, the bottom line includes a summary index that was computed by assigning frequency ratings to response categories for each of the fifteen items (0 = never, 1 = sometimes, 3 = often, and 4 very often) and averaging across items to yield a composite index value ($\alpha = 0.893$).

In thirteen of the fifteen contrasts shown in the table, ELH students experienced a lower exposure to disorder or violence than non-ELH

Table 8.7. Percent of ELH resident and nonresident children who witnessed selected instances of disorder and violence often or very often at school

Instance of Disorder and Violence	Nonresident Children	Resident Children
Students fighting	13.9	6.1
Students kissing or making out	41.6	51.6
Students being late for class	58.3	53.2
Students smoking	36.1	9.1 *
Students cutting class	50.0	15.2 *
Students cutting school	20.0	3.0 *
Students shouting at or threatening teachers or principals	16.7	3.0
Students pushing or hitting teachers or principals	2.8	0.0
Vandalism of school or personal property	17.1	3.1
Theft of school or personal property	2.8	3.0
Students consuming alcohol	16.7	3.0
Students taking illegal drugs	8.6	3.0
Students carrying knives	2.9	0.0
Students carrying guns	0.0	0.0
Robbery of students by other students	11.1	0.0
Index of Exposure to Disorder and Violence at School	2.17	1.69 **
Severity Weighted Disorder-Violence Index	45.5	34.1 *
Number of Students	30	28

**p < 0.01; *p < 0.05; +p < 0.10

students. The only two exceptions were witnessing "students kissing or making out," which 52 percent ELH students reported witnessing often or very often, compared with just 42 percent of nonresident students, and "students carrying guns," which no student in either group reported witnessing with any frequency (though 6 percent of children of nonresidents did admit to seeing students carrying guns rarely compared to no children of project residents). The most important differences for witnessing often or very often were with respect to students smoking (36 percent for nonresident students versus 9 percent for residents), students cutting class (50 percent versus 15 percent), and students cutting school (17 percent versus 3 percent), all of which were significant at the 5 percent level. Although the contrasts were not significant, rather large differences were also observed with respect to students fighting (14 percent for nonresidents versus 6 percent for residents), students threatening teachers (17 percent versus 3 percent), vandalism (17 percent versus 3 percent), consumption of alcohol (17 percent versus 3 percent), and robbery (11 percent versus 3 percent).

Considering average scores on the disorder and violence scale at the bottom of the table, we see that ELH students clearly are exposed to significantly less social disorder and violence than nonresidents. On average, residents scored 1.69 on the violence and disorder scale, whereas nonresidents scored 2.17 ($p < 0.01$). As with neighborhood disorder and violence, however, this simple summed index weights all infractions equally, whereas once again, some transgressions are much more serious (students pushing or hitting teachers, students consuming alcohol or drugs, students carrying knives or guns) than others (students making out, students being late for class, students cutting class). As described in appendix A6, we again used the Sellin-Wolfgang Crime Severity Index to choose scale values that most closely approximated the transgressions listed on our survey and multiplied the scale by the associated frequency before summing up to derive a severity-weighted crime and disorder scale ($\alpha = 0.864$).

This exercise also produced a scale of exposure to disorder and violence that differed significantly ($p < 0.05$) between nonresident children (45.5) and resident children (34.1). Figure 8.16 summarizes the results obtained when we include the dichotomous indicator of ELH residence in uncontrolled as well as unmatched and matched regressions with controls. All effects are in the expected direction, with ELH working to reduce children's exposure to disorder and violence at school, and in two of the three comparisons, the effect of ELH residence is significant. The most rigorous comparison is probably that done in the matched regression with controls, which yields an estimated effect of −12.5, which is significant at the 5 percent level and corresponds to a reduction of around 60 percent of a standard deviation.

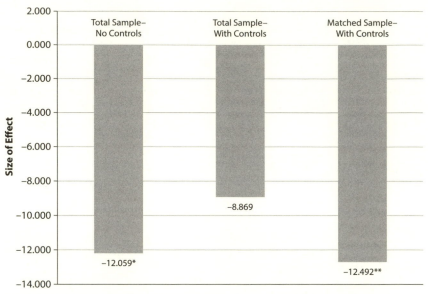

Figure 8.16. Effect of ELH on exposure to disorder and violence at school

Although the effect of ELH residence is also negative when time in the project is substituted for mere presence in ELH, as figure 8.17 shows, the effect is relatively small and insignificant statistically, implying that reduced violence is an immediate benefit that children attain upon entering the Mount Laurel school district, and not something that changes much over time after that. In qualitative interviews, some parents reported that the safer environment has led their children to become more eager, willing, and excited about going to school. In the course of interviewing one father, he told us, "I don't have to drag them out of their bed to go to school; you know what I'm saying? It's like, they're enjoying this; it's like a rush to them. It's a good school. And, that means a great deal to me. Seeing my sons, my kids just like that, eager to go back to school for some new acknowledgment, or whatever is going on, they like to be a part of it."

Educational Achievement

Because of practical and financial constraints, we are limited in our ability to assess educational achievement. Owing to this, we could not apply direct assessments of cognitive skills, and owing to confidentiality considerations, we could not gain access to student educational records. We

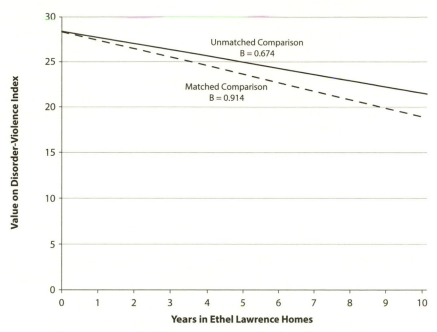

Figure 8.17. Effect of years in ELH on exposure to disorder and violence within schools

were thus left with the option of asking students to report their own grades, admittedly not an optimal strategy. We nonetheless asked each respondent to recall "the last report card that you received" and asked "how many of each grade did you get?" Students were then prompted with questions about the number of A's? number of B's? number of C's? number of D's? and number of F's? In other words, the question was quite specific in referring to a particular report card and an actual distribution of grades rather than simply asking students to report their GPA. Instead, we computed GPA from the specific distribution of grades students reported to us.

Grades do not measure actual learning, of course, or assess cognitive skills alone. They only roughly indicate the classroom achievement produced by a combination of effort, ability, difficulty, and grading conventions within specific school settings. Nonetheless, GPA is a powerful predictor of college achievement, generally outperforming cognitive tests such as the SAT in forecasting college grades and graduation rates, especially among minority students (see Massey and Probasco 2009). Given that the children of ELH residents have moved into higher-quality schools that are likely more difficult and more competitive scholastically, in which they will compete with students from far more educated and

socioeconomically advantaged family backgrounds, one might hypothesize ELH children to pay a penalty in terms of grades earned, receiving
lower marks than they would have had they remained in their former
schools.

We did not find this outcome to be the case, however. When we computed GPAs from the reported distribution of grades, we found a value of
2.86 for resident children and 2.63 for nonresident children. Thus children from the Ethel Lawrence Homes earned slightly *higher* grades, on
average, than comparable students not yet admitted to the project, though
the difference was not itself statistically significant. When we estimated
OLS regression equations that predicted GPA from individual, home, and
school characteristics, however, the effect of ELH residence went from
positive to negative in both the matched and unmatched analyses, suggesting perhaps that resident children did suffer a slight drop in grades,
other things being equal. Given these results, we entertained the possibility that attending more competitive schools did have a negative effect
on grades, but that these negative effects were offset by other positive
attributes of the children's new home and school environments. Put in a
different way, whereas the direct effect of ELH residence on grades may
indeed have been negative, the indirect effects through other variables
were positive.

Indeed, in equations predicting GPA from individual, home, and
school characteristics we found that three factors consistently predicted
grade achievement across model specifications (see appendix A7). Having a quiet place to study significantly increased grades, and exposure
to school disorder and violence decreased grades, in all model specifications, whether matched or unmatched and whether using ELH residence
or time in ELH to capture the effect of moving into the project. In addition, school quality predicted better grades in the unmatched regressions whether using the dichotomous indicator of project residence or the
cumulative time spent in the project.

Both parents and children described the positive effect that school
quality and resources had on educational performance. Here a mother
described how her child ended up in a special pre–first grade program:

> His kindergarten teacher had suggested it, and we went to the evaluation
> and, you know, she gave me a lot of information about it. I did some re-
> search myself. I asked folks, people, on a child study team and so forth and
> so on; and we just went with it. And we had the best—I shouldn't say the
> best, he had what I think was the best pre-first teacher ever—like, ever. It
> gave him time to mature, if that makes sense, at age five. It gave him time
> to kind-of find his pace with work, and um, and to just really get better, to
> get his feet a little more stable academically and to then build on that as he

has gone through first, second, third, and now fourth grade. [Now] he's a straight A–B student.

Thus despite the direct negative effect of entering a more competitive school, moving into ELH appears to improve grade performance indirectly, allowing students to access higher-quality schools with less violence and disorder, and enabling more of them to have their own room and a quiet place to study, outcomes that, in turn, increased grades. Our tentative conclusion, therefore, is that moving to ELH had no overall effect on the grades earned by the children of project residents, and that in the end the GPAs of children did not drop appreciably as a result of attending more academically competitive schools. They received better educations but nonetheless got the same grades.

New Life Trajectories

The evidence marshaled in this chapter indicates that moving into the Ethel Lawrence Homes not only enabled project residents to improve their neighborhood circumstances, but to reorient their lives toward greater mental health and more economic independence than would otherwise have been possible. At the same time, it allowed them to provide better conditions to ensure their children's educational success. Figure 8.18 summarizes findings for adults in the form of a path model. According to the diagram, ELH residence lowers residents' exposure to neighborhood disorder and violence, which in turn lowers the frequency of negative life events they experience, and both of these intervening

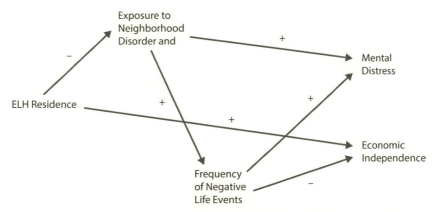

Figure 8.18. How moving to Ethel Lawrence Homes affected mental distress and economic independence among adults

effects serve to lower the degree of mental distress suffered by residents. Moving into ELH also increases the degree of economic independence achieved by residents, both directly and indirectly, by lowering their exposure to neighborhood disorder and violence, leading to fewer negative life events to undermine economic achievement.

Figure 8.19 offers a similar path diagram to summarize our findings for children. Moving into ELH created conditions that allowed parents to engage in more academically supportive behaviors with their children while enabling the children themselves to spend more time studying. In addition, the move also increased the likelihood that children had a quiet place to study at home while placing them in higher-quality schools with lower levels of social disorder and violence. Although the latter outcomes are benefits in and of themselves, they also act as intervening effects to raise grades indirectly. Moving into ELH allowed the children of residents to attend better, less violent schools and to find quiet places to study, which in turn led to improved grades. Although attending more competitive schools did negatively affect resident children's GPA's, this direct effect was counterbalanced by the foregoing indirect effects so that, overall, their grades did not suffer. The children received better educations while earning the same grades as before, putting them in a better position to attend college given the superior reputation of Mount Laurel's schools compared with those in Camden and other low-income communities around the state.

In an interview about the effect that moving to Ethel Lawrence has had on his family, one father reflected on the relationship between the

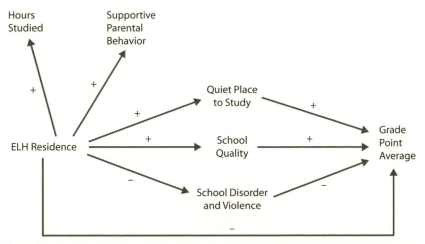

Figure 8.19. Path model showing effect of ELH residence on academic outcomes among children estimated from matched sample

stability of their housing and their growth as a family over the ten years they had lived in the complex, telling us that "they planted all the trees around here. It was so beautiful, different types of trees and all, and I remember looking out into the courtyard, how small it was because they were just planting them, and over the time, years, in which they've grown. Not only the trees, but I look at my kids and how much they've grown, and we're like, you know, putting down new roots. It's a beautiful thing."

CHAPTER 9

Affordable Housing

SUBURBAN SOLUTIONS TO URBAN PROBLEMS

The road to affordable housing in Mount Laurel, New Jersey, was long, winding, and fraught with obstacles that had to be overcome one by one in a tedious, seemingly endless process of litigation, negotiation, planning, and implementation. From the time the Springville Community Action Committee first formed in 1969 until Fair Share Housing Development finally opened up the second phase of units to residents in 2004, the Ethel Lawrence Homes were thirty-five years in the making. Over the decades, many fears were expressed and charges levied about the dire consequences of bringing affordable housing to Mount Laurel. Nonetheless the project was built and eventually opened. In this book we have told the story of how the Ethel Lawrence Homes came to be. We also conducted a systematic analysis of what happened in the wake of its opening. In doing so, we considered the project's consequences for the community, its effects on surrounding neighborhoods and their residents, and, of course, its influence on the lives of the tenants themselves. Here we review the principal findings of the Monitoring Mount Laurel Study and consider their implications, both for social science and public policy.

Fears That Never Materialized

Our review of work on the political economy of place highlighted a variety of reasons why debates about land use tend to be so emotional and overwrought, especially among those who have a stake in the outcome. In general, parties to land-use debates value real estate for either the utility it provides as a place to live or as a piece of property to be exchanged for material gain. Although use and exchange values sometimes coincide, in practice they often come into conflict with each other, and usually those protecting use values are different people from those promoting exchange values.

Neither use nor exchange values are inherently more right in any absolute sense, and the debate between them cannot be settled morally.

Rather, conflicts between use and exchange values must be adjudicated in the political realm. In the case of Mount Laurel, ELH tenants and neighbors both had strong interests in the use value of the residential area; but neighbors also had a strong interest in the exchange value of the neighborhood as homeowners and eventual home sellers, whereas ELH residents did not. Other Mount Laurel residents who were not neighbors, meanwhile, had little interest in the use value of the area and were solely focused on the project's potential effects on the exchange value of properties in the township. In the end, of course, the conflict of interests was settled, not entirely amicably, by the New Jersey State Supreme Court.

For most households in the United States, home equity is the largest single source of family wealth. Thus threats to home value become de facto threats to a family's economic status. It is a well-established principal of cognitive psychology that human beings experience the prospect of financial loss as extremely aversive and painful, a phenomenon known as "loss aversion" (Tversky and Kahneman 1991). As a result, people often behave quite "irrationally" in defending their economic interests (Kahneman, Knetsch, and Thaler 1991; Kahneman 2011). In addition, people tend to become emotionally attached to places in which they grow up, live, and raise their children, and when we consider that a place to live is not readily substitutable or renounced on the part of consumers, we begin to understand why conflicts over land use can be so divisive; and when one overlays issues of race and class onto land use, the mix can be downright combustible.

We certainly saw this combustibility in Mount Laurel. The proposal to build an affordable family housing project in the township met with strong, emotional, and vociferous opposition from very beginning. Over the course of a long series of court proceedings, newspaper editorials, letters to the editor, planning-board hearings, council meetings, and debates in other public forums, displays of vitriolic language, racist imagery, and venomous accusations were in common currency. Although some township residents rose to defend the project and its tenants, the public airwaves were dominated by the voices of opposition. Our survey of residents in neighboring subdivisions revealed, however, that although the public expression of negative emotion indeed reflected underlying racial animus, in the end the controversy was likely a "tempest in a suburban teapot" stirred by a small number of highly motivated, possibly racially antagonistic individuals who mobilized to oppose the project in the strongest possible terms. More than a decade after the first ELH residents moved in, however, most neighbors were either indifferent or positive toward the development.

Although future proposals for affordable housing in other communities will likely also encounter vitriolic opposition, we conclude that public officials might be well advised to discount the vehemence of the antidevelopment reaction as the actions of a highly motivated few against the indifference or favorable leanings of the many. Indeed, a decade after the opening of the Ethel Lawrence Homes, a fifth of the residents in neighboring subdivisions were unaware that an affordable housing project existed in the township; nearly a third did not know that a project existed in the neighborhood; almost three-quarters could not name the development; and nearly 90 percent had never interacted personally with a resident of the Homes. In sum, when the project finally opened it was not with a bang but a whimper.

Our research suggests that a whimper rather than a bang was indeed the appropriate reaction. In the controversy preceding the final approval of plans for ELH, township residents repeatedly expressed their fears of the dire consequences sure to follow in the wake of the project's opening—that crime would increase, that tax burdens would rise, and that property values would decline. Despite these fears, when we carefully assessed trends in crime, taxes, and home prices in the township and surrounding neighborhoods, we found no evidence whatsoever that the project's opening had any direct effect on crime rates, tax burdens, or property values. Moreover, the indirect effect on school expenditures was mitigated by the fact that the number of students was small (only thirty in a district of nearly three thousand students) and was scattered across separate primary, middle, and secondary schools. Given that the per-pupil cost was likely lower in Mount Laurel than in the school districts they came from, one could argue that the new arrangement represented a more efficient use of taxpayer's money to achieve better educational outcomes. In the end, the grievous externalities that so many predicted simply failed to materialize.

Moving to Opportunity

Our results therefore indicate that an affordable housing project for low- and moderate-income minority residents can indeed be developed in an affluent white suburb without imposing significant costs on the surrounding community or its residents. On the benefits side of the equation, we found that moving into the Ethel Lawrence Homes brought about a very clear improvement in the lives of project residents and their children. The effects we uncovered for adults are summarized graphically in figure 9.1, which replicates the path diagram shown in figure 8.18 after pairing each pathway with a parameter capturing the standardized effect size estimated from samples of ELH residents and nonresidents matched using propensity scores.

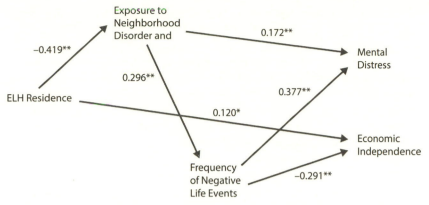

Figure 9.1. Path model showing effect of ELH residence on mental distress and economic independence among adults estimated from matched samples

As the path model clearly indicates, moving into ELH brought about a marked reduction in residents' exposure to social disorder and violence, which in turn produced a sharp reduction in the frequency of negative life events they experienced. As standardized effects, the path coefficients indicate the change in the dependent variable in terms of standard units (z-scores) produced by one standard deviation of change in the independent variable. Thus, increasing the likelihood of ELH residence by one standard deviation reduces a person's exposure to neighborhood disorder and violence by 0.419 standard deviations, which in turn reduces the person's incidence of negative life events by 0.296 standard units. Moving ahead in the causal chain, reducing neighborhood disorder and violence by one standard deviation, in turn, reduces the index of mental distress by 0.172 standard units, while a one standard deviation drop in the frequency of negative life events lowers the index of mental distress by 0.377 units, all substantial effects by the usual standards of social science.

The resulting set of direct and indirect effects of ELH residence on mental distress are summarized in the top two panels of table 9.1. Although the estimated direct effect of ELH residence on psychological distress is zero, the indirect effect through the reduction in exposure to disorder and violence and the lower frequency of negative life events is −0.119. The indirect effect is estimated by computing the product of the path coefficients along all routes connecting ELH residence to mental distress through intervening variables. Given the lack of a significant direct effect, this figure also represents the total causal effect of ELH residence on mental distress. As shown in the second column, very similar results are obtained when the set of equations is estimated using the unmatched samples, with indirect and total effects equaling a value of −0.126.

Table 9.1. Estimated direct and indirect causal effects of ELH residence on adult mental health, adult economic independence, and children's educational outcomes.

Effect of Ethel Lawrence Residence on:	Matched Samples	Unmatched Samples
Adults' Mental Distress*		
Direct	0.000	0.000
Indirect	–0.119	–0.126
Total	–0.119	–0.126
Adults' Economic Independence*		
Direct	0.120	0.147
Indirect	0.049	0.007
Total	0.169	0.154
Hours Studied**		
Direct	0.433	0.455
Indirect	0.000	0.000
Total	0.433	0.455
Supportive Parental Behavior**		
Direct	0.343	0.300
Indirect	0.000	0.000
Total	0.343	0.300
Children Having Quiet Place to Study**		
Direct	0.432	0.370
Indirect	0.000	0.000
Total	0.432	0.370
School Quality**		
Direct	0.444	0.474
Indirect	0.000	0.000
Total	0.444	0.474
School Disorder and Violence**		
Direct	–0.344	–0.208
Indirect	0.000	0.000
Total	–0.344	–0.208
Children's GPA**		
Direct	–0.327	–0.249
Indirect	0.389	0.414
Total	0.062	0.165

* Estimates hold constant the effect of subject's age, gender, race, education, marital status, percent female in the household, and propensity score (in the unmatched samples)

** Estimates control for child's age and gender as well as parent's age, gender, marital status, employment status, college education, and propensity (in the unmatched samples)

With respect to economic self-sufficiency, the path diagram shows that the direct effect of ELH residence on the index of economic independence, 0.120, is supplemented by an indirect effect through exposure to neighborhood disorder and violence and negative life events of .036 (obtained as the product of path coefficients: –0.419, .296, –0.291), thereby yielding a total effect of 0.156 in the matched sample, an estimate that is little different from the total effect of 0.154 estimated from unmatched sample, both strong and significant effects (p < 0.01). Thus a systematic comparison between ELH residents and a set of similarly self-selected nonresidents yields estimated causal effects that are rather strong by social science standards, whether or not one employs propensity score matching.

Figure 9.2 summarizes the causal effect of ELH residence on selected educational outcomes observed among adolescent children living in the Ethel Lawrence Homes by attaching parameter estimates derived from the matched sample analysis to each of the pathways shown in figure 8.19. The associated direct and indirect effects are summarized in the lower panels of table 9.1. Although ELH residence significantly increased the number of hours children spent studying and raised the degree of academically supportive behavior by parents, these two factors did not have any influence on grades once other factors were controlled. Thus the direct effect of ELH residence on hours studied is 0.433 and the direct effect of ELH residence on supportive parental behavior is 0.343. In

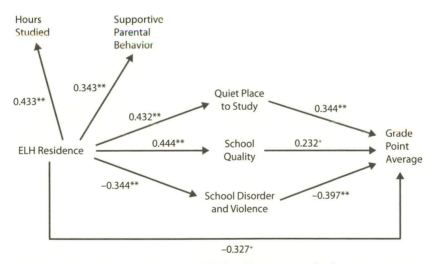

Figure 9.2. Path model showing effect of ELH residence on academic outcomes among children estimated from matched sample

other words, a one standard deviation increase in the likelihood of living in the Ethel Lawrence Homes would increase children's study time by 0.43 standard deviations and parents' index of supportive behavior by 0.34 standard deviations. As shown in table 9.1, the effect sizes are much the same at 0.455 and 0.300 when coefficients are estimated from the unmatched equations.

As shown in figure 9.2, ELH residence also has direct effects on the likelihood of having a quiet place to study, school quality, and school disorder and violence, with respective effects of 0.432, 0.444, and −0.344 when estimates are derived from the matched samples of residents and nonresidents. However, these variables also have their own effects on GPA of 0.344, 0.232, and −0.397, yielding indirect effects of ELH on GPA of 0.149, 0.103, and 0.137, for a total indirect effect of 0.389, which effectively counterbalances the direct effect of −0.327 to yield the small positive overall effect of 0.062. Results are little different when estimated using unmatched samples of residents and nonresidents.

These calculations confirm our tentative conclusions from the prior chapter, which was that ELH children's grades do not suffer because they attend more difficult and competitive schools after the move. Although the direct effect of ELH residence on GPA is indeed negative, this negative effect is offset by three important indirect effects that are positive. Even though students may be thrust into a more challenging educational environment as a result of moving, they also gain greater access to a quiet place to study (a room of their own or the project-sponsored homework club); they gain access to higher-quality schools with lower rates of disorder and violence; and all these gains lead to improvements in GPA that more than offset the negative effects of competing in a more demanding academic environment.

In order to show the total effect of these compensating direct and indirect effects on how grades changed with time spent in ELH, we used matched and unmatched regression equations to predict indices of school quality, school disorder, and the likelihood of having a quiet place to study given years of project residence, holding other variables constant at their means. We then inserted these predicted values into the regression to predict grades earned given time spent in ELH, again with other variables held constant at their mean values, to generate expected GPA values by years of residence. Figure 9.3 shows the results of this operation.

Although predictions from the unmatched models show a more pronounced rise in GPA with time spent in the project than those from the matched models, both sets of predictions indicate an improvement in grades earned with duration of project residence. According to the matched comparison, GPA rises from 2.85 initially to level off at around 3.08 after around four years, whereas in the unmatched comparison, GPA rises more

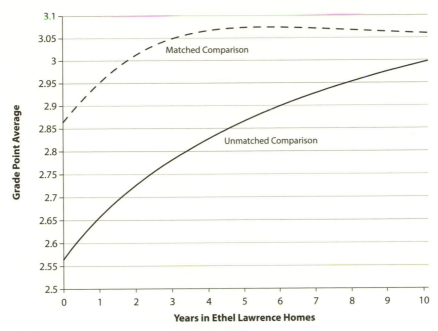

Figure 9.3. Effect of years in EHL on student GPA

steadily and sharply, going from an initial value of 2.57 to around 3.0 after ten years. Either way, the grade advantage improved over time for project residents through indirect channels, and at the very least we can conclude that moving into the Ethel Lawrence Homes had no detrimental effect on grades earned by students even though they received a much higher-quality education in more competitive and demanding schools.

Implications for Social Science and Social Policy

These findings have important substantive and theoretical implications for social science as well as practical implications for social policy. In terms of social science, a controversial discussion among scholars has focused on the existence and nature of "neighborhood effects." Social scientists continue to debate whether and how exposure to positive or negative circumstances within a residential area influence a person's life chances, above and beyond the influence of that person's individual and family circumstances. Although many studies have documented clear associations between neighborhood conditions and individual well-being along a variety of dimensions even after applying controls, cross sectional and even longitudinal regression models cannot really eliminate the alternative explanation of endogeneity—the hypothesis that unmeasured variables simultaneously cause poor people to move into poor neighborhoods and to express behaviors that disadvantage them.

Although recent quasi-experimental studies have sought to eliminate this rival hypothesis by comparing outcomes for treatment and control groups, earlier efforts have not been entirely successful. The two most important studies done to date were both based on housing-mobility programs, interventions that sought to move poor people into better neighborhoods and observe the consequences. In the Gautreaux Demonstration Project, public-housing residents were assigned to move out of projects and into city or suburban neighborhoods. In the Moving to Opportunity Demonstration Project, investigators sought to randomly allocate public-housing residents to high- and low-poverty. In the former study, however, assignment to treatment and control groups was not random at all, whereas in the latter, random assignment was undone by selective processes that unfolded after assignment. Although both studies found that moving into a better neighborhood indeed improved the conditions that people experienced in their daily lives and led to better mental health outcomes, the Gautreaux project generally found significant improvements in adults' economic status and children's educational outcomes whereas the MTO project did not.

Our study likewise arose out of a housing-mobility program—in this case an affordable housing development that was built to enable low- and moderate-income minority families to move into an affluent white suburb Using structurally equivalent treatment and comparison groups we were able to confirm the rather dramatic improvement in neighborhood conditions experienced by program participants as a result of entering Ethel Lawrence Homes. The improvement in neighborhood circumstances was documented statistically in two independent ways: (1) by comparing levels of neighborhood disorder and violence experienced by project residents before and after the move, and (2) by comparing ELH residents with a comparison group of nonresidents who also self-selected into the population of people seeking to enter an affordable housing project in an affluent white suburb, a group that we further equalized using propensity score matching. We thus have some assurance that the treatment and control groups are comparable despite a lack of random assignment. The same comparisons also confirmed that improved neighborhood circumstances did not come at the cost of interpersonal contact with friends or relatives or access to basic services need for daily living, which continued much the same after as before.

Having documented a sharp reduction in exposure to disorder and violence as a result of moving into ELH, we undertook a series of comparisons between matched and unmatched samples of ELH residents and a comparison group of nonresidents. We found that moving into the Ethel Lawrence Homes brought about a significant reduction in the incidence of negative life events, lowered levels of mental distress, increased employment and earnings, while decreasing welfare receipt, and generally producing a higher level of economic independence among participating adults. Among children, residence in ELH increased the quality of schools attended and reduced exposure to within-school violence and disorder, while providing more students with a quiet place to study and offering them more supportive parenting and an environment more conducive to studying. Having a quiet place to study and attending better schools with lower levels of violence and disorder, in turn, produced higher grades. Given the design of the study, we hold that these effects may be taken as causal, thus confirming the hypothesis that neighborhoods matter in explaining life trajectories and that neighborhood effects on socioeconomic outcomes are indeed real.

In terms of social policy, our results suggest that the development of affordable housing projects in affluent suburbs constitutes an efficacious means to lower levels of racial and class segregation while increasing social mobility for disadvantaged inner-city residents. Great strides in economic status were made by adults, and significant improvements in educational outcomes were achieved by children as a result of entering the Ethel Lawrence Homes, and these strides were accomplished without imposing significant social costs on project residents or economic costs on project neighbors or the suburban community in general.

The project also did not impose serious costs on the taxpayers of New Jersey or the Township of Mount Laurel (not counting the money wasted in litigation to block the project's construction). Designed so that all of its units were affordable to an unusually deep range of low- and moderate-income households, ELH is self-sustaining financially, with tenant rents (calibrated on income) and reserve funds covering its annual operating costs including the debt-service payments, which reflect a mix of subsidies made available for the project. ELH was financed and made possible mainly by funds from two principal sources: equity via the federal Low-Income Housing Tax Credit program and low-cost loans from the State of New Jersey through its Housing and Mortgage Finance Agency, the New Jersey Department of Community Affairs, and the Affordable Housing Program of the Federal Home Loan Bank. Our results suggest that these programs indeed constitute good investments of public funds to improve infrastructure (upgrading the housing stock), raise income and reduce dependency in the population (increasing average incomes and employment rates while lowering welfare use), and create new and better human capital (improving educational outcomes for children).

More specifically our results indicate that a 100 percent affordable rental development with a range of affordability between 10 and 80 percent of regional median income can be successfully developed anywhere, provided the necessary additional low-cost or no-cost financing is made available. The principal reason the Ethel Lawrence Homes were able to be built and occupied was the availability of funding through the Low-Income Housing Tax Credit program which, as noted in Chapter 3, constituted almost half of the project's total funding. Established by the Tax Reform Act of 1986, the LIHTC program has funded the construction of more than two million units in 33,000 projects since its creation, and of these units nearly 40 percent have been in suburbs (McClure 2006). Indeed, the fraction of LIHTC units developed in suburbs has been steadily rising over time, with 9,000–11,000 units placed in suburbs during the early 1990s; 17,000–29,000 during the middle 1990s; and 33,000–39,000 in the late 1990s and into the new millennium (McClure 2006).

What happened in Mount Laurel is really only part of a much larger phenomenon that is spreading throughout the country and carries the potential of constituting a major intervention into existing patterns of spatial segregation and offering a pathway out of poverty to many thousands of people. What is really unique about the Ethel Lawrence Homes is the range of affordability it offers to prospective renters. Whereas the vast majority of LIHTC-financed projects across the country are 100 percent affordable at 60 percent of median income, ELH offers units affordable to families earning between 10 and 80 percent of median income. Although LIHTC financing is sufficient to fund most affordable housing projects, whether constructed by a nonprofit or for-profit developer, it is usually not enough by itself to cover the total costs of projects with the range of affordability seen in Mount Laurel, and in plugging the gap, state funding was essential. Our results thus offer a ringing endorsement for the continuation and possible expansion of the LIHTC program as well as a plea for greater support at the state level to increase the range of affordability within suburban areas.

The great success of Ethel Lawrence Homes as a development, both for the people who inhabit it and the community that surrounds it, did not just happen, of course, but stemmed from the hard work, careful planning, and dedicated oversight of many people, especially those connected with Fair Share Housing Development, Inc., and the Fair Share Housing Center. Although it is not possible from the data at our disposal to pinpoint those elements of design and implementation that are primarily responsible for the success of the Ethel Lawrence Homes, several salient elements stand out.

First, the residents of ELH were both self-selected and filtered. All the tenants went out of their way to show up at the offices of the Fair Share

Housing Development to pick up, fill out, and turn in an application form for units that were advertised as being allocated on a first-come-first-served basis. Such people are almost by definition motivated to improve their lives and their neighborhoods and to increase their opportunities for socioeconomic advancement. In addition, all applicants were screened to pick people who are likely to be able to fit in socially, take advantage economically, and be "good tenants" who pay rent, get along with others, and maintain their units.

The Ethel Lawrence Homes thus do not necessarily provide a model of mobility for all poor and disadvantaged families in the United States. Those mired in substance abuse, criminality, family violence, and household instability are not good candidates for affordable housing developments. Their problems are likely to be complex, interconnected, manifold, and thus to require a more comprehensive intervention than simply providing a decent home in a peaceful neighborhood with good schools. Affordable housing developments do constitute an appropriate intervention, however, for the millions of low- and moderate-income families who are currently trapped in distressed urban neighborhoods for lack of anywhere else to go, but who nonetheless plug away to do the best they can at school and work hoping for a chance to advance. For such people, affordable housing developments such as the Ethel Lawrence Homes can dramatically divert life trajectories toward socioeconomic success, educational achievement, and real integration into the American middle class.

Another important factor is the range of affordability built into the project. During the 1950s and 1960s, public-housing projects were reserved for the neediest families, producing developments that virtually by definition concentrated poverty spatially to create an untenable social and economic environment. In contrast, units in ELH were designed to go to households earning a range of incomes, going from 10 percent of the county's median income for one person ($5,630) to 80 percent of the median income for a five-person family ($69,440). Even though all families were in a position to benefit from access to affordable housing, not all were abjectly poor, thus mitigating the pernicious consequences of concentrating economic deprivation that were all too evident in notorious projects such as the Robert Taylor Homes in Chicago (Venkatesh 2000) or the Pruitt Igoe Development in St. Louis (Rainwater 1970).

A third element was the careful attention to the project's design and aesthetics. Its physical layout was deliberately designed to mimic that prevalent in surrounding subdivisions, being situated around cul-de-sacs and public greens, set off from the main road and surrounded by fields and woodlands. The architectural style of its town houses was chosen to mimic styles found in surrounding neighborhoods and other affluent suburbs in the region, consisting of attractive town houses built using materials and painted with colors that blended seamlessly with adjoining areas such as Holiday Village across the street. In addition, the project from the start contained a development budget for landscape architecture and continues to have a line item in its operating budget for landscape maintenance, thereby ensuring the project will remain attractive and largely invisible to the surrounding community as "affordable housing." In this way, developers were able to blunt the reaction of neighbors when the project opened to the point where many do not even realize it is an affordable development. In so doing, they also avoided the visual stigma usually associated with "public housing" in the United States.

Finally, the management at the Fair Share Housing Development operates as much more than a simple rental agency. From the very beginning, social organization within the development was subject to deliberate design and careful planning. Thus the physical layout and building structures were planned with an eye to how they would influence patterns of social interaction and increase the possibilities for informal social control, with clear fields of vision that provide many of what Jane Jacobs (1969) calls "eyes on the street," people observing public spaces from individual units and stoops, along with inviting greens that attract children for play, and adults for leisure activities and socialization. Management intervenes actively to build internal social cohesion among project tenants, providing space and opportunities for them to meet both for formal discussions and for informal activities, sponsoring and helping to organize and sustain a Neighborhood Watch group, and offering a Homework Club for children, which simultaneously provides after-school child care to working parents and a vehicle for human-capital formation among children to enhance educational performance.

Whatever the precise reason for its success, the Ethel Lawrence Homes offers a proof of concept for the further development of affordable family housing, both as a social policy for promoting racial and class integration in metropolitan America and as a practical program for achieving poverty alleviation and economic mobility in society at large. Our results very clearly show that affordable housing for low- and moderate-income minority families can be built within an affluent white suburban environment without imposing significant costs on the host community or its residents, while simultaneously increasing the economic independence of project residents and improving educational achievement among their children, all with little or no cost to taxpayers in general. It is a win-win prospect for all concerned.

Appendices

Appendix A1: Survey of Residents in Neighborhoods
Adjacent to Ethel Lawrence Homes

Introduction. Hello. I am conducting a survey on behalf of investigators at Princeton University who are interested in housing conditions and needs in local neighborhoods. The survey will only take about ten minutes. Is there anyone aged 18 years or older at home who could talk about the neighborhood?

I can speak to about these issues? The survey will only take about ten minutes of your time.

1. What month and year did you move into your current home?

IF MOVED IN BEFORE 2000:

2a. Now, I want you to think about your neighborhood before and after the year 2000. By neighborhood I mean roughly a 2 block radius around your home. I am going to list a number of characteristics your neighborhood and I want you to tell me whether they are much less, somewhat less, about the same, somewhat greater, or much greater after the year 2000:

    a. Property Values. Are they much less, somewhat less, about the same, somewhat greater or much greater after 2000 than before?
    b. Local Traffic?
    c. Racial and Ethnic Diversity?
    d. Noise?
    e. Air Pollution?
    f. Frequency of Trash and Garbage Pick-Up?
    g. Frequency of Recycling Services?
    h. Graffiti?
    i. Test Scores in Public Schools?
    j. People hanging out on corners or loitering?
    k. Crime Rates?
    l. Overall Quality of Life?

3a. Now, I want you to think about conditions within Mount Laurel Township generally before and after the year 2000. I am going to list the same indicators and I want you to tell me whether they are much less, somewhat less, about the same, somewhat greater, or much greater after the year 2000:

a. Property Values. Are they much less, somewhat less, about the same, somewhat greater or much greater after 2000 than before?
b. Local Traffic?
c. Racial and Ethnic Diversity?
d. Noise?
e. Air Pollution?
f. Frequency of Trash and Garbage Pick-Up?
g. Frequency of Recycling Services?
h. Graffiti?
i. Test Scores in Public Schools?
j. People hanging out on corners or loitering?
k. Crime Rates?
l. Overall Quality of Life?

4a. Do you think the value of your home has decreased in the recent real estate downturn? If yes: by how much? If yes: by how much?

IF MOVED IN AFTER 2000:

2b. Now, I want you to think about your neighborhood since you moved in. By neighborhood I mean roughly a 2 block radius around your home. I am going to list a number of characteristics of your neighborhood and I want you to tell me whether they are much less, somewhat less, about the same, somewhat greater, or much greater since you arrived in the neighborhood:

a. Property Values. Are they much less, somewhat less, about the same, somewhat greater or much greater since moving?
b. Local Traffic?
c. Racial and Ethnic Diversity?
d. Noise?
e. Air Pollution?
f. Frequency of Trash and Garbage Pick-Up?
g. Frequency of Recycling Services?
h. Graffiti?
i. Test Scores in Public Schools?
j. People hanging out on corners or loitering?
k. Crime Rates?
l. Overall Quality of Life?

3b. Now, I want you to think about conditions within Mount Laurel Township generally since you moved in. I am going to list the same indicators and I want you to tell me whether they are much less, somewhat less, about the same, somewhat greater, or much since you arrived in the neighborhood:

a. Property Values. Are they much less, somewhat less, about the same, somewhat greater or much greater after 2000 than before?
b. Local Traffic?
c. Racial and Ethnic Diversity?
d. Noise?
e. Air Pollution?
f. Frequency of Trash and Garbage Pick-Up?
g. Frequency of Recycling Services?
h. Graffiti?
i. Test Scores in Public Schools?
j. People hanging out on corners or loitering?
k. Crime Rates?
l. Overall Quality of Life?

4b. Do you think the value of your home has decreased in the recent real estate downturn? If yes: by how much?

ALL RESPONDENTS:

5. Are you aware of any affordable housing developments that have been constructed or proposed for construction in Mount Laurel Township?

Yes____No____

6. Are you aware of any affordable housing developments that exist or have been constructed nearby, say within a mile of your home?

No____

If yes, then ask:

a. Can you tell me the name of that housing development?

No____Yes: Verbatim Response: _____

b. Where is it located?

Verbatim Response: _____

c. What are the first five words that come to mind to describe the residents of this development?

Verbatim Responses: _____

d. Do you personally know any residents of this development?

Yes____No____

e. Have you personally interacted with any residents of this development

Yes____No____

f. If respondent reports interaction: name all the places where you have interacted with residents of this development:

Record multiple responses verbatim: _____

g. If you have school-age children, have any of them made friends with kids from this development?

7. Thank you for sharing your perceptions with us. To conclude, we would just like to ask a few questions about yourself:

a. What is your age?
b. How would you identify your race or ethnicity?
c. Are you currently working at a job or looking for work?
   If working: Full time or part time?
   What is your current occupation?
d. How many years of school have you completed?

Number: _____

If they say: High school graduate: Record 12 years

College graduate: Record 16 years

Advanced Degree: Record 17

Closing. Those are all the questions we have. Thank you for your time.

Appendix A2: Guide for Interviewing Mount Laurel Public Officials

1. How long have you held your present job?

2. Do you know where the Ethel Lawrence Homes are located in Mount Laurel?

3. Before the year 2000, did you favor or oppose the construction of the Ethel Lawrence Homes in Mount Laurel?

4. Were you involved—either personally or professionally—in the review process for Ethel Lawrence Homes? In what capacity?

5. Have you heard of Fair Share Housing Development, Inc.? What can you tell me about this corporation?

6. Have you interacted with anyone from Fair Share Housing Development Corporation? In what context or capacity?

7. Have you interacted with any resident of the Ethel Lawrence Homes? In what context or capacity?

8. How would you describe the residents of Ethel Lawrence Homes?

9. To what degree to residents of Ethel Lawrence interact with other residents of Mount Laurel?

10. What have been the benefits to Mount Laurel of the construction and occupation of the Ethel Lawrence Homes?

11. What have been the costs to Mount Laurel of the construction and occupation of the Ethel Lawrence Homes, in general and for your agency?

12. Have your heard any negative comments from Mount Laurel residents about the Ethel Lawrence Homes?

13. Would you favor or oppose the construction of a similar development elsewhere in Mount Laurel? Why?

14. Would you favor or oppose the construction of a similar development in an adjacent township? Why?

15. Do the Ethel Lawrence Homes look similar to or different from other for-profit housing in the township?

16. Do you talk to officials in other municipalities about affordable housing issues?

Appendix A3: Questionnaire for Survey of Ethel Lawrence Homes Residents and Non-Resident Control Cases

Introduction. Hello. I am conducing a survey on behalf of investigators at Princeton University. They are interested in learning about conditions in the neighborhoods where you live now and in 1999, how they might have changed, and how you and your family may have adapted to these changes. The survey should take about a half hour of your time. May I ask you a few questions?

Respondent's Circumstances in 1999

To start out, I'd like you to think back to the household you occupied in December of 1999, right around the millennium celebration. Can you think about where and with whom you were living at that time? I'd like to find out a little about the family and neighborhood environments you experienced then.

1. Could you please tell me who was living with you in your household in December of 1999? Include *everyone* who lived in your home or apartment, even if they weren't a relative and even if they didn't spend the entire year with you. Please begin with yourself.

Relation to Respondent	Sex	Age	Enrolled in School?	School Years Completed	Working Part or Full Time?	Present All Year?

2. Thinking back to the specific area where you lived in 1999, I'd like you to estimate the percentage of African Americans, Latinos, and Asians in your neighborhood, say, within a three-block radius of your house or apartment.

   Estimated Percentage of African Americans or Blacks: _____

   Estimated Percentage of Latinos or Hispanics: _____

   Estimated Percentage of Asians: _____

3. When you lived in this neighborhood in 1999 how often do you recall seeing the following circumstances during that calendar year?

	Never	Rarely	Sometimes	Often	Very Often	Every Day
Homeless people on the street?						
Prostitutes on the street?						
Gang members hanging out on the street?						
Drug paraphernalia on the street?						
People selling illegal drugs in public?						
People using illegal drugs in public?						
People drinking or drunk in public?						
Physical violence in public?						
The sound of gunshots?						

4. When you lived in this neighborhood in 1999 how often do you recall interacting with the following people during that calendar year?

	Not Applicable	Never	Rarely	Sometimes	Often	Very Often	Every Day
Grand-mother?							
Mother?							
Father?							
Brother or Sister?							
Other family member?							
Next door neighbor?							
Best friend?							

5. When you lived in this neighborhood in 1999 how difficult was it for you to get to the following locations when you needed to?

	Not Applicable	Very Easy	Somewhat Easy	Neither Easy nor Hard	Somewhat Hard	Very Hard
The grocery store?						
The drug store?						
A place of work?						
Children's school?						
Day care?						
Doctor's office?						

6. When you made a trip to the following locations in 1999, about how long did it usually take you to get there?

    The grocery store?
    The drug store?
    Your job?
    Day care?

Children's school?
Doctor's office?

7. In general, how would you say your health was in 1999? Would you say it was excellent, very good, good, fair, or poor?

8. Can you recall the address where you lived in 1999?

Note Number, Street, Town or City, and Zip Code: _____

Respondent's Current Circumstances

9. Now I'd like to find out about the people who live with you now. Could you please tell me who lives in your household presently? As before, include *everyone* who lives in your home, even if they aren't a relative and even if they have not spent the entire year with you. Please be assured we will keep this information confidential. In particular, no one on the Ethel Lawrence staff will have access to the data. Please begin with yourself.

Relation to Respondent	Sex	Age	Enrolled in School?	School Years Completed	Working Part or Full Time?	Present All Year?

10. Thinking of your current place of residence, I'd like you to estimate the percentage of African Americans, Latinos, and Asians in your neighborhood, say, within a three-block radius of your house or apartment.

Estimated Percentage of African Americans or Blacks: _____

Estimated Percentage of Latinos or Hispanics: _____

Estimated Percentage of Asians: _____

11. Within the past 12 months how often do you recall seeing the following circumstances:

	Never	Rarely	Sometimes	Often	Very Often	Every Day
Homeless people on the street?						
Prostitutes on the street?						
Gang members hanging out on the street?						
Drug paraphernalia on the street?						
People selling illegal drugs in public?						
People using illegal drugs in public?						
People drinking or drunk in public?						
Physical violence in public?						
The sound of gunshots?						

12. In the past twelve months, how often do you recall interacting with the following people:

	Not Applicable	Never	Rarely	Sometimes	Often	Very Often	Every Day
Grandmother?							
Mother?							
Father?							
Brother or Sister?							
Other family member?							
Next door neighbor?							
Best friend?							

13. Within the past twelve months, how difficult has it been for you to get to the following locations when you needed to?

	Not Applicable	Very Easy	Somewhat Easy	Neither Easy nor Hard	Somewhat Hard	Very Hard
The grocery store?						
The drug store?						
A place of work?						
Children's school?						
Day care?						
Doctor's office?						

14. When you made a trip to the following over the past twelve months, about how long did it usually take to get there?

> The grocery store?
> The drug store?
> A place of work?
> Day care?
> Children's school?

15. In general, how would you say your health has been in the past twelve months? Would you say it has been excellent, very good, good, fair, or poor?

16. Please tell me how often you have each of the following conditions in the past twelve months?

	Never	A Few Times	About Once a Week	Almost Every Day	Every Day
A headache?					
A stomach ache or upset stomach?					
Feeling hot all over suddenly for no reason?					
Cold sweats					

	Never	A Few Times	About Once a Week	Almost Every Day	Every Day
Feeling physically weak for no reason?					
Sore throat or cough?					
Feeling very tired for no reason?					
Frequent or painful urination or peeing?					
Feeling really sick?					
Waking up feeling tired?					
Skin problems such as itching or pimples?					
Dizziness?					
Chest pains?					
A rapid pulse or heartbeat?					
Pains or soreness in muscles or joints?					
Poor appetite?					
Trouble falling or staying asleep?					
Trouble relaxing?					
Frequent crying?					
Fearfulness?					

17. What is the highest degree, diploma or certificate that you have received?

   Verbatim Response: _____

   a. In what year did you receive this degree, diploma or certificate? _____

18. Are you presently enrolled in school?

   No

   If yes, what grade? _____

19. Are you currently working for pay? We are interested even if your work is "off the books."

> No
>
> If yes:
>
> Number of hours worked per week: _____
>
> Wages or salary: _____ per _____
>
> Current occupation: _____
>
> Time in current position: _____years _____months

20. Do you presently own a motor vehicle?

> Yes____
>
> No ____ Do you have reliable access to a vehicle?

21. How many days per week do you make use of public transportation?

22. How good is public transportation service in this neighborhood? Very poor, poor, good, or very good?

23. What is your current marital situation?

> Married and living with spouse
> Married but separated from spouse
> Cohabiting with a romantic partner
> Divorced
> Never married
> Widowed

24. Within the past twelve months, how many times have the following events happened to you or someone who lives with you?

> Serious illness
> Serious injury
> Death
> Unexpected pregnancy
> Arrest by police
> Sentenced to jail or prison
> Expelled from school
> Loss of job
> Loss of home
> Robbery
> Burglary

25. Within the past twelve months, how many times have the following events happened to a relative or friend of yours?

Serious illness
Serious injury
Death
Unexpected pregnancy
Arrest by police
Sentenced to jail or prison
Expelled from school
Loss of job
Loss of home
Robbery
Burglary

Thank you. That's all the questions we have.

Appendix A4: Variables Used to Propensity Scores

To generate propensity scores for each applicant, we created a dependent variable equal to 1 if the participant had ever lived in the Ethel Lawrence Homes, and equal to 0 otherwise. We used Stata's psmatch2 command to generate propensity scores from the following set of variables:

Position on waiting list. All applicants to the Homes are placed on a waiting list in the order in which they submit their applications in person. Hence, lower numbers on the waiting list are more favorable for entry into the Homes. An applicant's position on the waiting list could thus be considered an indicator of both the applicant's real likelihood of being selected to move into the project and his/her motivation for being selected, since more-motivated applicants theoretically would submit their applications before less-motivated applicants. When management calls for a new round of applications, they begin a new waiting list, which means the applicants in our sampling frame were on one of five waiting lists: 2000, 2003, 2006, 2007, or 2010. Some waiting lists are much longer than others, which made it difficult to simply include applicants' waiting-list number in the regression equation—a position of "200" on the waiting list may be more or less favorable depending on how long the actual list for that particular year is. Thus, for each of the five application rounds, we split the list into quartiles and then generated a set of dummy variables indicating in which quartile a given applicant falls. These dummies were included in the model (reference = Quartile 1). There were also a handful of applicants (roughly 2.6 percent of all cases) that could not be found on a waiting list. Their application files were discovered when we were going through the applications that were archived at the Fair Share Housing Development. These cases were added to the sampling frame, but not assigned a waiting-list number. We assigned them a separate dummy indicating their status as "not assigned a waiting list number."

Number of bedrooms requested at Ethel Lawrence Homes. The Homes have 1-, 2-, and 3-bedroom units. According to management, the 3-bedroom units are in greatest demand, which means that a family requesting a 3-bedroom unit has a smaller probability of being selected to move in. We included a continuous variable, ranging from 1 to 3, indicating the number of bedrooms being requested.

Lives with a family member. To gauge an applicant's access to family resources, we included a binary measure of whether he/she was living with a family member at the time they applied to the Homes.

Female. We included a dummy variable indicating whether the applicant was female.

Relationship status. We generated four dummy variables indicating an applicant's status: never married (reference group), married, divorced/separated/estranged, and widowed.

Age. Age is coded as a continuous variable.

Has children. We included a dummy variable indicating whether (yes = 1) the applicant listed children under eighteen as potential residents on the application.

Income. Applicants were asked to self-report and provide documentation for their income, including nonwage income, like TANF or Social Security. Applicants who made it far enough in the application process also had their incomes verified by a Fair Share staff member. We drew on data from all available sources to create a measure of income at the time applicants applied to the Homes. For ease of interpretation, we standardized income for the propensity-score analysis. For each case missing on income, we imputed income to the mean annual income of other cases that shared the same relationship status, age, and sex. We include a variable in the model indicating whether a respondent's income was imputed (N = 8).

Neighborhood characteristics. Applicants were required to give a current address on their applications. Some applicants provided P.O. boxes; we assigned these applicants an address equal to the post office corresponding to this P.O. box. We then geocoded these addresses and attached relevant characteristics of applicants' census tracts. The final models included measures of percent black, percent Hispanic, percent vacant units, percent rental units, and percent below the federal poverty line.

Reasons for applying to Ethel Lawrence Homes. At the end of the application, applicants were asked to provide the reason they were applying to live in the project. Responses were open-ended and were used to create two dummy variables indicating residents' motivations for moving: housing-related needs (needs affordable housing, homeless, lease is up, needs more space, etc.); and reasons related to safety and opportunity (wants better school district, wants safer/better environment, wants a better life for family, etc.). We also created a dummy variable indicating whether respondents did not provide a response to this question. Lastly, we created an interaction variable between whether an applicant has children and whether they cited reasons related to safety and opportunity, under the assumption that applicants who have children and are concerned about safety issues may be particularly motivated to move.

Appendix A5: Questions for Resident and Non-Resident Household Members Aged 12–18

1. Line in household roster from Question 8 _____

2. Do you currently attend a public school, a private religious school, or a private nonreligious school?

    ( ) Public ( ) Private Religious ( ) Private Nonreligious ( ) Other (specify)

    What is the name of the school? _____

3. What grade are you currently attending? _____

4. On the last report card that you received, how many of each grade did you get?

    Number of A's: _____
    Number of B's: _____
    Number of C's: _____
    Number of D's: _____
    Number of F's: _____

5. On the last report card that you received, how many of each of the following courses did you take?

    English Courses _____
    Math Courses _____
    History Courses _____
    Science Courses _____
    Foreign Language Courses _____
    Vocational Courses _____

6. Thinking about the ethnic and racial composition of the school you currently attend, I'd like you to estimate the percentage of African Americans, Latinos, and Asians among students in the student body:

Estimated Percentage of African Americans or Blacks: _____
Estimated Percentage of Latinos or Hispanics: _____
Estimated Percentage of Asians: _____

7. During the last complete three months of school, how often do you recall witnessing the following behaviors on school property during school hours?

	Never	Rarely	Sometimes	Often	Very Often
Students fighting?					
Students smoking?					
Students kissing or "making out?"					
Students being late for class?					
Students cutting class?					
Students cutting school?					
Students shouting at or threatening teachers or principals?					
Students pushing or hitting teachers or principals?					
Vandalism of school or personal property?					
Theft of school or personal property?					
Students consuming alcohol?					
Students taking illegal drugs?					
Students carrying knives?					
Students carrying guns?					
Robbery of students by other students?					

8. Within the past twelve months, how often did your parents do the following:

	Never	Rarely	Sometimes	Often	Very Often	Always
Check if you'd done your homework?						
Help you with your homework?						
Participate in a Parent-Teacher Association?						
Talk with your friends?						
Talk with your friends' parents?						
Reward you for good grades?						
Punish you for bad grades?						
Punish you for disobedience?						
Limit your TV watching?						
Limit your playing of video games?						
Limit the time you spent with friends?						
Set an hour to return home at night?						
Ask you to do household chores?						
Take you to an art museum?						
Take you to a science center or museum?						
Take you to a library?						

9. Within the past three months, how often have you participated in the following activities?

	Never	Rarely	Sometimes	Often	Very Often
Organized sports at school?					
Organized sports outside of school?					
Playing pick-up games?					
Drama or theater activities?					
School band or orchestra?					
School debate?					
School cheerleading?					
Drill team?					
Pep club or related activities?					
Student government?					
Dance lessons?					
Private music lessons?					
Private art lessons?					
Scouting activities?					
Volunteer work in community?					

10. In the past three months, how often have you, yourself, made use of the following items:

	Never	Rarely	Sometimes	Often	Very Often
A daily newspaper?					
A Sunday newspaper?					
A weekly news magazine?					
An encyclopedia?					
A dictionary?					
An atlas?					
A computer?					
The internet?					
Pocket calculator?					
Piano?					
Other musical instrument?					

11. In the past twelve months, how often would you guess your mother make use of the following items:

	Never	Rarely	Sometimes	Often	Very Often
A daily newspaper?					
A Sunday newspaper?					
A weekly news magazine?					
An encyclopedia?					
A dictionary?					
An atlas?					
A computer?					
The internet?					
Pocket calculator?					
Piano?					
Other musical instrument?					

12. What is the latest you are currently allowed to stay out on a school night?

    Approximate Time: _____

13. What is the latest you are currently allowed to stay out on a weekend night?

    Approximate Time: _____

14. Do you presently have a bedroom of your own? Yes / No

    If no—with how many others do you share? _____

15. Do you have a specific place where you can study without being disturbed? Yes / No

16. During a typical seven-day week during the school year, please estimate the following about *yourself* (estimate all that apply):

    The number of hours you watched TV or videos
    The number of hours you played video games
    The number of hours you studied or did homework
    The number of hours you read for information or pleasure
    The number of hours you listened to music
    The number of hours you did chores or housework
    The number of hours you looked after brothers or sisters at home
    The number of hours you were employed outside the house
    The number of hours spent socializing with friends outside of school

17. In your current school, do you think your friends view the following behaviors as very uncool, somewhat uncool, neither cool nor uncool, somewhat cool, or very cool, where "cool" refers to behavior that is respected or admired by other students?

	Very Uncool	Somewhat Uncool	Neither Cool nor Uncool	Somewhat Cool	Very Cool
Studying hard outside of class?					
Asking challenging questions in class?					
Volunteering information in class?					
Answering teachers' questions in class?					
Solving problems using new and original ideas?					
Helping other students with their homework?					
Getting good grades in difficult subjects?					
Planning to go to college?					

18. Among the friends you hang out with these days, how important is it to:

	Not at All Important	A Little Important	Somewhat Important	Very Important
Attend classes regularly				
Study hard				
Play sports				
Get good grades				
Be popular or well-liked				
Finish high school				
Go to college				
Have a steady boyfriend or girlfriend				
Be willing to party and get wild				
Participate in religious activities				
Do community or volunteer work				
Hold a steady job				
Have a lot of money to spend				

19. To what extent do you agree with the following statements:

	Strongly Agree	Somewhat Agree	Somewhat Disagree	Strongly Disagree
Doing well in school helps you later in life				
I feel my future is limited				
What you are taught in school is pretty useless once you graduate				
There are better things to do than spend my time on school work				
Trying hard in school is a waste of time				

20. I want you now to think of your five closest friends at school. How many are:

Black?
Latino?
Asian?
White?
Other?

21. How well do you fit in at your current school? Do you fit in not well at all, not very well, reasonably well, very well, or extremely well?

22. Please think of *your very best friend* at school. To what extent are the following statements true about this person:

	Very Untrue	Somewhat True	Very True
Gets grades of B or better			
Is interested in school			
Studies hard			
Attends classes regularly			
Plans to go to college			
Is popular with others			
Plays sports			
Reads a lot			
Watches TV a lot			
Has had sexual intercourse			
Takes illegal drugs			
Gets drunk on alcohol			

23. The next few items assess how you feel about yourself. Please indicate how strongly you agree or disagree with each of the following statements.

	Strongly Disagree	Somewhat Disagree	Neither Agree nor Disagree	Somewhat Agree	Strongly Agree
I feel that I am a person of worth, equal to others					
I feel that I have a number of good qualities					
All in all, I am inclined to feel that I am a failure					
I am able to do things as well as most people					
I feel that I do not have much to be proud of					
I take a positive attitude toward myself					
On the whole, I am satisfied with myself.					
I wish I could have more respect for myself					
I feel useless at times					
At times, I think I'm no good at all					

24. Thinking about your life at the moment, please indicate how strongly you agree or disagree with each of the following statements.

	Strongly Disagree	Somewhat Disagree	Neither Agree nor Disagree	Somewhat Agree	Strongly Agree
I don't have control over the direction my life is taking					
In life, good luck is more important than hard work for success					
Every time I try to get ahead some-thing or somebody stops me					
When I make plans, I am almost certain I can make them work					
I feel left out of things going on around me					
If I work hard, I can do well					

25. In general, how would you say your health is? Would you say it is excellent, very good, good, fair, or poor?

26. Do you currently hold a job outside of school?

       If yes: Where do you work? _____

       How many hours per week?_____

       How much per hour?_____

Thank you. That's all the questions we have.

Appendix A6: Construction of Social Scales

Severity-Weighted Neighborhood Disorder Scale

Severity-weighted disorder scale = $\Sigma i \Sigma j$ (Xij * (j–1) * Wi), where
i refers to 1 to 9 indicators of neighborhood disorder
j refers to 1 to 6 response categories on frequency witnessed
Xi j = 1 if respondent picked response category j, 0 otherwise
Wi = Wofgang-Sellin Severity Score for item i
Reliability α = 0. 962

	Severity Weight
Homeless people on the street	0.3
Prostitutes on the street	2.1
Gang members hanging out on the street	1.1
Drug paraphernalia on the street	1.3
People selling illegal drugs in public	20.6
People using illegal drugs in public	6.5
People drinking or drunk in public	0.8
Physical violence in public	6.9
Hearing the sound of gunshots	2.1

Stress-Weighted Life Event Scale

Stress-Weighted Life Event Scale = Ei (Fi * Wi), where
i refers to 1 to 11 items on frequency of negative life events
Fi = frequency reported by respondent for life event i
Wi = Holmes-Rahe Stress Score
Reliability α = 0.874

The weights for each item are as follows:

Item	Weight
Serious illness	49
Serious injury	53
Death	82
Unexpected pregnancy	40
Arrest by police	37
Sentenced to jail or prison	63
Expelled from school	26
Loss of job	47
Loss of home	30
Robbery	29
Burglary	23

Scale of Neighbor Contact with ELH Residents

	No	Yes
Aware of affordable housing in the township	0	1
Aware of affordable housing in the neighborhood	0	1
Can correctly name the project	0	1
Has personally interacted with an ELH resident	0	1
Personally knows an ELH resident	0	1
Has children who knew children from ELH	0	1

Summary Scale 0–6
Reliability $\alpha = 0.778$

Scale of Degree to Which Neighbors Perceive Fears to Have Come True

	No	Yes
Respondent's own home value has decreased	0	1
Respondent's home value has fared worse than others in township	0	1
Respondent's home value has fared worse than others in the county	0	1
Property values are worse in the neighborhood	0	1
Property values are worse in the township	0	1
Crime is worse in the neighborhood	0	1
Crime is worse in the township	0	1
Crime is worse in the township	0	1
School test scores are getting worse	0	1

Summary Scale 0– 9
Reliability $\alpha = 0.641$

Scale of Residents Interaction with Social Others

Frequency of Interaction with	Never	Rarely	Sometimes	Often	Very Often	Every Day
Grandmother	0	1	2	3	4	5
Mother	0	1	2	3	4	5
Father	0	1	2	3	4	5
Brother or sister	0	1	2	3	4	5
Other family member	0	1	2	3	4	5
Next door neighbor	0	1	2	3	4	5
Best friend	0	1	2	3	4	5

Average Scale 0–5
Reliability $\alpha = 0.709$

Scale of Interaction with Family Members

Frequency of Interaction with	Never	Rarely	Sometimes	Often	Very Often	Every Day
Grandmother	0	1	2	3	4	5
Mother	0	1	2	3	4	5
Father	0	1	2	3	4	5
Brother or sister	0	1	2	3	4	5
Other family member	0	1	2	3	4	5

Average Scale 0–5
Reliability α = 0.613

Scale of Interaction with Non-Family Members

Frequency of Interaction with	Never	Rarely	Sometimes	Often	Very Often	Every Day
Next door neighbor	0	1	2	3	4	5
Best friend	0	1	2	3	4	5

Average Scale 0–5
Reliability α = 0.2768888

Scale of Access to Daily Services

How Difficult to Get to	Very Easy	Somewhat Easy	Neither Hard nor Easy	Somewhat Hard	Very Hard
The grocery store	0	1	2	3	4
The drug store	0	1	2	3	4
Your job	0	1	2	3	4
Children's school	0	1	2	3	4
Day care	0	1	2	3	4
Doctor's office	0	1	2	3	4

Average Scale 0–4
Reliability α = 0.893

Scale of Mental Distress

How Often In the Past 12 Months Have You Experienced	Never	A Few Times	Once a Week	Almost Every Day	Every Day
Trouble falling asleep	0	1	2	3	4
Trouble relaxing	0	1	2	3	4
Frequent crying	0	1	2	3	4
Fearfulness	0	1	2	3	4
Being very tired for no reason	0	1	2	3	4
Waking up tired	0	1	2	3	4

Average Scale 0–4
Reliability α = 0.764

Scale of Economic Self-Sufficiency

Factor-Weighted Sufficiency Scale = $\Sigma_i (Z_i * F_i)$, where
i refers to 1 to 4 economic variables (see below)
Z_i = the Z-Score for variable i
F_i = the factor loading for variable i
Reliability $\alpha = 0.924$

	Factor Loading
Working for pay	0.919
Income from work	0.956
Total income	0.827
Share of Income from work	0.927

Index of Parental Academic Support

In the Past 12 Months How Often Parents	Never	Rarely	Sometimes	Often	Very Often	Always
Checked homework	0	1	2	3	4	5
Helped with homework	0	1	2	3	4	5
Participated in PTA	0	1	2	3	4	5
Talked to other parents	0	1	2	3	4	5
Took child to library	0	1	2	3	4	5

Average Score 0–5
Reliability $\alpha = 0.763$

Factor Score of School Quality

Factor-Weighted Quality Scale = $\Sigma_i (Z_i * F_i)$, where
i refers to 1 to 9 school quality indicators (see below)
Z_i = the Z-Score for quality indicator i
F_i = the factor loading for variable i
Reliability $\alpha = 0.902$

	Factor Loadings	
	Middle School	High School
Average class size	0.719	0.731
Student mobility rate	0.846	0.824
% Students proficient on state language exam	0.959	0.984
% Students proficient on state math exam	0.950	0.942
Attendance rate	0.899	0.935
Average SAT Score	—	0.988
% Scoring 3+ on at least one AP exam	—	0.866
Dropout rate	—	0.926
Graduation rate	—	0.912

Severity Weighted School Disorder Scale

Severity-weighted school disorder scale = $\Sigma_i \Sigma_j (X_{ij} * (j-1) * W_i)$, where

i refers to 1 to 9 items on neighborhood disorder

j refers to 1 to 6 response categories on frequency witnessed

X_{ij} = 1 if respondent picked response category j, 0 otherwise

W_i = Wofgang-Sellin Severity Score for item i

	Severity Weight
Students fighting	6.20
Students kissing or making out	0.04
Students being late for class	0.06
Students smoking	0.08
Students cutting class	0.10
Students cutting school	0.20
Students shouting at or threatening teachers or principals	5.40
Students pushing or hitting teachers or principals	7.90
Vandalism of school or personal property	3.80
Theft of school or personal property	2.20
Students consuming alcohol	1.10
Students taking illegal drugs	6.50
Students carrying knives	2.40
Students carrying guns	4.60
Robbery of students by other students	4.40

Appendix A7: Equations for Comparative Analysis of ELH Residents and Non-Residents

Equation estimates for Figure 7.2: OLS models predicting neighborhood disorder index

Independent Variable	Unmatched	Unmatched	Matched
ELH Resident	–39.884**	–37.455**	–42.150**
	(6.030)	(6.412)	(6.066)
Male Household Head	–	9.578	–15.316
	(11.901)	(12.446)	
Head's Age	–	–0.727**	–0.954**
	(0.262)	(0.245)	
Head White	–	(11.036)	9.91
	(9.111)	(7.961)	
Head Other Race	–	–17.979*	–9.030
	(8.407)	(8.648)	
Married/Cohabiting	–	6.296	28.781**
	(9.422)	(9.708)	
Separated/Divorced	–	0.813	21.691**
	(7.266)	(6.760)	
Widowed	–	(5.490)	12.397
	(13.020)	(13.240)	
High School Graduate	–	–25.315*	–34.261**
	(10.331)	(10.757)	
Some College	–	–23.885*	–23.206*
	(9.706)	(10.610)	
College Graduate	–	–40.612**	–31.923*
	(12.370)	(12.630)	
% Female in Household	–	–14.204	–4.099
	(12.641)	(11.606)	
Propensity Score	–	6.335	–
	(16.712)		
Intercept	49.158**	111.251**	110.961**
	(4.340)	(17.524)	(15.078)
N	224	224	232
R-Squared	0.16	0.28	0.37

$**p < .01$; $*p < .05$; $^p < .10$ two tailed test

Equation estimates for Figure 7.4: OLS models predicting log of weighted stress index

Independent Variable	Unmatched	Unmatched	Matched
ELH Resident	−0.965**	−0.754*	−0.644^
	(0.333)	(0.366)	(0.353)
Male Household Head	−	0.421	0.886
	(0.679)	(0.724)	
Head's Age	−	0.002	0.024^
	(0.015)	(0.014)	
Head White	−	(0.284)	−0.927*
	(0.520)	(0.463)	
Head Other Race	−	(0.390)	−0.527
	(0.480)	(0.503)	
Married/Cohabiting	−	0.100	0.619
	(0.538)	(0.565)	
Separated/Divorced	−	0.148	0.499
	(0.415)	(0.393)	
Widowed	−	1.208	0.751
	(0.743)	(0.770)	
High School Graduate	−	0.643	1.182^
	(0.590)	(0.626)	
Some College	−	1.462**	2.428**
	(0.554)	(0.617)	
College Graduate	−	0.442	1.239^
	(0.706)	(0.735)	
% Female in Household	−	0.410	0.960
	(0.721)	(0.675)	
Propensity Score	−	−1.647^	−
	(0.954)		
Intercept	3.399**	2.740**	−0.494
	(0.240)	(1.000)	(0.877)
N	224	224	232
R-Squared	0.04	0.11	0.14

**p < .01; *p < .05; ^p < .10 two tailed test

Equation estimates for Figure 7.5: OLS models predicting log of weighted stress index

Independent Variable	Unmatched	Unmatched	Matched	Matched
ELH Resident	−0.754*	−0.401	−0.644^	−0.02
	(0.366)	(0.390)	(0.353)	(0.378)
Male Household Head	0.421	0.331	0.886	1.113
	(0.679)	(0.672)	(0.724)	(0.704)
Head's Age	0.002	0.009	0.024^	0.038**
	(0.015)	(0.015)	(0.014)	(0.014)
Head White	−0.284	−0.180	−0.927*	−1.074*
	(0.520)	(0.516)	(0.463)	(0.450)
Head Other Race	−0.39	−0.221	−0.527	−0.393
	(0.480)	(0.479)	(0.503)	(0.489)
Married/Cohabiting	0.1	0.04	0.619	0.192
	(0.538)	(0.532)	(0.565)	(0.558)
Separated/Divorced	0.148	0.14	0.499	0.177
	(0.415)	(0.410)	(0.393)	(0.390)
Widowed	1.208	1.259^	0.751	0.567
	(0.743)	(0.735)	(0.770)	(0.748)
High School Graduate	0.643	0.882	1.182^	1.690**
	(0.590)	(0.591)	(0.626)	(0.620)
Some College	1.462**	1.688**	2.428**	2.772**
	(0.554)	(0.555)	(0.617)	(0.605)
College Graduate	0.442	0.824	1.239^	1.712*
	(0.706)	(0.716)	(0.735)	(0.722)
% Female in Household	0.410	0.544	0.960	1.021
	(0.721)	(0.715)	(0.675)	(0.655)
Propensity Score	−1.647^	−1.707^	−	−
	(0.954)	(0.943)		
Weighted Disorder Scale	−	0.009*	−	0.015**
	(0.004)		(0.004)	
Intercept	2.740**	1.692	−0.494	−2.139*
	(1.000)	(1.079)	(0.877)	(0.950)
N	224	224	232	232
	0.11	0.13	0.14	0.20

**p < .01; *p < .05; ^p < .10 two tailed test

Equation estimates for Figure 7.7: OLS models predicting non-family interaction index

Independent Variable	Unmatched	Unmatched	Matched
ELH Resident	0.155	0.222	0.532**
	(0.160)	(0.177)	(0.170)
Male Household Head	–	0.063	0.031
	(0.328)	(0.349)	
Head's Age	–	–0.015*	–0.010
	(0.007)	(0.007)	
Head White	–	0.134	0.277
	(0.251)	(0.223)	
Head Other Race	–	–0.479*	–0.508*
	(0.233)	(0.244)	
Married/Cohabiting	–	0.500^	0.795**
	(0.260)	(0.272)	
Separated/Divorced	–	0.277	0.104
	(0.201)	(0.190)	
Widowed	–	0.484	0.234
	(0.362)	(0.373)	
High School Graduate	–	0.052	–0.517^
	(0.291)	(0.309)	
Some College	–	–0.180	–0.589^
	(0.273)	(0.305)	
College Graduate	–	–0.321	–0.733*
	(0.346)	(0.361)	
% Female in Household	–	0.405	1.048**
	(0.350)	(0.326)	
Propensity Score	–	–0.168	–
	(0.465)		
Intercept	2.676**	3.077**	2.428**
	(0.115)	(0.483)	(0.425)
N	223	223	231
R-Squared	0.00	0.07	0.16

**p < .01; *p < .05; ^p < .10 two tailed test

Equation estimates for Figure 8.2: OLS models predicting mental distress index

Independent Variable	Unmatched	Unmatched	Matched
ELH Resident	−0.221*	−0.213^	−0.132
	(0.110)	(0.122)	(0.115)
Male Household Head	–	−0.194	−0.147
	(0.226)	(0.237)	
Head's Age	–	−0.001	0.000
	(0.005)	(0.005)	
Head White	–	0.043	0.223
	(0.173)	(0.151)	
Head Other Race	–	−0.271^	−0.242
	(0.159)	(0.164)	
Married/Cohabiting	–	0.048	0.225
	(0.179)	(0.185)	
Separated/Divorced	–	0.176	0.515**
	(0.138)	(0.129)	
Widowed	–	0.161	0.069
	(0.247)	(0.252)	
High School Graduate	–	0.028	0.006
	(0.196)	(0.205)	
Some College	–	−0.024	−0.029
	(0.184)	(0.202)	
College Graduate	–	−0.325	−0.219
	(0.235)	(0.240)	
% Female in Household	–	0.133	0.270
	(0.240)	(0.221)	
Propensity Score	–	0.116	–
	(0.317)		
Intercept	1.102**	1.028**	0.742*
	(0.079)	(0.332)	(0.287)
N	224	224	232
R-Squared	0.02	0.07	0.16

**p < .01; *p < .05; ^p < .10 two tailed test

Equation estimates for Figure 8.3: OLS models predicting mental distress scale

Independent Variable	Unmatched	Unmatched	Matched	Matched
ELH Resident	−0.213^	0.038	−0.132	0.068
	(0.122)	(0.119)	(0.115)	(0.115)
Male Household Head	−0.194	−0.283	−0.147	−0.213
	(0.226)	(0.205)	(0.237)	(0.215)
Head's Age	−0.001	0.002	0.000	0.000
	(0.005)	(0.005)	(0.005)	(0.004)
Head White	0.043	0.124	0.223	0.310*
	(0.173)	(0.157)	(0.151)	(0.139)
Head Other Race	−0.271^	−0.148	−0.242	−0.151
	(0.159)	(0.146)	(0.164)	(0.149)
Married/Cohabiting	0.048	0.009	0.225	0.067
	(0.179)	(0.162)	(0.185)	(0.170)
Separated/Divorced	0.176	0.156	0.515**	0.392**
	(0.138)	(0.125)	(0.129)	(0.119)
Widowed	0.161	0.058	0.069	−0.060
	(0.247)	(0.226)	(0.252)	(0.228)
High School Graduate	0.028	0.075	0.006	−0.044
	(0.196)	(0.181)	(0.205)	(0.192)
Some College	−0.024	−0.071	−0.029	−0.265
	(0.184)	(0.173)	(0.202)	(0.193)
College Graduate	−0.325	−0.187	−0.219	−0.283
	−0.235	−0.219	−0.24	−0.222
% Female in Household	0.133	0.154	0.270	0.163
	(0.240)	(0.218)	(0.221)	(0.200)
Propensity Score	0.116	0.262	–	–
	(0.317)	(0.290)		
Weighted Disorder Scale	–	0.005**	–	0.003*
	(0.001)	(0.001)		
Log of Life Stress Scale	–	0.106**	–	0.124**
	(0.021)	(0.021)		
Intercept	1.028**	0.230	0.742*	0.489^
	(0.332)	(0.331)	(0.287)	(0.292)
N	224	224	232	232
R-Squared	0.07	0.25	0.16	0.32

**p < .01; *p < .05; ^p < .10 two tailed test

Equation estimates for Figure 8.4: OLS models predicting mental distress index

Independent Variable	Unmatched	Matched
Years in ELH	−0.025	−0.018
	(0.016)	(0.015)
Male Household Head	−0.203	0.153
	(0.226)	(0.237)
Head's Age	−0.001	0.000
	(0.005)	(0.005)
Head White	0.055	0.231
	(0.173)	(0.150)
Head Other Race	−0.290^	−0.256
	(0.159)	(0.162)
Married/Cohabiting	0.047	0.218
	(0.179)	(0.184)
Separated/Divorced	0.187	0.519**
	(0.138)	(0.128)
Widowed	0.184	0.081
	(0.248)	(0.253)
High School Graduate	0.044	0.022
	(0.196)	(0.205)
Some College	−0.011	−0.017
	(0.185)	(0.203)
College Graduate	−0.306	−0.203
	(0.235)	(0.241)
% Female in Household	0.110	0.252
	(0.240)	(0.218)
Propensity Score	0.036	–
	(0.306)	
Intercept	1.031	0.716*
	(0.333)	(0.284)
N	224	232
R-Squared	0.07	0.16

**p < .01; *p <. 05; ^p < .10 two tailed test

Equation estimates for Figure 8.5: OLS models predicting economic independence index

Independent Variable	Unmatched	Unmatched	Matched
ELH Resident	0.297*	0.334*	0.255*
	(0.118)	(0.129)	(0.114)
Male Household Head	–	–0.427^	–0.622**
	(0.225)	(0.217)	
Head's Age	–	–0.016**	–0.018**
	(0.005)	(0.005)	
Head White	–	(0.163)	(0.135)
	(0.173)	(0.206)	
Head Other Race	–	0.094	0.124
	(0.158)	(0.169)	
Married/Cohabiting	–	0.103	0.265
	(0.178)	(0.175)	
Separated/Divorced	–	(0.047)	0.180
	(0.137)	(0.140)	
Widowed	–	(0.195)	(0.149)
	(0.244)	(0.262)	
High School Graduate	–	0.538**	0.201
	(0.194)	(0.209)	
Some College	–	0.587**	0.232
	(0.183)	(0.201)	
College Graduate	–	0.660**	0.219
	(0.234)	(0.237)	
% Female in Household	–	–0.565*	–0.717**
	(0.239)	(0.228)	
Propensity Score	–	–0.172	–
	(0.251)		
Intercept	–0.154	0.534^	0.924**
	(0.085)	(0.307)	(0.300)
N	224	224	224
R-Squared	0.03	0.22	0.22

$**p < .01$; $*p < .05$; $^p < .10$ two tailed test

Equation estimates for Figure 8.6: OLS models predicting economic independence index

Independent Variable	Unmatched	Unmatched	Matched	Matched
ELH Resident	0.334*	0.280*	0.255*	0.267*
	(0.129)	(0.132)	(0.114)	(0.119)
Male Household Head	−0.427^	−0.384^	−0.622**	−0.574**
	(0.225)	(0.219)	(0.217)	(0.213)
Head's Age	−0.016**	−0.015**	−0.018**	−0.014**
	(0.005)	(0.005)	(0.005)	(0.005)
Head White	(0.163)	(0.192)	(0.135)	(0.193)
	(0.173)	(0.168)	(0.206)	(0.200)
Head Other Race	0.094	0.063	0.124	0.087
	(0.158)	(0.155)	(0.169)	(0.164)
Married/Cohabiting	0.103	0.104	0.265	0.194
	(0.178)	(0.172)	(0.175)	(0.168)
Separated/Divorced	(0.047)	(0.039)	0.180	0.131
	(0.137)	(0.133)	(0.140)	(0.136)
Widowed	(0.195)	(0.093)	(0.149)	(0.120)
	(0.244)	(0.237)	(0.262)	(0.252)
High School Graduate	0.538**	0.603**	0.201	0.370^
	(0.194)	(0.192)	(0.209)	(0.205)
Some College	0.587**	0.732**	0.232	0.516*
	(0.183)	(0.184)	(0.201)	(0.203)
College Graduate	0.660**	0.719**	0.219	0.401^
	(0.234)	(0.233)	(0.237)	(0.232)
% Female in Household	−0.565*	−0.518*	−0.717**	−0.644**
	(0.239)	(0.233)	(0.228)	(0.221)
Propensity Score	(0.172)	(0.250)	–	–
	(0.251)	(0.245)		
Weighted Disorder Scale	–	0.000	–	0.002
		(0.001)		(0.001)
Log of Life Stress Scale	–	−0.093**	–	−0.105**
		(0.024)		(0.024)
Mental Distress Scale	–	0.004	–	(0.008)
		(0.074)		(0.078)
Intercept	0.534^	0.685*	0.924**	0.740*
	(0.307)	(0.335)	(0.300)	(0.322)
N	224	224	224	224
R-Squared	0.22	0.28	0.22	0.30

$**p < .01$; $*p < .05$; $^p < .10$ two tailed test

Equation estimates for Figure 8.7: OLS models predicting economic independence index

Independent Variable	Unmatched	Matched
Years in ELH	0.040*	0.039*
	(0.016)	(0.016)
Male Household Head	−0.442*	−0.232
	(0.219)	(0.238)
Head's Age	−0.015**	−0.014**
	(0.005)	(0.005)
Head White	−0.220	−0.331*
	(0.167)	(0.154)
Head Other Race	0.072	0.041
	(0.155)	(0.163)
Married/Cohabiting	0.249	−0.022
	(0.172)	(0.185)
Separated/Divorced	−0.039	−0.012
	(0.133)	(0.134)
Widowed	−0.048	−0.243
	(0.241)	(0.252)
High School Graduate	0.620*	0.423*
	(0.192)	(0.210)
Some College	0.740**	0.724**
	(0.184)	(0.213)
College Graduate	0.713**	(0.843)
	(0.233)	(0.246)
% Female in Household	−0.505*	−0.322
	(0.232)	(0.219)
Propensity Score	−0.717*	–
	(0.298)	
Weighted Disorder Scale	0.000	0.000
	(0.001)	(0.001)
Log of Life Stress Scale	−0.107**	−0.100**
	(0.024)	(0.025)
Mental Distress Scale	0.024	−0.028
	(0.074)	(0.075)
Intercept	1.001**	0.535*
	(0.351)	(0.315)
N	224	232
R-Squared	0.30	0.30

**p < .01; *p < .05; ^p < .10 two tailed test

Equation estimates for Figure 8.8: Logit model predicting quiet place to study

Independent Variable	Unmatched	Unmatched	Matched
ELH Resident	1.199	2.263*	2.522*
	(0.752)	(1.033)	(1.058)
Age	–	0.244	0.210
	(0.211)	(0.237)	
Male	–	0.721	1.177
	(0.839)	(0.901)	
Parent's Age	–	−0.041	0.017
	(0.056)	(0.073)	
Parent Employed	–	−2.651^	−3.420*
	(1.474)	(1.479)	
Household Income	–	0.995	0.915
	(0.690)	(0.596)	
Propensity Score	–	−2.927	–
	(2.568)		
Intercept	0.999*	1.569	−1.423
	(0.442)	(3.857)	(5.427)
N	56	56	57
Log Likelihood	−24.90	−22.50	−20.54
Pseudo R-Squared	0.05	0.14	0.22

**p < .01; *p < .05; ^p < .10 two tailed test

Equation estimates for Figure 8.9: Logit model predicting undisturbed place to study

Independent Variable	Unmatched	Matched
Years in ELH	0.595*	0.787*
	(0.270)	(0.356)
Age	0.335	0.474
	(0.242)	(0.374)
Male	0.936	1.654
	(0.893)	(1.082)
Parent's Age	−0.023	0.059
	(0.056)	(0.098)
Parent Employed	−2.929^	−4.000*
	(1.570)	(1.607)
Household Income	1.050	1.136^
	(0.734)	(0.660)
Propensity Score	−3.017	–
	(2.704)	
Intercept	−0.489	−7.394
	(3.952)	(8.657)
N	56	57
Log Likelihood	−20.00	−16.93
Pseudo R-Squared	0.24	0.36

**p <. 01; *p < .05; ^p <. 10 two tailed test

Equation estimates for Figure 8.10: OLS models predicting parental support index

Independent Variable	Unmatched	Unmatched	Matched
ELH Resident	0.595*	0.565^	0.507*
	(0.244)	(0.303)	(0.222)
Age	–	–0.132^	0.001
		(0.068)	(0.056)
Male	–	–0.077	0.005
		(0.284)	(0.214)
Parent's Age	–	0.030^	0.033*
		(0.018)	(0.016)
Parent College Graduate	–	0.183	0.250
		(0.506)	(0.367)
Parent Married/Cohabiting	–	–0.159	0.082
		(0.525)	(0.423)
Parent Employed	–	0.230	0.248
		(0.472)	(0.357)
Household Income	–	–0.026	0.029
		(0.208)	(0.141)
Propensity Score	–	–0.989	–
		(0.794)	
Intercept	1.600**	2.755*	0.242
	(0.178)	(1.287)	(1.189)
N	56	56	57
Log Likelihood	–24.90	–22.50	–20.54
Pseudo R-Squared	0.10	0.23	0.24

$**p < .01$; $*p < .05$; $^p < .10$ two tailed test

Equation estimates for Figure 8.11: OLS models predicting parental support scale

Independent Variable	Unmatched	Matched
Years in ELH	0.084*	0.079**
	(0.034)	(0.026)
Age	−0.127^	0.003
	(0.067)	(0.054)
Male	−0.086	0.021
	(0.268)	(0.205)
Parent's Age	0.034^	0.033*
	(0.017)	(0.015)
Parent College Graduate	0.198	0.294
	(0.492)	(0.352)
Parent Married/Cohabiting	−0.252	0.078
	(0.514)	(0.406)
Parent Employed	0.346	0.288
	(0.434)	(0.327)
Household Income	−0.089	0.004
	(0.199)	(0.131)
Propensity Score	−0.614	–
	(0.702)	
Intercept	2.306^	0.168
	(1.255)	(1.137)
N	56	57
R-Squared	0.27	0.29

**p < .01; *p < .05; ^p < .10 two tailed test

Equation estimates for Figure 8.12: OLS models predicting hours studied per week

Independent Variable	Unmatched	Unmatched	Matched
ELH Resident	4.519*	6.359**	6.298**
	(1.742)	(2.245)	(2.021)
Age	–	–0.066	0.246
	(0.507)	(0.513)	
Male	–	2.137	1.183
	(2.109)	(1.945)	
Parent's Age	–	–0.027	0.037
	(0.131)	(0.145)	
Parent College Graduate	–	4.772	7.643*
	(3.749)	(3.337)	
Parent Married/Cohabiting	–	–1.529	–0.434
	(3.891)	(3.843)	
Parent Employed	–	–0.169	2.081
	(3.502)	(3.249)	
Household Income	–	–0.741	–1.870
	(1.540)	(1.278)	
Propensity Score	–	–8.431	–
	(5.886)		
Intercept	5.731**	9.918	–2.890
	(1.275)	(9.543)	(10.812)
N	56	56	57
Pseudo R-Squared	0.11	0.18	0.28

**p < .01; *p < .05; ^p < .10 two tailed test

Equation estimates for Figure 8.13: OLS models predicting hours studied per week

Independent Variable	Unmatched	Matched
Years in ELH	0.807**	0.874**
	(0.252)	(0.236)
Age	−0.049	0.216
	(0.497)	(0.492)
Male	1.738	1.219
	(2.004)	(1.882)
Parent's Age	0.015	0.037
	(0.126)	(0.140)
Parent College Graduate	4.938	8.189*
	(3.675)	(3.232)
Parent Married/Cohabiting	−2.293	−0.605
	(3.837)	(3.720)
Parent Employed	1.495	3.075
	(3.242)	(2.999)
Household Income	−1.464	−2.308^
	(1.483)	(1.198)
Propensity Score	−3.756	−
	(5.243)	
Intercept	5.318	−2.762
	(9.368)	(10.426)
N	56	57
Pseudo R-Squared	0.22	0.33

$**p < .01;\ *p < .05;\ ^p < .10$ two tailed test

Equation estimates for Figure 8.14: OLS models predicting factor index of school quality

Independent Variable	Unmatched	Unmatched	Matched
ELH Resident	0.982**	0.769**	0.540**
	(0.144)	(0.263)	(0.144)
Age	–	–0.041	–0.060
	(0.050)	(0.037)	
Male	–	–0.470*	–0.280*
	(0.209)	(0.139)	
Parent's Age	–	0.008	0.001
	(0.013)	(0.010)	
Parent College Graduate	–	–0.508	–0.905**
	(0.372)	(0.238)	
Parent Married/Cohabiting	–	0.177	0.057
	(0.386)	(0.274)	
Parent Employed	–	–0.054	–0.306
	(0.347)	(0.232)	
Household Income	–	0.093	0.240*
	(0.153)	(0.091)	
Propensity Score	–	0.528	–
	(0.584)		
Intercept	–0.519*	–0.077	1.179
	(0.133)	(0.946)	(0.772)
N	57	56	57
Pseudo R-Squared	0.35	0.46	0.55

$**p < .01$; $*p < .05$; $^p < .10$ two tailed test

Equation estimates for Figure 8.15: OLS models predicting factor index of school quality

Independent Variable	Unmatched	Matched
Years in ELH	0.077**	0.052**
	(0.026)	(0.018)
Age	−0.044	−0.073^
	(0.052)	(0.038)
Male	−0.564**	−0.304**
	(0.209)	(0.146)
Parent's Age	0.014	0.001
	(0.013)	(0.011)
Parent College Graduate	−0.488	−0.860**
	(0.383)	(0.250)
Parent Married/Cohabiting	0.127	0.023
	(0.400)	(0.288)
Parent Employed	0.202	−0.141
	(0.338)	(0.232)
Household Income	0.003	0.183^
	(0.155)	(0.093)
Propensity Score	1.163*	–
	(0.547)	
Intercept	−0.565	1.367^
	(0.977)	(0.807)
N	57	57
Pseudo R-Squared	0.43	0.51

**p < .01; *p <. 05; ^p <. 10 two tailed test

Equation estimates for Figure 8.16: OLS models predicting school disorder index

Independent Variable	Unmatched	Unmatched	Matched
ELH Resident	−12.059**	−8.869	−12.492**
	(5.578)	(7.703)	(5.175)
Age	−	0.480	0.699
	(1.597)	(1.315)	
Male	−	6.768	−0.890
	(6.646)	(4.981)	
Parent's Age	−	−0.272	0.361
	(0.412)	(0.371)	
Parent College Graduate	−	−13.390	−17.504*
	(11.812)	(8.545)	
Parent Married/Cohabiting	−	−6.043	−20.267*
	(12.259)	(9.841)	
Parent Employed	−	1.611	11.056
	(11.034)	(8.320)	
Household Income	−	2.116	−1.105
	(4.853)	(3.274)	
Propensity Score	−	−13.380	−
	(18.545)		
Intercept	32.236**	38.350	3.014
	(4.082)	(30.064)	(27.691)
N	56	56	57
Pseudo R-Squared	0.08	0.18	0.32

**$p < .01$; *$p < .05$; ^$p < .10$ two tailed test

Equation estimates for Figure 8.17: OLS models predicting school disorder index

Independent Variable	Unmatched	Matched
Years in ELS	−0.674	−0.914
	(0.819)	(0.647)
Age	0.576	1.144
	(1.611)	(1.347)
Male	8.324	0.005
	(6.502)	(5.156)
Parent's Age	−0.349	0.347
	(0.409)	(0.385)
Parent College Graduate	−13.603	−18.521*
	(11.924)	(8.857)
Parent Married/Cohabiting	−5.904	−19.185^
	(12.450)	(10.195)
Parent Employed	−1.900	6.127
	(10.518)	(8.216)
Household Income	3.183	0.506
	(4.812)	(3.284)
Propensity Score	−21.414	–
	(17.012)	
Intercept	43.262	−3.740
	(30.398)	(28.568)
N	56	57
Pseudo R-Squared	0.17	0.27

**p < .01; *p < .05; ^p < .10 two tailed test

References

Ahrentzen, Sherry. 2008. "How does affordable housing affect surrounding property values?" Research Brief No. 1, Housing Research Synthesis Project, Stardust Center for Affordable Homes and Families, Arizona State University.

Albright, Len. 2011. *Community Social Organization and the Integration of Affordable Housing Residents in a Suburban New Jersey Community*. Ph.D. Dissertation, Department of Sociology, University of Chicago.

Alonso, William. 1964. *Location and Land Use: Toward a General Theory of Land Rent*. Cambridge, MA: Harvard University Press.

Ariely, Dan. 2009. *Predictably Irrational: The Hidden Forces That Shape Our Decisions*. New York: Harper.

Babb, Carol, Louis Pol, and Rebecca Guy. 1984. "The Impact of Federally Assisted Housing on Single Housing Sales: 1970–1980." *Mid-South Business Journal* 4: 13–17.

Bauman, John F. 1987. *Public Housing, Race, and Renewal: Urban Planning in Philadelphia, 1920–1974*. Philadelphia, PA: Temple University Press.

Bertrand, Marianne, and Sendhil Mullainathan. 2004. "Are Emily and Greg More Employable than Lakisha and Jamal? A Field Experiment on Labor Market Discrimination." *American Economic Review* 94:991–1013.

Bowly, Devereux, Jr. 1978. *The Poorhouse: Subsidized Housing in Chicago 1895–1976*. Carbondale: Southern Illinois University Press.

Braun, Bob. 2011. "Braun: Mount Laurel low-income housing a success story." *Newark Star-Ledger*, July 25.

Brescia, Raymond H., 2009. "Subprime Communities: Reverse Redlining, the Fair Housing Act and Emerging Issues in Litigation Regarding the Subprime Mortgage Crisis." *Albany Government Law Review* 2 :164–216.

Briggs, Xavier de Souza, Joe T. Darden, and Angela Aidala. 1999. "In the Wake of Desegregation: Early Impacts of Scattered-Site Public Housing on Neighborhoods in Yonkers, New York." *Journal of the American Planning Association* 65: 27–49.

Briggs, Xavier de Souza, and Peter Dreier. 2008. "Memphis Murder Mystery? No, Just Mistaken Identity." *Shelterforce*. http://www.shelterforce.org/article/special/1043/.

Burchell, Robert W. 1985. *Mount Laurel II: Challenge and Delivery of Low-Cost Housing*. New Brunswick, NJ: Rutgers Center for Urban Policy Research.

Burgess, Ernest W. 1925. "The growth of the city: an introduction to a research project." Pp. 47–62 in Robert E. Park and Ernest W. Burgess, eds., *The City*. Chicago: University of Chicago Press.

———. 1928. "Residential Segregation in American Cities." *Annals of the American Academy of Political and Social Science* 140:105–15.

Bursick, Robert J., and Harold G. Grasmick. 1992. *Neighborhoods and Crime: The Dimensions of Effective Community Control*. Lanham, MD: Lexington Books.

Bush-Baskette, Stephanie R., Kelly Robinson, and Pater Simmons. 2011. "Residential and Social Outcomes for Residents Living in Housing Certified by the New Jersey Council on Affordable Housing." *Rutgers Law Review*, forthcoming. Available from the Social Science Research Network at http://ssrn.com/abstract=1865342.

Campbell, Donald T., and Julian Stanley. 1971. *Experimental and Quasi-Experimental Designs for Research*. New York: Wadsworth.

Capuzzo, Jill. 2001. "The Affordable Housing Complex That Works." *New York Times*, November 25, p. B1.

Carruthers, Bruce G., and Sarah L. Babb. 2000. *Economy/Society: Markets, Meanings, and Social Structure*. Thousand Oaks, CA: Pine Forge Press.

Charles, Camille Z. 2003. "The dynamics of racial residential segregation." *Annual Review of Sociology* 29: 67–207.

Charles, Camille Z., Mary J. Fischer, Margarita Mooney, and Douglas S. Massey. 2009. *Taming the River: Negotiating the Academic, Financial, and Social Currents in America's Selective Colleges and Universities*. Princeton, NJ: Princeton University Press.

Cisneros, Henry G., and Lora Engdahl. 2009. *From Despair to Hope: Hope VI and the New Promise of Public Housing in America's Cities*. Washington, DC: Brookings Institution Press.

Clampet-Lundquist, Susan. 2004a. "Moving over or moving up? Short-term gains and losses for relocated HOPE VI families." *Cityscape* 7: 57–80.

———. 2004b. "HOPE VI relocation: Moving to new neighborhoods and building new ties." *Housing Policy Debate* 15:415–47.

———. 2007. "No more 'Bois ball: The impact of relocation from public housing on adolescents." *Journal of Adolescent Research* 22:298–323.

———. 2010. "'Everyone had your back': Social ties, perceived safety, and public housing relocation." *City and Community* 9:87–108.

Clampet-Lundquist , Susan, and Douglas S. Massey. 2008. "Neighborhood Effects on Economic Self-Sufficiency: A Reconsideration of the Moving to Opportunity Experiment." *American Journal of Sociology* 114:107–43.

Council on Affordable Housing. 2010. "Proposed and Completed Affordable Units, 12/9/09." http://www.state.nj.us/dca/affiliates/coah/reports/units.pdf; accessed May 21, 2010. Updated to 2012 via email from COAH to David Kinsey, March 29, 2012.

Crowley, Sheila. 2009. "HOPE VI: What Went Wrong." Pp. 229–47 in *From Despair to Hope: HOPE VI and the New Promise of Public Housing in America's Cities*, edited by Henry G. Cisneros and Lora Engdahl. Washington, DC: Brookings Institution Press.

Danielson, Michael N. 1976. *The Politics of Exclusion*. New York: Columbia University Press.

Dehejia, Rajeev, and Sadek Wahba. 2002. "Propensity Score Matching Methods for Nonexperimental Causal Studies." *Review of Economics and Statistics* 84(1): 151–61.

DeMarco, Megan. 2012. "Christie Administration Asks Towns to Send Affordable Housing Money to State." *Newark Star Ledger*, July 24, 2012. http://www.nj.com/news/index.ssf/2012/07/christie_administration_asks_t.html.

DePalma, Anthony. 1988. "Mount Laurel: Slow, Painful Progress." *New York Times*, May 1, 1988.

DeSalvo, Karen B., Nicole Bloser, Kristi Reynolds, Jiang He, and Paul Muntner. 2006. "Mortality Prediction with a Single General Self-Rated Health Question: A Meta-Analysis." *Journal of General Internal Medicine* 21(3): 267–75.

de Souza Briggs, Xavier. 2005. *The Geography Of Opportunity: Race And Housing Choice in Metropolitan America*. Washington, DC: Brookings Institution Press.

de Souza Briggs, Xavier, Susan J. Popkin, and John Goering. 2010. *Moving to Opportunity: The Story of an American Experiment to Fight Ghetto Poverty*. New York: Oxford University Press.

Duany, Andres, Elizabeth Plater-Zyberk, and Jeff Speck, 2000. *Suburban Nation: The Rise of Sprawl and the Decline of the American Dream*. New York: North Point Press.

Duncan, Otis D., and Beverly Duncan. 1957. *The Negro Population of Chicago: A Study of Residential Succession*. Chicago: University of Chicago Press.

Edin, Kathryn, and Laura Lein. 1997. *Making Ends Meet: How Single Mothers Survive Welfare and Low-Wage Work*. New York: Russell Sage Foundation.

Evans, Peter B. 1995. *Embedded Autonomy: States and Industrial Transformation*. Princeton, NJ: Princeton University Press.

Fair Share Housing. 2010. What is the Mount Laurel Doctrine?" Accessed 7/25/11. http://fairsharehousing.org/mount-laurel-doctrine/.

Fischel, William A. 2004. "An economic history of zoning and a cure for its exclusionary effects." *Urban Studies* 41:317–40.

Fischer, Claude S., Gretchen Stockmayer, Jon Stiles, and Michael Hout. 2004. Distinguishing the Geographic Levels and Social Dimensions of U.S. Metropolitan Segregation, 1960–2000." *Demography* 41:37–59.

Fischer, Mary J., and Douglas S. Massey. 2004. "The Social Ecology of Racial Discrimination." *City and Community* 3:221–43.

Fligstein, Neil. 2001. *The Architecture of Markets: An Economic Sociology of Twenty-First Century Capitalist Societies*. Princeton, NJ: Princeton University Press.

Fogelson, Robert M. 2005. *Bourgeois Nightmares: Suburbia 1870–1930*. New Haven: Yale University Press.

Fong, Eric. 1994. "Residential Proximity Among Racial Groups in American and Canadian Neighborhoods." *Urban Affairs Quarterly* 30(2): 285–97.

———. 1996. "A Comparative Perspective of Racial Residential Segregation: American and Canadian Experiences." *Sociological Quarterly* 37(2): 501–28.

———. 2006. "Residential Segregation of Visible Minority Groups in Canada." Pp. 51–75 in Eric Fong, ed., *Inside the Mosaic*. Toronto: University of Toronto Press.

Fong, Eric, and Kumiko Shibuya. 2005. "Multi-Ethnic Cities in North America." *Annual Review of Sociology* 31:285–304.

Freedman, Matthew, and Emily Owens. 2011. "Low-Income Housing Development and Crime." *Journal of Urban Economics*, forthcoming.

Freeman, L., and Botein, H., 2002. "Subsidized Housing and Neighborhood Impacts: A Theoretical Discussion and Review of the Evidence." *Journal of Planning Literature* 16:359–78.

Friedman, Samantha, and Gregory D. Squires. 2005. "Does the Community Reinvestment Act Help Minorities Access Traditionally Inaccessible Neighborhoods?" *Social Problems* 52(2): 209–31.

Funderburg, Richard, and Heather MacDonald. 2010."Neighbourhood Valuation Effects from New Construction of Low-income Housing Tax Credit Projects in Iowa: A Natural Experiment." *Urban Studies* 47:1745–71.

Galster, George C. 2004. "The effects of affordable and multifamily housing on market values of nearby homes. Pp. 176–201 in Anthony Downs, ed. *Growth Management and Affordable Housing: Do They Conflict?* Washington, DC: Brookings Institution Press.

Galster, George C., Peter A. Tatian, Anna M. Santiago, Kathryn L. S. Pettit, and Robin E. Smith. 2003. *Why Not in My Backyard? Neighborhood Impacts of Deconcentrating Assisted Housing.* New Brunswick, NJ: Rutgers Center for Urban Policy Research.

Getlin, Josh. 2004. "Low-income housing wins a beachhead in the 'burbs ." *Seattle Times*, November 14, B1.

Glaeser, Edward L., and Joseph Gyourko. 2003. "The impact of zoning on housing affordability." *Economic Policy Review* 9:23–39.

———. 2008. *Rethinking Federal Housing Policy: How to Make Housing Plentiful and Affordable.* Washington, DC: AEI Press.

Glaeser, Edward L., Joseph Gyourko, and Raven Saks. 2005. "Why have house prices gone up?" *American Economic Review* 95:329–33.

Glaeser, Edward L, Jenny Schuetz, and Bryce Ward. 2006. *Regulation and the Rise of Housing Prices in Greater Boston.* Cambridge, MA: Pioneer Institute for Public Policy Research and Rappaport Institute for Greater Boston.

Glaeser, Edward L., and Bryce Ward. 2006. "The causes and consequences of land use regulation: Evidence from Greater Boston." NBER Working Paper No. W12601. Cambridge, MA: National Bureau of Economic Research.

Goering, John, and Judith Feins. 2003. *Choosing a Better Life? Evaluating the Moving to Opportunity Experiment.* Washington, DC: The Urban Institute Press.

Goetz, Edward G. 2003. *Clearing the Way: Deconcentrating the Poor in Urban America.* Washington, DC: The Urban Institute Press.

Goldstein, Ira, and William L. Yancey. 1986. "Public Housing Projects, Blacks, and Public Policy: The Historical Ecology of Public Housing in Philadelphia." Pp. 262–89 in John M. Goering, ed., *Housing Desegregation and Federal Policy*. Chapel Hill: University of North Carolina Press.

Goleman, Daniel. 2006. *Emotional Intelligence: Why It Can Matter More Than IQ.* New York: Bantam.

Griffiths, Elizabeth, and George Tita. 2009. "Homicide in and Around Public Housing: Is Public Housing a Hotbed, a Magnet, or a Generate of Violence for the Surrounding Community?" *Social Problems* 56: 474–93.

Guillen, Mauro F. 2001. *The Limits of Convergence: Globalization and Organizational Change in Argentina, South Korea, and Spain*. Princeton, NJ: Princeton University Press.

Guo, Shenyang Y., and Mark W. Fraser. 2009. *Propensity Score Analysis: Statistical Methods and Applications*. Thousand Oaks, CA: Sage Publications.

Gyorko, Joseph E., Albert Saiz, and Anita A. Summers. 2008. "A new measure of the local regulatory environment for housing markets: Wharton Residential Land Use Regulatory Index. *Urban Studies* 45:693–729.

Haar, Charles M. 1996. *Suburbs Under Siege: Race, Space, and Audacious Judges*. Princeton, NJ: Princeton University Press.

Haddock C. K., W. S. Poston, S. A. Pyle, R. C. Klesges, M. W. Vander Weg, A. Peterson, and M. Debon. 2006. "The Validity of Self-Rated Health as a Measure of Health Status Among Young Military Personnel: Evidence from a Cross-Sectional Survey." *Health and Quality of Life Outcomes* 4:57–66.

Hall, Peter A., and David Sockice. 2001. *Varieties of Capitalism: The Institutional Foundations of Comparative Advantage*. Oxford: Oxford University Press.

Hanley, Robert. 1984. "Some Jersey towns, giving in to courts, let in modest homes." *New York Times*, February 29, p. A1.

Hasse, John, John Reiser, and Alexander Pichacz. 2011. "Evidence of Persistent Exclusionary Effects of Land Use Policy within Historic and Projected Development Patterns in New Jersey: A Case Study of Monmouth and Somerset Counties." Unpublished Paper, Geospatial Research Laboratory, Rowan University.

Hays, R. Allen. 1985. *The Federal Government and Urban Housing: Ideology and Change in Public Policy*. Albany: State University of New York Press.

Hirsch, Arnold R. 1983. *Making the Second Ghetto: Race and Housing in Chicago, 1940–1960*. Cambridge: Cambridge University Press.

Hirsch, Deborah. 2009. "Report ranks Camden most dangerous U.S. city." *Cherry Hill Courier Post*, Nov. 24, p. 1.

Holmes, T. H., and M. Masuda. 1974. "Life Change and Illness Susceptibility." Pp. 45–72 in B. S. Dohrenwend and B. P. Dohrenwend, eds., *Stressful Life Events: Their Nature and Effects*. New York: Wiley.

Holmes, T. H., and R. H. Rahe. 1967. "The Social Readjustment Rating Scale." *Journal of Psychosomatic Research* 11:213–18.

Holzman, Harold R., 1996. "Criminological Research on Public Housing: Toward a Better Understanding of People, Places, and Spaces." *Crime and Delinquency* 42:351–78.

Hunt, R. Bradford. 2009. *Blueprint for Disaster: The Unraveling of Chicago Public Housing*. Chicago, IL: University of Chicago Press.

Husock, Howard. 2003. *America's Trillion-Dollar Housing Mistake: The Failure of American Housing Policy*. Lanham, MD: Ivan R. Dee.

Iceland, John, Daniel A Weinberg, and Erika Steinmetz. 2002. *Racial and Ethnic Residential Segregation in the United States: 1980–2000*. Washington, DC: U.S. Census Bureau.

Idler, Ellen L., and Yael Benyamini. 1997. "Self-Rated Health and Mortality: A Review of Twenty-Seven Community Studies." *Journal of Health and Social Behavior* 38(1): 21–37.

Jackson, Kenneth T. 1985. *Crabgrass Frontier: The Suburbanization of the United States.* New York: Oxford University Press.

Jacobs, Jane. 1969. *The Death and Life of Great American Cities.* New York: Modern Library. Jencks, Christopher, and Susan E. Mayer. 1990. "The Social Consequences of Growing Up in a Poor Neighborhood." Pp. 111–86 in Laurence E. Lynn, Jr., and Michael G. H. McGeary, eds., *Inner City Poverty in the United States.* Washington, DC: National Academy of Sciences.

Jones, E. Michael. 2004. *The Slaughter of Cities: Urban Renewal as Ethnic Cleansing.* South Bend, IN: St. Augustine's Press.

Kahneman, Daniel. 2011. *Thinking Fast and Slow.* New York: Farrar, Straus and Giroux.

Kahneman, Daniel, Jack L. Knetsch, Richard H. Thaler. 1991. "Anomalies: The Endowment Effect, Loss Aversion, and Status Quo Bias." *The Journal of Economic Perspectives* 5(1): 193–206

Katznelson, Ira. 2005. *When Affirmative Action Was White: An Untold History of Racial Inequality in Twentieth-Century America.* New York: W. W. Norton.

Kaufman, Julia E., and James Rosenbaum. 1992. "The education and employment of low- income black youth in white suburbs." *Educational Evaluation and Policy Analysis* 14:229–40.

Keels, Micere, Greg Duncan, Stefanie DeLuca, Ruby Mendenhall, and James Rosenbaum. 2005. "Fifteen years later: can residential mobility programs provide a long-term escape from neighborhood segregation, crime, and poverty?" *Demography* 42 (1): 51–73.

Kirp, David L., John P. Dwyer, and Larry A. Rosenthal. 1995. *Our Town: Race, Housing, and the Soul of Suburbia.* New Brunswick, NJ: Rutgers University Press.

Kling, Jeffrey R., Jeffrey B. Liebman, and Lawrence F. Katz. 2007. "Experimental analysis of neighborhood effects." *Econometrica* 7:83–119.

Koebel, Theodore C., Robert E. Lang, and Karen A. Danielsen. 2004. *Community Acceptance of Affordable Housing.* Washington, DC: National Association of Realtors. http://www.vchr.vt.edu/pdfreports/Community%20Acceptance%20of%20Affordable%20Housing.pdf. Accessed 7/17/11.

Lareau, Annette. 2000. *Home Advantage: Social Class and Parental Intervention in Elementary Education.* Lanham, MD: Rowman and Littlefield.

———. 2011. *Unequal Childhoods: Class, Race, and Family Life, Second Edition with an Update a Decade Later.* Berkeley: University of California Press.

Lawrence-Halley, Ethel A. 2007. "Biography of Ethel Robinson Lawrence." The Richard C. Godwin Lecture in Honor of Ethel Lawrence, Rutgers Camden. http://goodwinlecture.rutgers.edu/lawrence.htm.

Ledoux, Joseph. 1996. *The Emotional Brain: The Mysterious Underpinnings of Emotional Life.* New York: Simon and Schuster.

———. 2002. *Synaptic Self: How Our Brains Become Who We Are.* New York: Viking.

Lee, Chang-Moo, Dennis P. Culhane, and Susan M. Wachter. 1999. "The Differential Impacts of Federally Assisted Housing Programs on Nearby Property Values: A Philadelphia Case Study." *Housing Policy Debate* 10:75–93.

Levine, Jonathan. 2005. *Zoned Out: Regulation, Markets, and Choices in Transportation and Metropolitan Land Use.* Oxford: RFF Press.

Logan, John, and Harvey Molotch. 1987. *Urban Fortunes: The Political Economy of Place.* Berkeley: University of California Press.

Lomnitz, Larissa. 1977. *Networks and Marginality: Life in a Mexican Shantytown.* New York: Academic Press.

Lord, Richard. 2004. *American Nightmare: Predatory Lending and the Foreclosure of the American Dream.* Monroe, ME: Common Courage Press.

Ludwig, Jens., Jeffrey Liebman, Jeffrey Kling, Greg Duncan, Lawrence Katz, Ronald Kessler, and Lisa Sanbonmatsu. 2008. "What Can We Learn about Neighborhood Effects from the Moving to Opportunity Experiment?" *American Journal of Sociology* 114:144–88.

Ludwig, Jens, Lisa Sanbonmatsu et al. 2011. "Neighborhoods, Obesity, and Diabetes—A Randomized Social Experiment." *New England Journal of Medicine* 365:1509–19.

Lundberg, Olle, and Kristiina Manderbacka. 1996. "Assessing Reliability of a Measure of Self-Rated Health. *Scandinavian Journal of Public Health* 24:218–24.

Malpezzi, Stephen. 1996. Housing prices, externalities, and regulation in U.S. metropolitan areas." *Journal of Housing Research* 7:209–41.

Massey, Douglas S. 1995. "Getting Away with Murder: Segregation and Violent Crime in Urban America." *University of Pennsylvania Law Review* 143(5):1203–32.

———. 1996. "The Age of Extremes: Concentrated Affluence and Poverty in the 21st Century." *Demography* 33:395–412.

———. 2001. "The Prodigal Paradigm Returns: Ecology Comes Back to Sociology." Pp. 41–48 in Alan Booth and Ann C. Crouter, eds., *Does it Take a Village? Community Effects on Children, Adolescents, and Families.* Mahwah, NJ: Lawrence Erlbaum Associates.

———. 2004. "Segregation and Stratification: A Biosocial Perspective." *The DuBois Review: Social Science Research on Race* 1:1–19.

———. 2005a. *Return of the L-Word: A Liberal Vision for the New Century.* Princeton: Princeton University Press.

———. 2005b. *Strangers in a Strange Land: Humans in an Urbanizing World.* New York: Norton.

———. 2008. *Categorically Unequal: The American Stratification System.* New York: Russell Sage Foundation.

Massey, Douglas S., Jere R. Behrman, and Magaly Sanchez. 2006. *Chronicle of a Myth Foretold: The Washington Consensus in Latin America.* Thousand Oaks, CA: Sage Publications.

Massey, Douglas S., and Adam Bickford. 1992. "Segregation in the Second Ghetto: Racial and Ethnic Segregation in American Public Housing. 1977." *Social Forces* 69:1011–38.

Massey, Douglas S., Camille Charles, Garvey Lundy, and Mary J. Fischer. 2003. *Source of the River: The Social Origins of Freshmen at America's Selective Colleges and Universities*. Princeton: Princeton University Press.

Massey, Douglas S., and Nancy A. Denton. 1985. "Spatial Assimilation as a Socioeconomic Outcome." *American Sociological Review* 50:94–105.

———. 1988. "The Dimensions of Residential Segregation." *Social Forces* 67: 281–315.

———. 1993. *American Apartheid: Segregation and the Making of the Underclass*. Cambridge, MA: Harvard University Press.

Massey, Douglas S., and Mitchell E. Eggers. 1990. "The Ecology of Inequality: Minorities and the Concentration of Poverty 1970–1980." *American Journal of Sociology* 95:1153–88.

———. 1993. "The Spatial Concentration of Affluence and Poverty During the 1970s." *Urban Affairs Quarterly* 29:299–315.

Massey, Douglas S., and Mary J. Fischer. 2003. "The Geography of Inequality in the United States 1950–2000." Pp. 1–40 in William G. Gale and Janet Rothenberg Pack, eds., *Brookings-Wharton Papers on Urban Affairs 2003*. Washington, DC: Brookings Institution.

Massey, Douglas S., and Shawn M. Kanaiaupuni. 1993. "Public Housing and the Concentration of Poverty." *Social Science Quarterly* 74:109–23.

Massey, Douglas S., and Garvey J. Lundy. 2001. "Use of Black English and Racial Discrimination in Urban Housing Markets: New Methods and Findings." *Urban Affairs Review* 36:470–96.

Massey, Douglas S., and Brendan P. Mullan. 1984. "Processes of Hispanic and Black Spatial Assimilation." *American Journal of Sociology* 89:836–73.

Massey, Douglas S., and LiErin Probasco. 2010. "Divergent Streams: Race-Gender Achievement Gaps at Selective Colleges and Universities." *The DuBois Review: Social Science Research on Race* 7(1): 219–46.

Massey, Douglas S., Jonathan T. Rothwell, and Thurston Domina. 2009. "Changing Bases of Segregation in the United States." *Annals of the American Academy of Political and Social Science* 626:74–90.

McClure, Kirk. 2006. "The Low-Income Housing Tax Credit Goes Mainstream and Moves into the Suburbs." *Housing Policy Debate* 17(3): 419–46.

McNulty, Thomas L., and Steven R. Holloway. 2000. Race, Crime, and Public Housing in Atlanta: Testing a Conditional Effect Hypothesis." *Social Forces* 79:707–29.

Mendenhall, Ruby, Stefanie DeLuca, and Greg Duncan. 2006. "Neighborhood Resources, Racial Segregation, and Economic Mobility: Results from the Gautreaux Program." *Social Science Research* 35:892–923.

Metcalf, George R. 1988. *Fair Housing Comes of Age*. New York: Greenwood Press.

Miller, Shazia. 1998. "Order and Democracy: Trade-offs between Social Control and Civil Liberties at Lake Parc Place." *Housing Policy Debate* 9:757–73.

Mills, Edwin S., and Bruce W. Hamilton. 1997. *Urban Economics* (5th ed.). Boston: Addison-Wesley.

Molz, Michelle. 2003. "Hundreds apply for low-cost homes." *Cherry Hill Courier-Post*, September 16. http://www.southjerseynews.com/issues/september/m091603j.htm.

Molz, Michelle, and Michael T. Burkhart. 2002. "S. J. housing project shines." *Cherry Hill Courier-Post*, May 5, 2002. http://www.southjerseynews.com/issues/may/m050502a.htm#.

Morenoff, Jeffrey, Robert J. Sampson, and Stephen Raudenbush. 2001. "Neighborhood Inequality, Collective Efficacy, and the Spatial Dynamics of Urban Violence." *Criminology* 39:517-60.

Morgan, Stephen L., and Christopher Winship . 2007. *Counterfactuals and Causal Inference: Methods and Principles for Social Research*. New York: Cambridge University Press.

Morris, Martina, and Bruce Western. 1999. "Inequality in earnings at the close of the twentieth century." *Annual Review of Sociology* 25: 623-57.

Murphy, Alexandra K., and Danielle Wallace. 2010. "Opportunities for Making Ends Meet and Upward Mobility: Differences in Organizational Deprivation Across Urban & Suburban Poor Neighborhoods." *Social Science Quarterly* 91(5): 1164-86.

Nelson, Arthur C., Thomas W. Sanchez, and Casey J. Dawkins. 2004. "The effect of urban containment and mandatory housing elements on racial segregation in U.S. metropolitan areas, 1990-2000. *Journal of Urban Affairs* 26:339-50.

New Jersey Department of Community Affairs. 2010. "Proposed and Completed Affordable Units. Trenton: Department of Community Affairs. Accessed online January 2010. http://www.state.nj.us/dca/affiliates/coah/reports/units.pdf.

———. 2011. "About DCA." Trenton: Department of Community Affairs. Accessed online October 19, 2011. http://www.nj.gov/dca/about/index.html.

New Jersey Department of Education. 2011. 2009 Department of Education School Report Card File. Trenton: New Jersey Department of Education. Accessed September 7-8 at http://education.state.nj.us/rc/rc09/index.html.

New Jersey Division of State Police. 1990-2009. *Uniform Crime Report: State of New Jersey*. West Trenton: New Jersey Division of State Police. Accessed August, 15-16 at http://www.state.nj.us/njsp/info/stats.html.

New Jersey Division of Taxation. 2010a. "Average Residential Sale Price." Accessed online January 2011. http://www.state.nj.us/treasury/taxation/lpt/class2 avgsales.shtml.

———. 2010b. "General Tax Rates by County and Municipality." Accessed online January 2011. http://www.state.nj.us/treasury/taxation/lpt/taxrate.shtml.

New Jersey Housing and Mortgage Finance Agency. 2011. "About the HMFA." Trenton: Housing and Mortgage Finance Agency. Accessed October 19, 2011. http://www.nj.gov/dca/hmfa/.

Newman, Oscar. 1972. *Defensible Space: Crime Prevention Through Urban Design*. New York: Macmillan.

Nguyen, Mai Thi. 2005. "Does affordable housing detrimentally affect property values? A review of the literature." *Journal of Planning Literature* 20:15-26.

North, Douglas C. 1990. *Institutions, Institutional Change and Economic Performance*. Cambridge: Cambridge University Press.

O'Flaherty, Brendan. 1996. *Making Room: The Economics of Homelessness*. Cambridge, MA: Harvard University Press.

Orfield, Myron. 2002. *American Metropolitics: The New Suburban Reality*. Washington, DC: Brookings Institution Press.

O'Sullivan, Arthur. 2008. *Urban Economics* (7th ed.). New York: McGraw Hill.

Park, Robert E. 1926. "The Urban Community as a Spatial Pattern and A Moral Order." Pp. 3–18 in Ernest W. Burgess, ed., *The Urban Community*. Chicago: University of Chicago Press.

Patterson, Kelly L., and Robert M. Silverman. 2011. *Fair and Affordable Housing in the U.S.: Trends, Outcomes, Future Directions*. Leiden: Brill.

Pearsall, R., and Wahl, J. 2000. "Complex provides a new start." *Cherry Hill Courier Post*, pp. 1A, 5A, November 20.

Pendall, Rolf. 2000. "Local land-use regulation and the chain of exclusion." *Journal of the American Planning Association* 66:125–42.

Pendall, Rolf., Robert Puentes, and Jonathan Martin. 2006. "From traditional to reformed: A review of land use regulations in the nation's 50 largest metropolitan areas." Brookings Institution Research Brief, Washington, DC.

Piketty, Thomas, and Emmanuel Saez. 2003. "Income Inequality in the United States, 1913–1998." *Quarterly Journal of Economics* 158:1–16.

Pizarro, Max. 2009. "Christie all but drives a stake through COAH in Monmouth County remarks." Politicker NJ. Accessed 7/25/2011. http://www.politickernj.com/max/ 27179/christie-all-drives-stake-through-coah-monmouth-county-remarks.

Polikoff, Alexander. 2006. *Waiting for Gautreaux: A Story of Segregation, Housing, and the Black Ghetto*. Evanston, IL: Northwestern University Press.

Popkin, Susan J., Victoria E. Gwiasda, Lynn M. Olson, and Dennis P. Rosenbaum. 2000. *The Hidden War: Crime and the Tragedy of Public Housing in Chicago*. New Brunswick, NJ: Rutgers University Press.

Popkin, Susan J., Bruce Katz, Mary K. Cunningham, Karen D. Brown, Jeremy Gustafson, and Margery A. Turner. 2004. A *Decade of HOPE VI: Research Findings and Policy Challenges*. Washington, DC: The Urban Institute and the Brookings Institution.

Portes, Alejandro. 2010. *Economic Sociology: A Systematic Inquiry*. Princeton, NJ: Princeton University Press.

Portes, Alejandro, and Erik Vickstrom. 2011. "Diversity, Social Capital, and Cohesion." *Annual Review of Sociology* 37:461–79.

Purnell, Thomas, William Idsardi, and John Baugh. 1999. "Perceptual and Phonetic Experiments on American English Dialect Identification." *Journal of Language and Social Psychology* 18:10–30.

Putnam, Robert D. 2000. *Bowling Alone: The Collapse and Revival of American Community*. New York: Simon and Schuster.

———. 2007. "E Pluribus Unum: Diversity and Community in the 21st Century: The 2006 Johan Skytte Prize Lecture." *Scandinavian Political Studies* 30(2): 137–74.

Rabiega, William A., Ta-win Lin, and Linda M. Robinson. 1984. "The Property Value Impacts of Public Housing Projects in Low and Moderate Density Residential Neighborhoods." *Land Economics* 60:174–79.

Rabinowitz, Alan. 2004. Urban Economics and Land Use in America: The Transformation of *Cities in the Twentieth Century*. New York: M. E. Sharp.

Rainwater, Lee. 1970. *Behind Ghetto Walls: Black Families in a Federal Slum*. Chicago: Aldine, Atherton.

Reardon, Sean F., and Kendra Bischoff. 2011a. "Income Inequality and Income Segregation." *American Journal of Sociology* 116(4), 1092–153.

———. 2011b. Growth in the Residential Segregation of Families by Income, 1970–2009. American Communities Project, Brown University. www.s4 .brown.edu/us2010/Data/Report/report111111.pdf.

Roncek, Dennis W., Ralph Bell, and Jeffrey M. A. Francik. 1981. "Housing Projects and Crime: Testing a Proximity Hypothesis." *Social Problems* 29: 151–66.

Rose, Jerome G., and Robert E. Rothman 1977. *After Mount Laurel: New Suburban Zoning.* New Brunswick, NJ: Rutgers Center for Urban Policy Research.

Rosenbaum, James E. 1991. "Black Pioneers: Do Their Moves to the Suburbs Increase Economic Opportunity for Mothers and Children?" *Housing Policy Debate* 2:1179–213.

Rosenbaum, James E., Marilyn J. Kulieke, and Leonard S. Rubinowitz. 1987. "Low-income Black Children in White Suburban Schools: A Study of School and Student Responses." *Journal of Negro Education* 56:35–43.

Rosenbaum, James E., and Susan J. Popkin. 1990. Economic and Social Impacts of Housing Integration: A Report to the Charles Stewart Mott Foundation. Evanston, IL: Center for Urban Affairs and Policy Research.

———. 1991. "Employment and Earnings of Low-income Blacks who Move to Middle-class Suburbs," in Christopher Jencks and Paul Peterson, eds. *The Urban Underclass.* Washington, DC: The Brookings Institution.

Rosenbaum, James E., Susan J. Popkin, Julia E. Kaufman, and Jennifer Rusin. 1991. "Social Integration of Low-income Black Adults in Middle-class White Suburbs." *Social Problems* 38:448–61.

Rosin, Hanna. 2008. "American Murder Mystery." *The Atlantic,* July/August 2008. http://www.theatlantic.com/magazine/archive/2008/07/american-murder -mystery/6872/.

Ross, Stephen L., and Margery A. Turner. 2004. "Other Things Being Equal: A Paired Testing Study of Discrimination in Mortgage Lending." *Journal of Urban Economics* 55:278–97.

Rossi, Peter H. 1980. *Why Families Move.* Thousand Oaks, CA: Sage Publications.

Rothwell, Jonathan T. 2011. "Racial Enclaves and Density Zoning: The Institutionalized Segregation of Racial Minorities in the United States." *American Law and Economics Review* 13(1): 290–358.

———. 2012. "The Effects of Racial Segregation on Trust and Volunteering in U.S. Cities." *Urban Studies* 49(10): 2109–36.

Rothwell, Jonathan T., and Douglas S. Massey. 2009. "The Effect of Density Zoning on Racial Segregation in U.S. Urban Areas." *Urban Affairs Review* 44:799–806.

———. 2010. "Density Zoning and Class Segregation in U.S. Metropolitan Areas." *Social Science Quarterly* 91:1123–43.

Rubin, Donald B. 2006. *Matched Sampling for Causal Effects.* New York: Cambridge University Press.

Rubinowitz, Leonard S., and James E. Rosenbaum. 2000. *Crossing the Class and Color Lines: From Public Housing to White Suburbia.* Chicago: University of Chicago Press.

Rugh, Jacob S., and Douglas S. Massey. 2010. "Racial Segregation and the American Foreclosure Crisis." *American Sociological Review* 75(5): 629–51.

———. 2012. Residential Isolation by Race and Class: Trends in the United States since 1970. Working Paper, Office of Population Research, Princeton University.

Sampson, Robert J. 1990. "The Impact of Housing Policies on Community Disorganization and Crime." *Bulletin of the New York Academy of Medicine* 66:526–33.

———. 1993. "The Community Context of Violent Crime." Pp. 259–86 in *Sociology and the Public Agenda*, edited by William Julius Wilson. Newbury Park, CA: Sage.

———. 2008. "Moving to Inequality: Neighborhood Effects and Experiments Meet Social Structure." *American Journal of Sociology* 114:189–231.

———. 2009. "Racial Stratification and the Durable Tangle of Neighborhood Inequality." *Annals of the American Academy of Political and Social Science* 621:260–80.

———. 2012. *Great American City: Chicago and the Enduring Neighborhood Effect.* Chicago: University of Chicago Press.

Sampson Robert J., Jeffrey Morenoff, and Felton Earls. 1999. "Beyond Social Capital: Spatial Dynamics of Collective Efficacy for Children." *American Sociological Review* 64: 633–60.

Sampson, Robert J., J. Morenoff, and T. Gannon-Rowley. 2002. "Assessing Neighborhood Effects: Social Processes and New Directions in Research." *Annual Review of Sociology* 28:443–78.

Sampson, Robert J., Stephen Raudenbush, and Felton Earls. 1997. "Neighborhoods and Violent Crime: A Multilevel Study of Collective Efficacy." *Science* 277:918–24.

Sampson, Robert J., and Patrick Sharkey. 2008. "Neighborhood Selection and the Social Reproduction of Concentrated Racial Inequality." *Demography* 45:1–29.

Sampson, Robert J., Patrick Sharkey, and Stephen Raudenbush. 2008. "Durable Effects of Concentrated Disadvantage on Verbal Ability among African-American Children." *Proceedings of the National Academy of Sciences* 105, No. 3: 845–53.

Sampson, Robert J., and William Julius Wilson. 1995. "Toward a Theory of Race, Crime, and Urban Inequality." In *Crime and Inequality*, edited by John Hagan and Ruth Peterson. Stanford, CA: Stanford University Press.

Santiago, Anna M., George C. Galster, and Peter Tatian. 2001. "Assessing the Property Value Impacts of the Dispersed Housing Subsidy Program in Denver." *Journal of Policy Analysis and Management* 20(1): 65–88.

Schwartz, Alex F. 2006. *Housing Policy in the United States* (2nd ed.). New York: Routledge.

Shaw, Clifford, and Henry McKay. 1969. *Juvenile Delinquency and Urban Areas.* Chicago: University of Chicago Press.

Skogan, Wesley G. 1990. *Disorder and Decline: Crime and the Spiral of Decay in American Neighborhoods.* New York: Free Press.

Small, Mario Luis. 2004. *Villa Victoria: The Transformation of Social Capital in a Boston Barrio.* Chicago, IL: University of Chicago Press.

Small, Mario L., and Katherine Newman. 2001. "Urban Poverty after the Truly Disadvantaged: The Rediscovery of the Family, the Neighborhood, and Culture." *Annual Review of Sociology* 27:23–45.

Smeeding, Timothy M., Jeffrey P. Thompson, Asaf Levanon, and Esra Burak. 2011. Inequality, and Poverty over the Early Stages of the Great Recession. Pp. 82–126 in David B. Grusky, Bruce Western, and Christopher Wimer, eds., *The Great Recession*. New York: Russell Sage Foundation.

Smith, Robin, and Michelle DeLair. 1999. "New Evidence from Lender Testing: Discrimination at the Pre-Application Stage." Pp. 23–41 in Margery A. Turner and Felicity Skidmore, eds., *Mortgage Lending Discrimination: A Review of Existing Evidence*. Washington, DC: Urban Institute.

Smothers, Ronald. 1997a. "Decades Later, Town Considers Housing Plan for the Poor." *New York Times*, March 3, p. B1.

———. 1997b. "Low-Income Houses and a Suburb's Fear." *New York Times*, April 5, p. 25.

———. 1997c. "Ending Battle, Suburb Allows Homes for Poor." *New York Times*, April 12, p. 21.

Spector, Paul E. 1981. *Research Designs*. Thousand Oaks, CA: Sage Publications.

Spoto, Mary Ann. 2012. "N.J. Supreme Court: Christie Can't Abolish Council of Affordable Housing." *Newark Star-Ledger*, June 11. http://www.nj.com/news/index.ssf/2012/06/nj_supreme_court_christie_cant.html.

Squires, Gregory D. 1994. *Capital and Communities in Black and White: The Intersections of Race, Class, and Uneven Development*. Albany: SUNY Press.

———. 1997. *Insurance Redlining: Disinvestment, Reinvestment, and the Evolving Role of Financial Institutions*. Washington, DC: Urban Institute Press.

———. 2004. *Why the Poor Pay More: How to Stop Predatory Lending*. Westport, CT: Praeger/Greenwood Publishing Group.

———. 2007. "Overcoming Discrimination in Housing, Credit, and Urban Policy," *Buffalo Public Interest Law Journal* 25:81–95.

Squires, Gregory D., and Jan Chadwick. 2006. "Linguistic Profiling: A Tradition of the Property Insurance Industry." *Urban Affairs Review* 41(3): 400–15.

Stack, Carol. 1974. *All Our Kin: Strategies for Survival in a Black Community*. New York: Harper.

Suttles, Gerald D. 1968. *The Social Order of the Slum: Ethnicity and Territory in the Inner City*. Chicago: University of Chicago Press.

Taeuber, Karl E., and Alma F. Taeuber. 1965. *Negroes in Cities: Residential Segregation and Neighborhood Change*. Chicago: Aldine.

Telles, Edward E. 1992. "Residential Segregation by Skin Color in Brazil." *American Sociological Review* 57(2): 186–97.

———. 2004. *Race in Another America: The Significance of Skin Color in Brazil*. Princeton, NJ: Princeton University Press.

Termine, Matthew. 2010. "Promoting Residential Integration through the Fair Housing Act: Are Qui Tam Actions a Viable Method of Enforcing 'Affirmatively Furthering Fair Housing' Violations?" *Fordham Law Review* 79(3): 1367–427.

Tiebout, Charles M. 1956. "A Pure Theory of Local expenditures." *Journal of Political Economy* 64:416–24.

Tienda, Marta. 1991. "Poor People, Poor Places: Deciphering Neighborhood Effects on Poverty Outcomes." Pp. 244–62 in Joan Huber (ed.), *Macro-Micro Linkages in Sociology*. Newbury Park, CA: Sage Publications.

Tighe, J. Rosie. 2010. "Public Opinion and Affordable Housing: A Review of the Literature." *Journal of Planning Literature* 25:3–17.

Turner, Margery A., Fred Freiberg, Eerin B. Godfrey, Carla Herbig, Diane K. Levy, and Robert E. Smith. 2002. *All Other Things Being Equal: A Paired Testing Study of Mortgage Lending Institution*. Washington, DC: U.S. Department of Housing and Urban Development.

Turner, Margery A., Susan J. Popkin, and Lynette A. Rawlings. 2008. *Public Housing and the Legacy of Segregation*. Washington, DC: Urban Institute Press.

Tversky, Amos, and Daniel Kahneman. 1991. "Loss Aversion in Riskless Choice: A Reference-Dependent Model." *Quarterly Journal of Economics* 106(4): 1039–61.

U.S. Census Bureau. 2009. U.S. Decennial Census—Profile of Selected Housing Characteristics & Profile of Selected Social Characteristics. Accessed online June 2009. http://factfinder.census.gov/home/saff/main.html.

———. 2011a. Income Inequality: Historical Statics. Census Web Page. http://www.census.gov/hhes/www/income/data/historical/inequality/index.html.

———. 2011b. *American Fact Finder*. Accessed 7/25/11. http://factfinder2.census.gov/faces/nav/jsf/pages/index.xhtml.

Varady, David P., and Carole C. Walker. 2007. *Neighborhood Choices: Section 8 Housing Vouchers and Residential Mobility*. New Brunswick, NJ: Rutgers Center for Urban Policy Research.

Vernarelli, Michael J. 1986. "Where Should HUD Locate Assisted Housing?: The Evolution of Fair Housing Policy." Pp. 214–34 in John M. Goering, ed., *Housing Desegregation and Federal Policy*. Chapel Hill: University of North Carolina Press.

Venkatesh, Sudhir A. 2000. *American Project: The Rise and Fall of a Modern Ghetto*. Cambridge, MA: Harvard University Press.

Weatherburn, Don, Bronwyn Lind, and Simon Ku. 1999. "'Hotbeds of Crime?' Crime and Public Housing in Urban Sydney." *Crime and Delinquency* 45: 256–71.

Wilson, James Q. 1983. *Thinking About Crime*. New York: Basic Books.

Wilson, James Q., and George L. Kelling. 1982. "Broken Windows." *The Atlantic Monthly*, March, pp. 29–38.

Wilson, William Julius. 1987. *The Truly Disadvantaged: The Inner City, the Underclass, and Public Policy*. Chicago: University of Chicago Press.

Wolf, L. A., B. S. Armour, and V. A. Campbell. 2008. "Racial/Ethnic Disparities in Self-Rated *Morbidity & Mortality Weekly Report* 57(39):1069–73.

Wolff, Edward N. 2004. "Changes in household wealth in the 1980s and 1990s in the U.S." Working Paper No. 407. Annandale-on-Hudson, NY: The Levy Economics Institute of Bard College.

———. 2010. "Recent trends in household wealth in the United States: Rising debt and the middle-class squeeze—an update to 2007." Working Paper No. 589. Annandale-on-Hudson, NY: The Levy Economics Institute of Bard College.

Wolfgang, Marvin E., Robert M. Figlio, Paul E. Tracy, and Simon I. Singer. 1985. *The National Survey of Crime Severity*. Washington, DC: U.S. Government Printing Office

Yinger, John. 1995. *Closed Doors, Opportunities Lost: The Continuing Costs of Housing Discrimination*. New York: Russell Sage.

Index

Page numbers in italics refer to figures, illustrations, and tables.